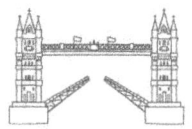

# GATEWAY ENGLISH

How to Boost your English Word Power
and Unlock New Languages

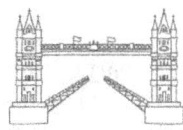

# GATEWAY ENGLISH

How to Boost your English Word Power
and Unlock New Languages

### Dr Michael Arnheim
Barrister at Law
Sometime Fellow of
St John's College, Cambridge

All rights reserved. No part of this publication may be reproduced, stored in a retrieval system or transmitted, in any form or by any means, electronic, mechanical, photocopying, recording or otherwise, without the prior permission of the publishers.

Dr Michael Arnheim has asserted his right under the Copyright, Designs and Patents Act, 1988 to be identified as the author of this work.

Paperback edition: ISBN 978-1-911369-09-7
eBook edition: ISBN 978-1-911369-45-5

First edition

Copyright © 2020 Dr Michael Arnheim
Layout and design: Copyright @ 2020 LinguaBooks

A CIP catalogue record for this book is available from the British Library.

Every effort has been made to trace the holders of intellectual property rights and the publishers will be happy to correct any mistakes or omissions in future editions.

This book is sold subject to the condition that it shall not, by way of trade or otherwise, be lent, resold, hired out or otherwise circulated without the publisher's prior consent in any form of binding or cover other than that in which it is published and without a similar condition including this condition being imposed on the subsequent purchaser.

LinguaBooks
Elsie Whiteley Innovation Centre
Hopwood Lane
Halifax HX1 5ER

www.linguabooks.com

| POSUI DEUM ADIUTOREM MEUM |

**To the sacred memory of
my beloved parents**

**Dr Wilhelm Arnheim (1901–75)**
A wise medical doctor and true polymath,
with the driest sense of humour

**and**

**Mrs Vicky Arnheim (1905–90)**
A brilliant musician, gifted teacher,
dedicated social organizer,
great cook, and loving mother

**And to the sacred memory of my
beloved grandmother, "Oma"**

**Mrs Martha Arnheim (1875–1965)**
An eternally cheerful and optimistic, courageous spirit
who taught me German and whose wonderful humorous
tales of the old Germany will remain with me always.

# About the Author

DR MICHAEL ARNHEIM (commonly known as "Doctor Mike") is a practising London barrister, Sometime Fellow of St John's College, Cambridge, and author of 22 published books to date, this being the twenty-second.

As a 14-year-old schoolboy he was picked to join the "Quiz Kids" team of five capped and gowned teenagers appearing every Friday evening on South Africa's Springbok Radio, of which he became a stalwart member, "retiring" at the age of eighteen.

He entered Johannesburg's University of the Witwatersrand at the age of 16, taking a first-class B.A. in History and Classics at the age of 19, first-class Honours in Classics at 20 and an M.A. with distinction at the age of 21.

Michael Arnheim then went up to St John's College, Cambridge, on a National Scholarship (later converted to a St John's College Scholarship supplemented by a Strathcone Travel Exhibition). He was awarded a Cambridge Ph.D. in 1969 in record time, and in 1972 his doctoral dissertation was published by Oxford University Press under the title "The Senatorial Aristocracy in the Later Roman Empire." In the meantime, he was elected into a Fellowship of St John's College, Cambridge, where he combined research with a great deal of teaching in Classics and Ancient History for a number of colleges.

At the age of 31, Michael Arnheim was invited to take up the position of full Professor and Head of the Department of Classics back at his old university in South Africa. During his time in that position he devised a new system of learning Latin, for which he wrote a series of Latin stories titled "The Adventures of Marcus." He also taught his students Spanish under the title of "Modern Latin," using etymological links with English, along the lines described in this book.

Despondent about the future of South Africa, Dr Arnheim returned to Britain, where he was called to the Bar by Lincoln's Inn in 1988, combining his practice of law with the writing of books, a combination that is still continuing.

For further information on Michael Arnheim, you may consult the Wikipedia article on him at:

en.wikipedia.org/wiki/Michael Arnheim.

You are also welcome to contact him by email at:

Counsel@arnheim-law.com.

# Preface

THIS BOOK, MY twenty-second published book to date, has had a very long gestation period, originating in the days when I was a doctoral student at St John's College, Cambridge. I was encouraged to embark on this project by the ebullient polyglot "Joppy" Jopson, the emeritus Professor of Comparative Philology, who lamented that the subject had taken what he considered to be an unduly pedantic turning. "I can't understand all that algebra," he would say in his characteristically charitable manner.

Comparative philology, or comparative linguistics, as it is now more usually labelled, is concerned with comparing languages and establishing "family" relationships among them. Closely involved with this is *etymology,* which is the study not only of the *origins* of words but also of their *essential core meanings.* This indeed is why *etymology* is so called, coming ultimately as it does from the Greek word *eteos,* meaning "true, real." This sense was captured by the great Roman writer and thinker (and failed politician) Marcus Tullius Cicero, who translated Greek *etymologia* into Latin as *veriloquium,* literally, "speaking the truth, true speech."

Etymology should therefore be a valuable tool for native English speakers to improve their word power and also to learn other related languages – and that is the purpose of this book. It is all the more necessary as etymology has rather fallen between two or even three stools (if that is possible). On the one hand there is the tendency of the academic study of comparative linguistics to turn into what Joppy light-heartedly disparaged as "algebra." Secondly, there is no shortage of popular books on English etymology, which, however, treat the subject as a form of entertainment and tend to concentrate on quirky, odd words and word histories. Neither of these approaches is much concerned with language learning.

Thirdly, however, there are language-learning courses, in both print and online formats, that make much of purely artificial "links" between words in different languages. One such language-learning course that I discuss in this book is based on a mnemonic "method" associating similar-sounding words, such as learning the Spanish word *flor* meaning "flower" by picturing a rose lying on the *floor*. There is of course no connection between Spanish *flor* and English **floor** other than a similarity in pronunciation. Under this language learning "method" learners would need the imagination of a Shakespeare coupled with a prodigious memory to create artificial "links" of this kind for every new word that they came across. Instead of that, would it not be so much easier and more enjoyable to learn Spanish *flor* by associating it with actual related words in English, such as **floral**, **florist**, **florid**, which are all connected with the concept of "flower," have a close resemblance to the Spanish word, and actually share a common origin with it (as indeed even the English word **flower** does as well).

This book is intended to combine practicality with enjoyment. This cunning plan has inevitably resulted in a certain amount of overlap between the chapters, which enables the book to have something of a *modular* character, so that, as far as possible, each chapter is independent of the rest. So, in order to understand chapter 16, for example, you would not need to read your way through all the previous chapters, though it would certainly help to follow up any cross-references in that chapter itself. However, you should certainly read Chapter 1 before you immerse yourself in any of the other chapters, because that chapter explains how this book should be used to obtain maximum benefit from it.

To my former student and long-time friend Tom Malnati of Florida I owe a tremendous debt of gratitude (and a lot of IHOP breakfasts) for proofreading the whole book and suggesting certain amendments and additions. All errors remaining are my own responsibility alone.

The people whose assistance I have received over the years are too numerous to mention. But I cannot omit to mention my friend Jack Ward, whose repeated badgering me to finish what he called my "dictionary book" has probably brought it to fruition sooner than would otherwise have been the case. The numerous etymological discussions with my friend Paul Jones have probably also done no harm.

In Cambridge, besides my gratitude to "Joppy" Jopson and Sir Harold Bailey, Professor of Sanskrit, with his library stacked a foot high on the floor, I owe a great deal to my mentor, friend and colleague, Professor John Crook, whose linguistic facility was such that he even translated into English a Danish academic treatise on Ancient Athens. My earliest exposure to Classical etymology was thanks to my two predecessors as Jan Hofmeyr Professor of Classics and Head of Department at the University of the Witwatersrand, the late Theo Haarhoff and Simon Davis.

Not least, I must thank my publisher, Dr Maurice Claypole for suggesting the title for this book. I was originally intending to call it *Angel Tongue*, on the basis of the (apocryphal) story related in Chapter 2. But, when a cover sketch was produced showing two angels, I realized that that title was likely to be misleading. It was then that Maurice Claypole came up with the idea of "Gateway English" combined with the original explanatory subtitle. And thanks, too, to my friend Ryan Eyre of Seattle, who did the hard work of preparing the two indexes in record time.

Any reader of this book is welcome to contact me with queries or comments at: Counsel@arnheim-law.com.

Dr Michael Arnheim
29 February 2020

# Contents

| | | |
|---|---|---:|
| | About the Author | 6 |
| | Preface | 8 |
| | Introduction | 13 |
| 1 | HOW TO USE THIS BOOK | 22 |
| 2 | NOT ANGLES BUT ANGELS | 38 |
| 3 | A FISTFUL OF FALLACIES | 44 |
| 4 | THE TOWER OF BABEL | 60 |
| 5 | SEMANTIC DRIFT | 72 |
| 6 | THE FRENCH CONNECTION | 82 |
| 7 | A ROMAN TRIUMPH | 94 |
| 8 | A GRIMM TALE | 105 |
| 9 | THE GERMANIC COUSINHOOD | 122 |
| 10 | A LATIN ROMANCE | 141 |
| 11 | A GREEK DRAMA | 159 |
| 12 | LOAN OR THEFT? | 166 |
| 13 | WORDS AS METAPHORS | 170 |
| 14 | SOUND MOVES | 179 |
| 15 | TOPS AND TAILS | 184 |
| 16 | IT'S ALL IN YOUR GENES | 194 |
| 17 | A BURNING QUESTION | 197 |
| 18 | TO THE EGRESS | 199 |
| 19 | LOVE IS ALL YOU NEED | 201 |

| 20 | MONEY MAKES THE WORLD GO ROUND | 209 |
| 21 | WHEN DOES A CONVICTION NOT LAND YOU IN JAIL? | 213 |
| 22 | TERM LIMITS | 216 |
| 23 | THE PEASANTS ARE REVOLTING | 219 |
| 24 | OUR BUSINESS IS RUBBISH | 224 |
| 25 | DO NOT GIVE ANY MONEY TO SOLICITORS | 227 |
| 26 | TRUST ME, I'M A DOCTOR | 229 |
| 27 | BEAR WITH ME | 231 |
| 28 | A BATHROOM WITHOUT A BATH | 236 |
| 29 | WATER, WATER EVERYWHERE | 241 |
| 30 | A FEW CONTRANYMS | 243 |
| 31 | ALL THAT ALGEBRA | 249 |
| 32 | ENVOI | 258 |
| | **Glossary** | 259 |
| | **References** | 263 |
| | **English Word Index** | 265 |
| | **Subject and Name Index** | 281 |

# Introduction

AN APOCRYPHAL STORY is told of a new Polish recruit to the Prussian army under King Frederick the Great of Prussia (reigned 1740–86). Warned that the King would shortly be doing his annual inspection of the troops, the young soldier was concerned, because he could not speak any German. His fears were allayed when his comrades told him that the King always asked the same three questions in the same order, so the young Pole could be coached in advance. The three questions were: (a) How old are you? (b) How long have you been in my army? And (c) Do you drink or smoke? But on this occasion the King changed his routine slightly. The first question he asked was: "How long have you been in my army?" To which the luckless rookie replied, "Eighteen years, Your Majesty." Slightly puzzled, the King then asked: "How old are you?" "Six months, Your Majesty," replied the recruit amidst suppressed laughter from his comrades in arms. The last question was, "Are you satisfied with your conditions of pay and service?" "Neither," came the reply. It is not known how the story ended, but, as the King actually disliked the German language, preferring French, the young recruit probably escaped unscathed.

## Quanto? and troppo

The moral of the story is the importance of the knowledge of foreign languages. Native English speakers often assume that foreigners all speak or at least understand English, so, as long as you speak English loudly enough you will be understood, and there is no need for native English speakers to learn any foreign language themselves. There are many anecdotes reflecting this attitude, like that of the frequent

English visitor to Italy who proclaimed that to tour Italy you only needed to know two words: *quanto?* meaning "how much?" and *troppo* meaning "too much."

## Decline in popularity of language courses

Despite the welter of foreign language courses now available both in live classes and on the internet, the study of foreign languages at school and university has declined sharply in both Britain and America. The BBC reported in February 2019 that "Foreign language learning is at its lowest level in UK secondary schools since the turn of the millennium, with German and French falling the most."[1] The BBC quoted figures published by the Joint Council for Qualifications, which revealed a 67% drop between 2002 and 2018 in the number of takers of German and a 63% drop in French at GCSE (taken by students aged 15–16). The BBC also reported that "Business organizations have expressed concern at the lack of language skills in the UK. Matthew Fell, chief UK policy director for business group CBI (Confederation of British Industry), said: 'Employer demand for French, German and Spanish skills have significantly increased over the last few years. The decline in language learning in schools must be reversed, or else the UK will be less competitive globally and young people less prepared for the modern world.'"

## Language study "difficult"

What is particularly striking is the reason given for this decline. Of the 2,048 mainstream secondary schools in the UK which responded to a BBC survey "most said that the perception of languages as a difficult subject was the main reason behind a drop in the number of

---

[1] Branwen Jeffreys, "Language learning: German and French drop by half in UK schools," *BBC News*, 27 February 2019.

pupils studying for exams."[2] If teenagers find languages "difficult," this is a reflection on the teaching methods involved.

The position in the US is similar. Despite the importance of a knowledge of foreign languages to America's national security and diplomacy, it was reported in February 2019 that "according to the US Government Accountability Office, nearly one in four Foreign Service officers do not meet the language proficiency requirements that they should meet to do their jobs."[3]

The same article reports that "researchers at the Modern Language Association recently found that colleges lost 651 foreign language programs from 2013 to 2016." Only 20% of students study a foreign language at K-12 level, and at college level this figure drops to just 7.5%, a percentage that has been "steadily declining in recent years." "This may stem," it is suggested, "from knowledge of the fact that English is widely spoken and studied throughout the world. However, the fact remains that 75% of the world population does not speak English."[4]

Even high-level government representatives of English-speaking countries tend to address international conferences and meetings in English, while foreign leaders frequently do so in what is to them a foreign language – English. The United Nations, the European Parliament and the Davos World Economic Forum are cases in point.

**Most language courses lump all learners together**

Most language courses, whether in live classes or as an online program, treat all learners the same. An Italian language course, for example, will be the same for all learners no matter whether their

---

[2] Ibid.

[3] "Foreign language classes becoming more scarce." theconversation.com/foreign-language-classes-becoming-more-scarce-102235, February 6, 2019.

[4] Ibid.

home language (L1) is English, French, Turkish or Chinese. The fact that English and French are related to Italian while Turkish and Chinese are not is simply ignored. Some of these language programs claim to be based on the "natural" way a child acquires fluency in its native tongue, but all that generally amounts to is just to expose the learner to speech in the target language (L2) without any translation or explanation.

It is a serious fallacy to expect an adult learner to be able to learn a language like a young child. There is some doubt whether children's well-documented ability to soak up and absorb their native tongue is the product of some feature of the immature human brain or whether it is just by dint of their total immersion in their native language and culture in their home environment 24 hours a day every day. If the former, then it will simply not be possible for an adult learner to emulate a child's language learning experience. If the latter is the case, an adult learner would have to be immersed in the L2 language and culture as completely as an infant for a period of months or even years, which, though theoretically possible, would not normally be practical. So, in either case, it is not very helpful to treat an adult learner like a child.

## "Listen and learn"

A common complaint about "listen and repeat" programs generally is that they tend to be boring. Some of these programs do go beyond pure repetition and require the learner to create their own individual variations. But these methods, different though they are from one another, are still mostly based on memorizing words and phrases, whether the course is all conducted in the target language or with the aid of translation from the learner's home language. The use of translation means that learners will be thinking in their native language rather than in the target language. But avoiding translation will not necessarily facilitate thinking in the target language either. In a review of Rosetta Stone, one of the leading brands of language courses, Nick Dahlhoff, the creator of All Language Resources, comments: "Rosetta Stone ... completely removes English from the lessons. Instead, everything is taught with pictures and your target language ... while I understand the appeal of a somewhat immersive learning environment without any English, I'm not necessarily sold on it. Using pictures work [sic] great for simple things (like 'dog') but it's less clear for more abstract ideas (like 'decision' or 'hope')."[5]

## Rosetta Stone

Examples from the Rosetta Stone Spanish course displayed in the review include a picture of a man in shirtsleeves sitting at a desk, with the caption: "*El médico está escribiendo.*" But the fact that no translation is provided does not prevent the learner from figuring out the meaning of the caption by translating it anyway, as: "The doctor is writing." And the absence of any explanation, another feature of Rosetta Stone courses, does not draw the learner's attention to the distinction between the wording of this caption and "*El medico escribe*" ("The doctor writes"). The first caption is an example of the "present continuous" or "present progressive" – technically a combination of the present *tense* with the continuous *aspect* – which would be familiar to a native English speaker, because a similar construction exists in English: "The doctor is writing," as against: "The doctor writes." The first sentence describes an activity that is going on right now, while the second is more general. But a lot of languages, including German, for example, lack a continuous form. So, in German, "*Der Arzt schreibt*" can mean either "The doctor writes" or "The doctor is writing." And a German learning a language like English or Spanish that does have the continuous form needs to be made aware of the distinction. A native English or Spanish speaker learning German needs to know not only that German lacks a continuous

---

[5] alllanguageresources.com.pimsleur-vs-rosetta-stone-or-possibly-neither.

construction, but also that there are other ways around it, for example by using the word *gerade* ("just," "just now"), as in: *"Der Arzt schreibt gerade."* This only underlines the problem of lumping all learners together regardless of their individual language background and also the problem, found in some leading language courses, of deliberately eschewing any explanation in the learner's native language. A very common difficulty experienced by Germans learning English is to do with expressions in the past tense. Why, for example, is it wrong to say, "I have seen him yesterday"? The literal equivalent in German is perfectly correct: *"Ich habe ihn gestern gesehen."* You can also say, using the simple past tense (technically known as the preterite): *"Ich sah ihn gestern."* But that tense tends to be used mostly in writing rather than in conversation.

### *Ser* and *estar* in Spanish

To return to the picture of the doctor in the Rosetta Stone Spanish course, you may have noticed that the caption used the verb *estar* to create the present continuous: *"El médico está escribiendo"* ("The doctor is writing"). The word *está* literally means "(he) is" – but Spanish also has another way of saying "(he) is," namely *es*, from the verb *ser* ("to be"). So, could you say *"El médico es escribiendo"*? No, but a Rosetta Stone learner would not be alerted to any of this, as the program contains no explanations and is all in the target language. If you wanted to say, "Pedro is a doctor," then *es* would be appropriate: *"Pedro es médico."* But "Pedro is in the living room" is *"Pedro está en la sala."* Any clue yet on the difference between *ser* and *estar*? The rules governing the use of these two important verbs are quite complex, but, in short, *ser* is used for a permanent or lasting attribute, whereas *estar* is for being in a (generally temporary) state or location. This is where etymology comes in. *Ser* is from Latin *esse* ("to be"), from which "he, she or it is" is *est*, not a million miles away from Spanish *es*. But Latin has only one way of saying "he is," so where does Spanish *estar* come from? The initial [e-] in Spanish *estar* is a common feature before [sc-], [st-] or [sp-] in most Romance languages.⁶ So, it doesn't take a great deal of ingenuity to figure out that it is from Latin *sto, stare, statum* ("to stand") from which comes English **state**, as in "to be in a state of anger, denial, chaos, flux." That is why *estar* is used in Spanish to indicate a state – which also explains why it is used in the present continuous, as in our old friend, *"El médico está escribiendo."* Needless to say, there are some exceptions, one of which is in connection with the word *muerto* ("dead"), Spanish from Latin *mortuus* ("dead", from which come English **mortal**, etc.) So, in Spanish "The king is dead" is *"El rey está muerto"* – death being a state, though generally considered to be a permanent state!

## Pimsleur

Pimsleur, a leading competitor of Rosetta Stone, also eschews grammar, as they proclaim in their own promotional literature:

"Learn grammar by listening – not studying. You don't need to study grammar to speak correctly. Your internal language center intuitively knows when something sounds correct. For example, if someone said, 'Him and I goed to the store' you would automatically know it isn't correct."⁷

Really? A native speaker of English might possibly know "automatically" that *\*goed* is a no-go expression (excuse the feeble pun!) in English – though even that is by no means guaranteed. To take another example, it is common (in both senses of the word) for native English speakers to converse routinely in expressions like: "Where was you yesterday?" For the most part, however, accurate grammar is not a prerequisite to understanding or even speaking a language, which is one of the reasons why this book concentrates very heavily on vocabulary rather than grammar. And over-punctilious attention

---

⁶ See Chapter 14, SOUND MOVES.
⁷ Quoted by Nick Dahlhoff at: alllanguageresources.com. pimsleur -vs-rosetta-stone-or-possibly-neither.

to grammatical niceties can also result in some amusing howlers. As a barrister I once encountered a solicitor whom I dubbed "Mr Whom," because, not being sure whether to use "who" or "whom" but assuming that "whom" was the more "genteel" term, he would use "whom" all the time, as in: "I don't know *whom* is representing the defendant" instead of: "I don't know *who* is representing the defendant." The point is that the words "who is representing the defendant" form a separate clause, of which "who" is the subject. "Whom" would be wrong here, because it is used only for objects, not subjects. So, in being extra-careful to demonstrate his grammatical accuracy, this solicitor only succeeded in revealing himself to be an ignoramus.

**Language Transfer**

Unfortunately, language courses that set out to avoid the pitfalls of the leading programs are not necessarily any better. One that comes highly recommended by some of the critics of the big brands is Language Transfer, which describes itself as "The Thinking Method," and "promises you an instant sense of progress, and an ensuing learning journey like none [sic] other!" It is not too encouraging to encounter this solecism right at the outset. The program is supposedly based on conversation. Two of the earliest phrases to which the learner is introduced in the French course are: *Je veux le gâteau* ("I want the cake") and *Tu veux le gâteau* ("You want the cake"). Both are technically correct, but not very practical. The setting for this type of phrase is a restaurant or café, where it would be as impolite in French as in English to say "I want," rather than, for example, "I would like," which in French is *"Je voudrais."* Moreover, as most conversations that language learners are likely to need will be with strangers, the first word for "you" to which they should be introduced is the polite term, *vous*. The familiar form, *tu*, which is the one used from the outset in the Language Transfer course, is applicable only to conversations between children, teenagers, students, family and friends, or when an adult is speaking to a child, an animal – or God.

To be on the safe side, you should use *vous*, which should therefore take pride of place in any French language learning course.

But even the phrase *"Je voudrais le gâteau"* is not particularly idiomatic, which is important in a course geared to conversation. Unless you are wanting to buy a whole cake and pointing it out to the shop assistant, the relevant phrase should be *"Je voudrais du gateau,"* meaning "I would like some cake," literally, "I would like of the cake" – "of the..." being a very common French idiom for "some." As cake plays such a prominent part right at the start of the Language Transfer course, it might have been relevant and interesting to point out that the English phrase "It's a piece of cake," meaning that something is easy, is inverted in French. *"Ce n'est pas de la tarte,"* literally, "It's not tart" or "It's not pie," means "It's not easy," so the concept of cake, tart or pie as representing something pleasant is the same in both languages, but the viewpoint is different.

The Language Transfer French course actually refers occasionally to etymological links between French and English words, but, as the program is purely audio, the relevant words have to be spelt out, which greatly reduces the value of this feature. Links between words have to be seen in print in order to make any real impression on the memory, especially in a language like French, which is not exactly phonetic (or phonemic).

There is certainly no shortage of potential pitfalls in learning a new language, but there is also no reason why it should not be fun. One of the most enjoyable and valuable language learning tools, but one that is sadly neglected, is etymological links between words. The English language is perfectly positioned for this purpose, having a foot, so to speak, in both the Germanic and the Romance linguistic camps, enabling easy access to a wide range of European languages as well as a fun way to improve your English vocabulary, regardless whether you are a native English speaker, the speaker of English as a second language, or a learner of English. If this book assists your language development in any way, it will have achieved its objective.

# CHAPTER 1

# HOW TO USE THIS BOOK

THIS BOOK IS titled *Gateway English – How to boost your English word power and unlock new languages*. But exactly how can the book be used to help you to achieve these two goals? It has to be emphasized that this book is not concerned with pronunciation, grammar or syntax, only vocabulary. Is that because I don't consider those other aspects of language learning important? Not at all. But pronunciation, which is of very great importance, can't be taught by a book. As for structure, or grammar and syntax, I do believe they should be subordinated to vocabulary, differing in this (as in practically everything else) from Noam Chomsky and his preoccupation with grammar and syntax – even to the point of his insisting – against clear evidence to the contrary – that every language must have "recursion," the ability to combine clauses with one subordinate to another. I discuss this more fully elsewhere in the book.

**Pronunciation**

As mentioned above, learning pronunciation from a book is practically impossible. Even such aids as the International Phonetic Alphabet (IPA) and other phonetic ways of representing sounds are of very little practical use. And the IPA has the added problem that it is daunting to most ordinary people, almost like a whole new language in itself. It is essential to listen to native speakers' pronunciation, or at least to recordings, and to repeat the sounds that you hear. But beware, it is just as possible to be "tone deaf" in regard to language as it is in music, where someone thinks they are repeating a particular sound but in fact are not. A friend of mine with a degree in German was incredulous when I pointed out to him that the German word *Mann* is not pronounced the same as its English equivalent, **man**, and that the /a/ sound in English **man** doesn't exist in German at all!

Certain sounds are undoubtedly difficult for foreigners to replicate, e.g. the guttural sounds in Dutch, the German, /ch/ after /e/ or /i/, the French uvular /r/, the Polish /Ł/, or the clicks in certain African languages. But most mispronunciations are easily avoided, resulting from sticking too closely to the spelling of the written word read as if it were English. An example is the common mispronunciation by English speakers of the German or Dutch [v] as equivalent to the English [v], when the correct pronunciation is like the English [f]. Similarly, the mispronunciation of German or Dutch [w] as equivalent to English [w] instead of as English [v]. The name *Volkswagen* is a good example, which is routinely mispronounced even by TV presenters and others who should know better as "Volkswaggon" (just as if that was an English word) instead of as "Folksvahgen."

As Mario Pei put it in his *How to Learn Languages and What Languages to Learn* (1966), "French is a language of beautiful but difficult sounds, so far as a speaker of English is concerned." (p. 160). Though, as I have said, pronunciation cannot be learnt from a book, the books on learning French seem to want to prove the point. They generally say that a [c] is pronounced like a [k] except before an [e] or [i] and that a [p] is pronounced as in English. They also don't always mention that a [d] after an [r] is silent. Yet to the English ear the French family name *Picard* will probably sound something like "Bigar." Those are the easy sounds. Of course, any French learner will be introduced to:

- The pronunciation of French [u], [eu] and [oeu].
- The nasalization of vowels before an [n], as in *action*, *nation* or *association*.

- The *"liaison"* between a final consonant and an initial vowel, as in *nous avons* "we have," which is pronounced *"noo-zah-vong"* or *deux ans* "two years," pronounced *"der-zang."*

## Structure: grammar and syntax

If you want to ask the way to the nearest toilet in a foreign language, you only need to know the word for "toilet," and you will be understood regardless of your grammatical accuracy. But that does not mean you should ignore grammar altogether. A friend of mine with a keen interest in language makes a beeline to the formation and use of the subjunctive in any new language that he comes across, and the more tenses of the subjunctive there are the better, as far as he is concerned! In learning most languages the subjunctive can safely be left to a later stage, unless you want to replicate the quirks of a particular dialect. In Irish English, for example, it is considered polite to use circumlocutory expressions such as: "Would you be wanting a mineral water with your lunch?" The basic structure of a language is all you need to begin with. You can always graduate to the pluperfect subjunctive later on if need be!

The gender of nouns in most languages is another overblown problem. There is the apocryphal story that I relate elsewhere in the book about the customer in a French restaurant who, spotting a fly in his soup, alerts the waiter in his best French: *"Garçon, il y a un mouche dans ma soupe"* ("Waiter, there's a fly in my soup"). *"Une mouche, Monsieur,"* retorts the waiter. "What damned good eyesight those Frenchies have!" remarks the customer to his fellow diners." The point of course is that the waiter was merely correcting the customer's grammar, because *mouche*, French for "fly," is feminine, while the customer thought the waiter was identifying the sex of that particular fly. According to some adherents of the Sapir-Whorf school, according to which the language you speak affects or shapes the way you think, the grammatical gender of a noun will have an effect on the way you think about it. As it happens, the word for "fly" in Romance and Germanic languages is feminine, whereas in Hebrew, for example, the word for "fly," *zvuv,* is masculine. Do Hebrew speakers really have a different concept of "fly" from, say, French speakers? And what about someone who is bilingual in, say, Hebrew and German? The word for "fly" is masculine in Hebrew but feminine in German, so does their perception of "fly" change according to whether they are speaking one language or the other? This sort of reasoning is heavily redolent of irrational political correctness.

The real point of the story about the fly in the soup is that the waiter understood the customer perfectly despite his grammatical faux pas. And that will generally be the case. There are a few words in some languages which exist in both a masculine and feminine form, with different meanings. But there is rarely any danger of misunderstanding, though a slight chance of embarrassment – and the French, in particular, can be quite cruel in that respect. Here are a few examples of such doublets:

- ❖ *Un livre* (masculine) means "a book," while *une livre* (feminine) is "a pound" either in reference to the British currency or to a pound weight, for, though France pioneered the metric system, the term *livre* is still used in common parlance to refer to half a kilogramme, which is actually a little more than a pound in weight; in Canada the pound is still used as a weight side by side with the metric system. But the chances of mistaking a pound weight or money for a book are zero. Blame the duplication on the French tendency to shorten Latin words. In Latin the two words are quite distinct: *liber, libri* "book" as against *libra, librae* "pound" (the Roman pound of 12 ounces).

- ❖ *Un tour* (masculine) means "a turn, a tour," as in *Le Tour de France,* the famous cycle race, from Latin *torno, tornare, tornatum,* "to turn on a lathe, to polish," from which come English **tour, detour, attorney, turn, return**. *Une tour* (feminine) means "a tower" as in *La Tour Eiffel,* from Latin *turris* "tower," giving rise to both English **tower** and **turret**. Here, too, there is little chance of confusion between the masculine and feminine French *tour.*

- ❖ *Un voile* (masculine) is "a veil," also now used for "hijab," while *une voile* (feminine) is "a sail." Both come from Latin *velum* "a cloth, curtain," the plural of which, *vela,* meant "a sail." Latin *velum* is neuter, so its plural is *vela*, but this was mistaken in Vulgar Latin for a feminine singular. Hence the two variants in French.

❖ *Un moule* (masculine), from Latin *modulus* "a measure," diminutive of Latin *modus* ("measure"), means "a mould/mold" and hence "a baking tin/pan," while *une moule* (feminine), almost invariably found only in the plural, *moules*, as in that signature French dish, *moules marinières*, is from Latin *musculus* ("a muscle," actually a diminutive of Latin *mus* "mouse"!), and means "a mussel." Once again, not much chance of confusion here!

In some languages it is quite usual for the subject of the verb not to be expressed at all, because the subject is clearly indicated by the verb ending. These languages, known technically as "null-subject" or "pro-drop" (for "pronoun-dropping") languages, include Latin, Italian, Spanish and Portuguese, Catalan, Romanian, Greek, the Slavic languages and Hindi in the Indo-European family, plus Basque, Hungarian, Finnish, Estonian, Arabic, Hebrew, Chinese, Japanese, Korean and many more, e.g. Latin: *Veni, vidi, vici* ("I came, I saw, I conquered"). Julius Caesar's famous boast is *the* classic example of the pro-drop feature par excellence! Caesar was not only a brilliant general, a popular politician and a skillful author, but also a learned grammarian and the author of a book on Latin grammar, which however (fortunately perhaps) has perished. It will be noticed that the word *ego* ("I"), the subject of all three verbs is missing in Caesar's terse slogan. It is always possible to add the subject for emphasis, but it is not needed for clarity, and this is one of the features that gave Latin its lapidary character. Another almost equally famous Latin tag is Descartes's *Cogito ergo sum* ("I think, therefore I am"), which again omits the subjects of both verbs. Here we have an interesting comparison, because Descartes wrote it first in French, which is not a pro-drop language and in which it is: *Je pense, donc je suis,* which is not nearly as memorable as the Latin version. Portuguese: *Tenho muito frio* ("I am very cold"); *Faça favor de falar mais devagar* ("Please speak more slowly"); *Não deixes para amanhã o que podes fazer hoje* (translation of Benjamin Franklin's advice: "Don't put off until tomorrow what you can do today"). Italian: *Ho venti anni* ("I am twenty years old"); *Da quanto tempo aspetta?* ("How long have you been waiting?"); *Piove sul bagnato* (lit. "It rains on wet ground," so "It never rains but it pours"). The subject pronouns of all these sentences are omitted because they are clearly indicated by the verb endings.

French differs from the other Romance languages in needing the subject always to be expressed. The reason for this is the French tendency to swallow verb endings, in the sense that they are often silent. But this is actually an advantage to the learner, as the verb endings can often be ignored in conversation. Take for example *parler,* "to speak," the conjugation of the present tense of which runs as follows: *je parle, tu parles, il/elle parle,* **nous parlons, vous parlez***, ils/elles parlent.* With the exception of the two shown in bold, all the verb forms are pronounced the same, simply as "parl."

In the Germanic languages, including English, the subject pronoun must always be expressed. The need for this in English is pretty obvious, as verb endings are not very helpful, e.g. **I move, you** (singular) **move, he/she/it moves, we move, you** (plural) **move, they move**. Here all forms of the verb have the same ending except for the third person singular, and in the past tense all forms are exactly the same: **I/you/he/she/it/we/you/they moved**.

Grammar and syntax contain many twists and turns, which can be quite daunting and most of which can be learnt gradually. However, there are a few basics that really need to be assimilated early on and a few common mistakes to be guarded against. Though English has largely shed its inflections, those few inflections that have survived should be mastered. As I mentioned in the introduction, a surprising number of native English speakers are guilty of the most elementary grammatical errors all the time, such as saying, "Where was you yesterday?"

Another common error emanating from the mouths and even the pens of people who should know better, is this kind of remark: "Best wishes from my wife and I," which not only grates on the ear but reveals a complete misunderstanding of a really basic feature. Those guilty of this kind of solecism would never make the mistake of saying "Best wishes from I." They would say, quite correctly, "Best wishes from me." So they have to be taught that adding another person in does not change this, and they must say: "Best wishes from my wife and me." But going to the opposite extreme of overly pedantic grammatical correctness can be almost as irritating – and is usually a sign that the perpetrator is not a native speaker of English. What I mean is phrases like "It is I." This is perfectly correct grammatically, because "It" and "I" refer to the same person, or, to put it in technical language, "It" is the subject and "I" is the **complement** (because it "completes" the sentence, not **compliment**, although that is really a misspelling of the same word.) In French you could never say *"C'est je"* for "It's me," but, as King Louis XIV is reputed to have said, *"L'état c'est moi,"* (lit. "The state it's me," or "I am the state"). In German, on the other hand, "It's me" becomes *"Das bin ich."*

## Learning vocabulary through etymology

Once you have a rough idea of the basic structure of the language that you are learning – or even before – you can tackle vocabulary, which is far more enjoyable than grammar provided you do it the right way. That is where this book comes in – word-building by means of etymological links – as distinct from "memory palaces," other mnemonic aids or random links, as promoted in so many different language learning courses.

**Etymology** is not just the study of word origins but also of the true, essential meaning of words, a pure Greek word, *etymologia*, from *etymos*, meaning "true, real, actual," from Greek *eteos* "true, real." Cicero coined the Latin term *veriloquium* (lit. "speaking the truth") as a translation of Greek *etymologia*. Words change their meaning over time, sometimes quite radically, but a word's essential kernel of meaning is rarely lost. It is this core meaning or essence that is revealed by a word's etymology. Take for example the English word

**conventional**, in the sense of "ordinary, commonplace, unoriginal, traditional." It is obviously from **convention**, which means "custom, tradition, rule of conduct" as in: "Driving on the left was a **convention** rejected by the French Revolution." But **convention** can also means "an official meeting, assemblage," as in: "This year's Democratic Party **convention** will be held in Chicago." Now it is not hard to trace **convention** back to Latin *con-* "together" + *venio, venire, veni, ventum* "to come," so literally "a coming together," But how does the concept of "a coming together" relate to that of **conventional** as "unoriginal"? A **conventional** style of architecture, for example, is so called because it was originally accepted, agreed upon – a form of "coming together." So, a **convent**, as a house occupied by a community of nuns, is quite literally "a coming together," and **convenient** essentially means "agreeable," well illustrated by this extract from Starkey's *England* (1538) as quoted in the OED: "The best kind of lyfe and most **convenyent** to the nature of man." The same concept is found in cognates in the Romance languages, like Spanish *convenir*, "to agree" *conveniente* "suitable, advisable," *convenio* "agreement," *convento* "convent, (in Argentina) tenement house", is particularly well illustrated by the French homonym *convention,* as in the phrase *convention de vente,* "a contract of sale," a contract being a "meeting of minds."

## Learning vocabulary – wrong approach

Before turning to the right approach, let me knock on the head a typical "random links" method currently available, namely Olly Richards's Iwillteachyoualanguage.com. Here is an example of his "method" (from email dated 07-02-20):

> Take the Spanish verb 'caber' (to fit). 'Caber' looks very
> different from the English word 'fit', right? Well, yes, until you
> break it down:
>     – cab
>     – ber
> Now what do you see?

A cab and a bear!
Now, ask yourself: "How on Earth can a **cab** *fit* a **bear** inside???"
....and you've got a striking mental image that means you'll never forget the verb *to fit* in Spanish.
Need to remember how to say "to fit" in Spanish? Just ask yourself if a *cab* can **fit** a bear inside?
Cab > bear > cab-bear = *caber*!

This example of Olly Richards's "memory technique" is illustrated by a photograph of a large brown bear leaning out of the window of a New York taxi, which is certainly a memorable image. But is this really a practical a way of learning vocabulary? Here are a few reasons why I believe it is nothing of the kind:

- ❖ Memorable though the image is, why should it mean "to fit"? It could equally well be remembered as meaning "drive," "roar" or "passenger." And the bear does not actually fit in the taxi anyway: it's far too big! So "fit" is unlikely to be uppermost in the learner's mind.
- ❖ And why should you remember it as cab + bear anyway? Why not as taxi + bear or bear + taxi, or maybe even as bear + escape?
- ❖ Olly Richards provides a graphic image for this one word, but he evidently expects his "students" to conjure up suitable images in their own minds for other words. You would need to have the imagination of a Shakespeare to visualize a suitable image for every new word!
- ❖ In what sense does *caber* mean "to fit" anyway? The English word has a variety of meanings, some transitive (with an object) and some intransitive (without an object), e.g. (a) These jeans don't **fit** me any more. (b) The tailor **fitted** him for a new suit. (c) Your conclusion does not **fit** the facts. (d) This car has been **fitted** with a new gearbox. (e) He did not **fit** in with the other team members. Olly Richards gives no indication of which of these meanings *caber* would "fit" (pun intended).
- ❖ Not a single sentence or phrase is given to show how *caber* is used.
- ❖ *Caber* means "to fit," so, grammatically speaking, it is an infinitive. But how do you say, "it fits," "they used to fit," "it is fitted," to take just a few examples? Olly Richards provides no guidance.

## HOW TO USE THIS BOOK

❖ The pronunciation is seriously misleading. The [a] in *caber* is not pronounced like the [a] in English **cab**, as Olly suggests. That sound does not even exist in Spanish. Instead, the way that [a] is pronounced is similar to the [u] in English "cub." And to assume, as Olly Richards appears to do, that the [b] in *caber* is pronounced the same as the [b] in English **cab** is also incorrect. The Spanish [b], when followed by a vowel, is pronounced midway between English /b/ and /v/. That is why, for example, the city known in English as "Havana" is spelt "Habana" in Spanish.

❖ *Caber* does mean "to fit," but only in a restricted sense – intransitive in respect of fitting into a space or a gap (Collins Spanish Dictionary, 2011). When it comes to "fit" meaning matching facts, the same Dictionary gives three other words: *cuadrar* or *corresponder* or *coincidir con* – but not *caber*.

❖ However, there is an important Spanish idiomatic phrase with *caber*: *no cabe duda* "there is no doubt about it." Needless to say, Olly does not mention this.

❖ This phrase has nothing to do with "fitting," but it gives us an important clue about *caber*.

❖ *Caber* is actually derived from one of the most basic and important of all Latin verbs: *capio, capere, cepi, captum*, meaning "to take, grasp, seize, occupy." It does not take much to figure out this connection and you don't need any imagination to make the connection. The original meaning of *no cabe duda* was presumably literally something like "there is no taking of doubt," hence "there is no room for doubt." With the use of **etymology** – which, remember, means "the true meaning" of a word (see above) – we are able to penetrate to the real essence of *caber*. Another idiomatic use of *caber* is: *Cabe que venga más tarde* ("He may possibly come later"), which again gives us some insight into the true meaning of *caber* as indicating what we might call "wiggle room," hence possibility. A similar concept is discernible in Portuguese, where *caber* has a slightly wider range of meaning than in Spanish and where *Cabe a ela decidir* means "It's up to her to decide."

Knowledge that *caber* is from Latin *capio, capere, captum* opens up a huge vista of other related words: English derivatives from *capio*: **capacity**, **capacious**, **capture**, **caption** and, noting the change of the [a] in *capio* when compounded with a prefix: **accept, deceive, except, exception, receive, reception**.

This opens up a whole Indo-European panorama, because Latin *capio* is cognate with words in other Indo-European languages, including Greek *kapto, kaptein* "to swallow," and a whole host of Germanic words including German *haben*, Dutch *hebben*, Afrikaans *hê*, Danish *har*, Norwegian *ha*, Swedish *ha* – and English **have, heave, heavy, haven**. How come these Germanic words all have an [h] instead of the Latin [c] or Greek [k]? All these words descend from an unrecorded Proto-Indo-European (PIE) word, whose reconstructed root is *\*kap*, meaning essentially "to grasp." Latin and Greek retain the original initial /k/ sound, while in the Germanic family this underwent a sound shift to an /h/ sound, as is explained by Grimm's Law.[8]

Which is better, to rack (or even wrack) your brains to come up with some quirky random image for each new word that you want to learn – or to link the word in question effortlessly with other words related to it, unlocking not only the meaning of that particular word but also many other words as well, both in English and, if you so wish, in other languages into the bargain?

The decision of which of these two routes to choose is, I would suggest, a no-brainer. The etymological route is not only far easier but more interesting and more productive as well, while Olly Richards's and other similar mnemonic devices place great strain on the memory and are, not to put too fine a point on it, a hard slog. Why, then, do so many language learning courses push "memory palaces" and other artificial mnemonic devices?

An important reason is the demise of comparative philology, the professional, non-pedantic and practical study of etymology, which has now all but disappeared from universities across the globe. Associated with that is the development in academia of two areas,

---

[8] See Chapter 8, A GRIMM TALE.

neither of which is concerned with practical language learning: namely, Chomskyan linguistics, which is fixated on abstruse theories of grammar and syntax, and non-Chomskyan linguistics, which, in an attempt to claim the title of "science" has developed its own complex terminology – aptly but disparagingly labelled "algebra" by critics like the late Professor "Joppy" Jopson of Cambridge – and shows no interest in the teaching or learning of actual languages.

## Learning vocabulary through etymology – the right approach

Here are the major steps involved in building up your vocabulary in any language, whether you have some knowledge of that language already or not:

(1) Identify to what language family and sub-family the language belongs. This book concentrates on the Indo-European family and the Romance and Germanic sub-families.

(2) This classification will lead you to certain telltale features. If it is a Romance language, that means it's a daughter language of Latin, its relationship with which is determined by certain rules. You don't need to know any Latin to figure this out: there are more than enough close Latin derivatives in English for this purpose. So, if you are trying to remember, say, either the English or the French word fragile "breakable, easily broken," it would not take you long to recognize the close connection between the two words which, as it happens, share not only the same spelling (though not the same pronunciation), but also very much the same meaning.

(3) Going further into it, you will find that both the English and the French words are from Latin *fragilis,* "breakable, easily broken, brittle, fragile, frail (physically or mentally)," from Latin *frango, frangere, fregi, fractum* "to break." Latin verbs are generally listed in dictionaries with four "principal parts," representing the present tense, the present infinitive, the perfect tense and the perfect participle (the "supine"), respectively, to give you the different stems for forming all the tenses and moods of the verb in this highly inflected language. In this book, I generally give only the first, second and fourth principal parts of Latin

verbs, because the third principal part is not relevant for derivatives, which come only from the present stem or the supine stem.

(4) Though Latin *fragilis* is from *frango*, you will notice that the [n] in *frango* has dropped out, as the [n] presumably essentially represents a nasalization, and the [n] is also absent from the third and fourth principal parts of the verb as well. And in the supine the [g] turns to [c]. This is for euphony, as it is almost impossible to pronounce a /g/ sound followed by a /t/ sound. Try it! And always remember that spelling is merely an attempt to represent the sounds of the spoken language – at least initially. (There are of course some languages, notably Greek, in which the pronunciation has undergone a fundamental shift while the orthography (spelling) still reflects a much earlier version of the spoken language).

(5) Both English and French have other derivatives from Latin *frango*: (a) **frangible**, the same in both written form (but not pronunciation) and meaning, "easily breakable." (b) English and French **fragment**, "a part broken off." (c) English **infringe** – note how the [a] has changed to [i] – a common shift when a word is compounded with a prefix (cf. Latin *facio, facere, factum* "to do, make," from which come English **deficient, efficient, sufficient**). (d) English **fraction, fracture**.

(6) It is important to recognize certain major sound shifts that have taken place from Latin to French, such as, notably, the dropping of the intervocalic consonant (the consonant between two vowels). In the case of *fragilis*, this gave rise to Old French *fraile* (Modern French *frêle*) "weak, infirm," from which we get English **frail** "(of people) physically weak, infirm."

(7) Applying Grimm's Law, we find that Latin *frango, frangere, fractum* has Germanic cognates, all meaning "to break," including German *brechen*, Dutch *breken*, Afrikaans *breek* – and English **break** and **breach**, as in "breach of contract."[9]

---

[9] See Chapter 8, A GRIMM TALE.

## Applied etymology

Using etymological links to grow your English vocabulary and unlock new Indo-European languages requires the **application** of the steps outlined above. And the words **apply** and **application** are very apt in this regard – as in this digital age the abbreviation "**app**" for "**application**" now seems to **apply** (pun intended) to practically any computer program designed for a particular purpose.

An apocryphal school principal pondering how to treat an unruly student sent to him to be disciplined, concluded that this called for **applied** psychology. "So," he reminisced, "I reached for the biggest **applied psychology** book on my bookshelves – and **applied** it." That kind of discipline is no longer allowed, but it highlights the words **apply** and **application**, now abbreviated to "**app**," which has become so ubiquitous. The English words **apply** and **application** have a wide range of meanings, which it is important to know and understand. The following are all perfectly good English sentences using **apply** and **application** in a number of different ways:

- For a clearer complexion, **apply** this cream twice a day.
- Your **application** for the vacant post was successful.
- I **applied** for that position, but they said I was over-qualified.
- That description does not **apply** to you.
- When following another car too closely, **apply** your brakes.
- You really need to **apply** yourself more diligently to your studies.

In all these examples **apply** and **application** are used in a figurative sense. Their origin is Latin *applico, applicare, applicatum* "to attach, join, connect," from Latin *ad-* "to, towards" + *plico, plicare, plicatum* "to fold," probably from PIE *\*plek-* "to plait, twine," and hence "to fold" (de Vaan), cognate with "suffixed form" *\*plek-t-e/o-* "to plait, twine" (AHDIER), giving rise to Latin *plecto, plectere, plexum* "to plait, twist," cognate with Greek *pleko*, "to plait, twine, twist, weave, braid." So the basic underlying meaning is a physical one of plaiting or folding, which has given rise to a large number of derivatives, most of which are generaly used in a figurative sense. The following English derivatives reveal the imagery or metaphor involved: **simple, simplicity, duplex, duplicate, duplicitous, duplicity, complex, complicate, complicit, complicity, accomplice, implicate, implicit, explicit, explicate, replica, replicate, multiple, multiplicity, plexus**. There is also another layer of derivatives, chiefly via French: **plait, pleat, ply, plywood, pliant, pliable, comply, splay, deploy, display, employ, employer, employee, employment, imply, multiply, reply**.

- ❖ **Plexus**, from the perfect participle (supine) of Latin *plecto, plectere, plexum*,"twisted, braided," used chiefly in the phrase **solar plexus**, referring to the network of nerves in the abdomen, "the pit of the stomach," the adjective **solar** from Latin *sol, solis* "the sun," presumably because of its central position.

- ❖ From **simple**, from Latin *simplex* lit. "with one fold," it is easy both to figure out the meaning of all the other derivatives and also to build your vocabulary around this concept. German *Einfach*, lit. "one fold" hence "simple", and Dutch and Afrikaans *eenvoudig*, lit. "one folded," so "simple," share the same image. English **manifold** as an adjective, meaning "many and various," also shares this image, while **manifold** as a noun is often used in a technical sense referring to a pipe fitting with several outlets, or a "pipe running from a carburetor to the cylinders in an internal combustion engine of an automobile" (EOL) – a return to a more literal image of "with many folds."

- ❖ **Duplex** in the sense of a two-storey apartment likewise retains the literal image, but then **duplicate** draws slightly away from the literal image to mean "to copy." The image underlying **duplicitous** and **duplicity** is a slight further extension, namely "double-dealing," hence "dishonesty, deception."

- ❖ **Complex, complicated**, (from complicate), from Latin *com-* ("with, together" or just with intensive effect) + *plecto, plectere, plexum* ("to plait, twist, weave"), so "intertwined," hence "intricate, difficult to explain, made of interlocking parts." In psychology, a term coined by Carl Gustav Jung, which he described as "a node in the unconscious," so "a knot of unconscious feelings and beliefs," or "a connected group of repressed desires," as in Oedipus complex, inferiority complex, God complex.

- **Implicate**, lit. "to fold in," so "to involve someone in a crime or misdeed," but **imply**, **implicit** and **implication** extend the concept of "folding in" into the realm of speech, as in: "The news report implied that he was murdered." Not to be confused with **infer**, as in: "We infer from the evidence that he was murdered." **Infer** means "to deduce from facts" while **imply** means "to hint at."[10] **Infer**, also of Latin origin, comes from another large family, the irregular Latin verb *fero, ferre, tuli, latum* "to bear, carry," with derivatives including **confer**, **conference**, **defer**, **deference**, **differ**, **difference**, **differential**, **ferret**, **indifferent**, **offer**, **prefer**, **proffer**, **refer**, **reference**, **suffer**, **transfer**, **vociferous**, with Germanic cognates **bear**, **birth**, **burden** and derivatives from Greek cognate *phoros* "bearer" from Greek *phero* "to bear, carry," including **metaphor**, **euphoria**, **phosphorus**.

- "Simple" in other European languages: There are four main roots among European languages for the concept of "simple": (a) that represented by English **simple**, French *simple*, Italian *semplice*, Spanish *simple*, Portuguese *simples*, Romanian *simplu* – all from Latin *simplex* (see above) (b) that represented by German *einfach*, Dutch and Afrikaans *eenvoudig*, Greek *haplos* – all of which also mean literally "one fold" (c) that represented by Danish, Norwegian and Swedish *enkel* literally "one, only" plus a similar suffix to Latin *singulus* "single, apiece, one each, and (d) that represented by Russian *prostój*, Bulgarian *prost*, Polish *prosty*, Czech and Slovak *prostý*, Serbian and Croatian *prőst*, Slovene *prost*, Lithuanian *paprastas* – all of which mean "straight, simple."

---

[10] Merriam-Webster.

# CHAPTER 2

# NOT ANGLES BUT ANGELS

ONE DAY IN about the year 586 a Roman nobleman happened to spot some good-looking, blond young boys for sale in the slave market in Rome. On enquiring where they were from, he was told that they were Angles, members of one of the Germanic tribes that had migrated to Britain after the collapse of the western Roman Empire. "*Non Angli sed angeli,*" the nobleman is reputed to have said: "Not Angles but angels." And when this same nobleman became Pope Gregory I, he despatched a mission to England to convert the slave boys' fellow countrymen to Christianity.

The language spoken by the young boys was a minor Germanic dialect, Anglo-Saxon or Old English, which was destined to take wing and become the most influential political, commercial and educational medium of communication in the world – the English language – with a vast vocabulary drawn chiefly from French, Latin and Greek successively piled on top of its Germanic foundation.

Although only about a quarter of English words are of Germanic origin, these words form the bedrock of the English language, which is why English is classified as a Germanic language. This Germanic substratum has provided the language with much of its most basic vocabulary, including **head, heart, father, mother, brother, tree, fire, work, new, young, eat, water**. As a Germanic language, English is related to the rest of the Germanic family of languages, which in turn all form part of a huge interlocking superfamily of Indo-European languages.

But, before venturing into that exciting territory, let us concentrate for a moment on English and its Germanic cousins, which include Dutch, Afrikaans, German, Danish, Swedish, Norwegian (both Bokmål and Nynorsk) and Icelandic.

English contains a common stock of Germanic words which can be used to learn other Germanic languages. Here for example are the opening words of the Bible in four Germanic languages:

**English**: In the beginning God created the heaven and the earth.
**Dutch**: *In den beginne schiep God den hemel en de aarde.*
**Danish**: *I Begyndelsen skabte Gud Himmelen og Jorden.*
**German**: *Am Anfang schuf Gott Himmel und Erde.*

The only non-Germanic feature of the English version is the word **create**, which is of Latin origin. All the other Germanic languages use *schaffen* (German) or a related word. The English words **shape** and **shave** are related to these but have developed divergent meanings. The word has a cognate (that is, a word with a common origin) in Latin *scabies* ("itch, mange"), which is also now found in English. The connection between "itch" and "create" may not be immediately obvious, but Latin *scabies* refers not so much to the condition as to the sufferer's reaction to it, by scratching. And, from "scratch" it is not a big jump to "scrape" and then to "shape" and finally to "create."

Written English contains a higher proportion of Latin-based words than spoken or colloquial English, and formal, academic and scientific vocabulary is even more Latinate than ordinary written English. Words of Germanic Anglo-Saxon origin, forming as they do the bedrock of the English language, are literally the most down-to-earth – short, direct and unpretentious. Words coming from French tend to be more formal, while direct Latin borrowings are likely to be more elevated in tone, less familiar and more pretentious. A drowning man does not shout "**Assist! Assist!**" (Latin via French) or even "**Aid! Aid!**" (French indirectly from Latin) but "**Help! Help!**" (Anglo-Saxon).

## To have and to hold

"To have and to hold, from this day forward ... until death do us part" – traditional Christian marriage vows.

According to wordfrequency.info, **have** is the most frequently used verb (and the eighth most frequently used word altogether) in American English, and, I presume, in British English as well, although this rating is owed quite largely to the use of **have** to form the present perfect tense, as in **"I have eaten." "Have you seen the wolf?" "We have never voted." Hold** is rather less frequent, checking in at number 214. Like all the most frequently used English words, both these words are of Germanic origin. Other related words to **have** include **heave**, "to lift, throw," used either literally or figuratively, as in "to heave a sigh of relief," also **heave-ho**, colloquially in the sense of "dismissal," as in "he was given the old **heave-ho**." Derivatives from **have** include **behave**, lit. "to handle, conduct oneself (properly)," **behoove** ("to be fit or proper"), the prefix **be-** being a common English intensive or causative prefix, as found in **berate, becalm, belittle, befuddle, besmirch**. The words for "to have" in the other Germanic languages are all closely related to **have**: German *haben*, Dutch *hebben*, Danish *har*, Norwegian *ha*, Swedish *ha*.

**Hold** likewise has cognates in the other Germanic languages: German *halten*, Dutch *houden*, Afrikaans *hou*, Danish and Norwegian *holde*, Swedish *hålla*, all meaning "to hold." English **hold** has derivatives such as **behold**, often used in a jocular sense, as in "lo and behold," and also **beholden**, used chiefly in a formal legal sense, meaning "obliged, obligated." Its first appearance in print was in about 1340: "I am highly **beholden** to you and ever more will be servant to yourselves." (spelling modernized – *Sir Gawain and the Green Knight*). **Hold**, both as a verb and as a noun, is found in a number of common compounds and phrases, e.g. **holdup, stranglehold, hold on, hold off, hold down, hold your own, hold your horses, hold your tongue, hold water.**

In the 14th century Middle English "chivalric romance" *Sir Gawain and the Green Knight,* the word **knight** is sometimes replaced by the word *****gome**. Both are Germanic words. English **knight** is related to German *Knecht,* meaning "a servant, laborer, farm-hand." The German word has retained the lowly status of the original, while the English word, starting out from Anglo-Saxon *cniht,* "boy, servant," became the term for a military servant or follower of the king, and from there a member of an order of chivalry. In a Parliament Roll of 1411, quoted in the OED, knights are listed above esquires and yeomen.

The word *****gome** meaning "man," which is now obsolete, is last cited by the OED in 1515. Coupled with **bride**, we find *****bridegome**, meaning "a newly married man," in Middle English down to 1340 (OED), but in Tyndale's translation of the Bible of 1526 we find the word spelt "**brydegrome**" and in 1580 as "**bridegroome**." The change in spelling was influenced by the word **groom**, which originally meant "boy, young man" or "male servant, attendant on the king or nobleman," and now chiefly "employee who looks after horses." None of the other Germanic languages added that intrusive [-r-] in their equivalent of **bridegroom**: German *Bräutigam,* Dutch and Afrikaans *bruidegom,* Danish and Norwegian *brudgom,* Swedish *brudgum.* English **groom** as a verb has a wide range of meanings, from "tidying up someone's appearance" to "coaching a political candidate" to "pretending to befriend a child with a view to sexual abuse."

An important cognate of *****gome** is Latin *homo, hominis* ("man, human being") as in **homo sapiens** (lit. "wise man"). Latin *homo* gave rise to *humanus,* which means the same as its English derivative **human** and is probably related to Latin *humus,* "earth, ground, soil." So Latin *homo* is literally "earthling." Cf. the similar conceptual link between "earth" and "man" in Hebrew, where *adam* means "man" – hence the name of the first man, Adam – and *adamah* means "earth." Of course, there is no etymological link between Hebrew *adam/adamah* and Latin *homo/humus.* And there is no link of any kind between Latin *homo* ("man") and the English slang abbreviation **homo** for **homosexual**, the **homo-** part of which is from Greek *homos* ("common, the same, equal, similar"), which has been used to construct many English words, e.g. **homogeneous** ("of the same kind"), **homeopathy** and those three stooges, **homonyms**, **homophones** and **homographs**.

It is also worth pointing out that Greek *homos* is related to Greek *hama* meaning "together with, at the same time," which is cognate with English **same** and words in the other Germanic languages meaning "together": German *zusammen*, Dutch *samen*, Afrikaans *saam*, Danish and Norwegian *sammen*, Swedish *tillsammans*. English **seem**, **seemly**, **some** and **-some** as in **threesome**, **handsome**, **winsome**, are from the same origin.

Another cognate with Greek *hama* is Latin *similis*, from which we get English **similar**, which also shares its meaning, together with **simulate**, **simultaneous**, **simple**, **single**, **singular**, **singlet**, **singleton**. How, you may well ask, can Greek *hama* be related to Latin *similis* or English **same**? The equivalence of what we represent as an initial [h-] in Classical Greek (really, just a rough breathing and silent in Modern Greek) with an initial [s-] in Latin and the Germanic languages is certainly curious but occurs on a regular basis.[11]

## "Hold, enough!"

> Lay on, Macduff,
> And damn'd be him that first cries, 'Hold, enough!'
> – Shakespeare, *Macbeth*, Act 5, Scene 8.

Germanic languages are of course a branch of the vast Indo-European family of languages, which also includes the Romance, Celtic, Hellenic, Slavic, Baltic and Indo-Iranian languages. **Hold** does not have any known cognates in the non-Germanic branches. **Have**,

---

[11] See Chapter 11, A GREEK DRAMA.

however, does have cognates in Latin and other Indo-European languages. But, contrary to what one might have expected, it is not related to Latin *habeo, habere, habitum* "to have," despite the similarity in both form and meaning. An initial [h] in Germanic languages corresponds to an initial [c] in Latin, in accordance with Grimm's Law.[12] So the Latin word that is cognate with English **have** is actually *capio, capere, captum* "to take," together with its derivatives, such as *captivus* "prisoner" and *capax* "capable." The Roman historian Tacitus described the Emperor Galba as "*omnium consensu capax imperii, nisi imperasset*" ("By universal agreement capable of ruling, if he had not ruled"). In other words, he appeared likely to be a competent emperor, but that illusion was shattered once he took power.

Latin *capio, capere, captum* has innumerable compounds such as *accipio, accipere, incipio, incipere* and *recipio, recipere*, all of which have direct or indirect (through French) English derivatives. Notice how, when compounded, the [a] in the present stem of *capio, capere* changes to an [i] and the [a] in the supine stem, *captum*, changes to an [e]. So, the relevant principal parts of *accipio* are *accipio, accipere, acceptum*. The English derivatives follow suit, e.g. **accept, incipient, inception, recipient, receptive, recipe**.

---

[12] See Chapter 8, A GRIMM TALE, where this is explained.

# CHAPTER 3

# A FISTFUL OF FALLACIES

### Equating language and alphabet

IT IS COMMONLY mistakenly assumed that related languages are written in the same alphabet. In fact, it is possible to write any language in any alphabet or using any writing system. So just because two languages share the same alphabet does not mean that they are related, and the opposite is also true: just because two languages are written in different alphabets does not necessarily mean that they are unrelated. Western colonialism has resulted in many languages being written in the Roman alphabet that are unrelated to any European language. Vietnamese, Malay and Indonesian are examples of this, as are many African languages, including Swahili, Yoruba and Zulu.

Turkish, which used to be written in the Arabic alphabet, now uses a (slightly modified) Roman alphabet, although Turkish is neither a Semitic language (like Arabic) nor an Indo-European language. The motive for the change was essentially political. It was part of the drive of Mustafa Kemal Atatürk (1881–1938), the founder of modern Turkey, to westernize his country. He was always portrayed, even on postage stamps, wearing white tie and tails, the ultimate statement of western sartorial elegance. The version of the Latin alphabet introduced by Atatürk in 1928 consists of 29 instead of the standard 26 letters, including modified versions of the [c], [s], [g], [i], [o], and [u]. One of the most puzzling is the letter [ğ], which is pronounced similarly to English [w] as in **water**. This symbol is topical because it happens to occur in the name of Turkish President, Recep Tayyip Erdoğan.

## A FISTFUL OF FALLACIES

Before they were expelled in 1492, the Jews of Spain spoke a language usually called Ladino, a form of Medieval or Old Spanish interspersed with words from other languages, especially Hebrew. It was usually written in the Hebrew alphabet, with which the Jews were most familiar. This is still the case today. Ladino is now spoken by about 150,000 Sephardic Jews, mostly in Israel, where there are even two Ladino newspapers.

Yiddish is a parallel example in regard to Ashkenazic Jews. It is essentially German with an admixture of Hebrew and some Slavic words and written in a modified Hebrew alphabet. The Hebrew alphabet itself has no vowels, but Yiddish improvised, giving vowel quality to certain consonants, notably aleph and ayin, that in Hebrew are silent and take on sound colouring from vowel points written underneath or (more usually) omitted. On the eve of World War II, there were between 11 and 13 million Yiddish speakers. The number is now down to about 2 million, mostly made up of ultra-orthodox Jews, but Yiddish classes in America are booming and there is something of a revival of the Yiddish theatre there. Ultra-orthodox Jews, or Haredim, regard Hebrew as too sacred to use in everyday conversation, so they use Yiddish as their first language instead, even in Israel. Though the vocabulary of Yiddish is chiefly drawn from German, Yiddish speakers had trouble pronouncing some German sounds and modified them accordingly. The popular Yiddish song, *"Bei Mir Bistu Shein"* ("To Me You're Beautiful") composed in 1932 became a hit in Nazi Germany under its teutonified title, *"Bei mir bist Du schön"* – until its Jewish provenance was discovered.

The use of the Latin or Roman alphabet, with various modifications, has grown exponentially, aided by the computer revolution. The English alphabet differs slightly from the alphabet used in Classical Latin. For one thing, the [w] did not exist in the Latin alphabet but came into use in Middle English and Middle German in about 1300. Classical Latin was written all in block capitals. The [J] and the [U] did not exist, but were written as [I] and [V] respectively. So the name "Julius" would have been written IVLIVS. Phonetically, an initial [i] followed by a vowel would tend to be pronounced like the [y] in English **yet**, which eventually came to be represented by the letter [j], Similarly, an initial [u] in Latin followed by another vowel would originally have been pronounced like the [w] in English **wood** and came to be represented by the letter [v], the pronunciation of which gradually hardened into a sound similar to that of the [v] in English **voice**. There was a longstanding dispute among Classicists on the pronunciation of the initial [V] in Latin. The Romance languages all pronounce it similarly to the [v] in English **voice** (and in Spanish it veers to midway between that sound and the sound of the [b] in English **bear**, e.g. The capital of Cuba, Havana, which in Spanish is *La Habana*). So why should it have been pronounced differently in Latin? Unfortunately, the tape recordings of Cicero's speeches are a bit scratchy! But it makes sense to start from the assumption that words were originally spelt phonetically. So, Julius Caesar's famous slogan, *veni, vidi, vici* ("I came, I saw, I conquered") would probably have been originally pronounced something like: *oo-eni, oo-idi, oo-iki*. If you say that fast enough, it sounds like *weni, widi, wiki*, which may well be how it actually sounded at the time. It does sound rather weak (no pun intended), so I prefer the stronger pronunciation of the [v] as a modern English, French or Italian [v], though that is probably historically incorrect.

The Roman alphabet was a heavily modified version of the Etruscan alphabet, which was based on a variant of the Greek alphabet, which in turn came ultimately from the Phoenician alphabet, from which the Hebrew alphabets also arose – the palaeo-Hebrew alphabet, a variant of which is still used by the Samaritans, and the square Aramaic script, which is used to write Hebrew today. This just shows how careful you have to be not to associate writing systems with languages, because while the Hebrew and Phoenician languages are classified as Semitic, Greek and Latin are Indo-European, and the Etruscan language is not related to any other known language. It's a pity that we have lost any proper names for the letters of the alphabet. In English the letter B is pronounced "bee", C is "see", D is "dee," and so on, which makes it difficult to understand the spelling out of words without resorting to some such convention as the ICAO or NATO phonetic alphabet: Alfa, Bravo, Charlie, Delta, Echo, Foxtrot, etc. But these "names" have no relationship to the appearance of the letters, which was the case originally. The Hebrew letters all have names that originally were reminiscent of the shape of the letters concerned, e.g. *bet* = house, *gimmel* (Hebrew *gamal* = camel. English **camel** is itself derived from the Hebrew or Phoenician word); *dalet* (Hebrew *delet* = door); *ayin* = eye. When the Greeks took over and adapted the Phoenician alphabet the letters were given names similar to their original names, which however had no meaning in Greek. The shape of the Greek letter delta, Δ, however, is strikingly reminiscent of a tent-flap, a primitive form of door, from which the Phoenician letter got its name. The Greek word *delta* had no meaning, but, because of its shape it was used by the Greek historian Herodotus (c. 484–425 BCE) to describe the mouth of the River Nile, and it is now used in English for any river mouth irrespective of shape.

## "My language is not related to any other language."

A number of languages have been touted as "language isolates" over the years, usually wrongly. Those correctly identified as such include the ancient Sumerian language and Etruscan, both extinct, and, among living languages Korean, the Ainu language of Northern Japan, and, alone in Europe, Basque, spoken in NW Spain and the adjacent area of France on the other side of the Pyrenees. Many attempts have been made to link it to one or other language family, but so far to no avail. Basque is the only Pre-Indo-European language that is still extant in western Europe.

The Basques are probably the descendants of the people known to the Romans as *Vascones*. The names are clearly related, even though the [V] was probably pronounced like the English [w] in "water", as discussed above and as confirmed by the geographer Strabo (64 BCE– c. 24 CE), who named them in Greek as *Ouaskones*. In modern

Spanish the Basques are called *Vascos*, pronounced almost like "*Bascos*." Genetic research published by the National Geographic Society Genographic Project in 2012 found through detailed DNA analysis that Basques share unique genetic patterns that distinguish them from the surrounding non-Basque Indo-European populations. Not only do the Basques differ genetically from their neighbours: they have also been living where they are now a lot longer. The study concluded that "our data provide support for the hypothesis of a partial genetic continuity of contemporary Basques ... with the earlier settlers of their homeland since pre-Neolithic times."[13] The Neolithic or New Stone Age began around 10,000 BCE, while the Indo-Europeans did not arrive on the scene in western Europe until about 3,000 BCE at the earliest, though these dates are by no means certain. The point is that the Basques were there long before the arrival of the Indo-Europeans.

It is important to remember that peoples cannot simply be equated with languages. Not all people who identify as Basque, for example, are Basque speakers. In fact, it is estimated that the Basque language is spoken by less than 30% of Basques, amounting to some 700,000 people, the overwhelming majority of whom are bilingual in either Spanish or French.[14] Basque, or Euskara, to give it its Basque name, is a highly complex language, of which there are five main dialects. Here is the first verse of the book of Genesis in Basque: *"Hastapenean, Jaincoac ezdeusetaric eguin içan cituen cerua eta lurra."* ("In the beginning God created heaven and earth"). Although Basque has been influenced by Spanish to some degree, there is no indication of that here!

So, unless the language of the person claiming to speak a unique language unrelated to any other is Korean, Ainu or Basque, he or she is probably mistaken.

---

[13] http://eltsov.org/mtphyLaspx.
[14] Wikipedia: "Basque Language."

## "My language is the granddaddy of all other languages."

This is the opposite fallacy to the previous one, but equally false. In the comedy movie *My Big Fat Greek Wedding*, the father of the bride, Gus, insists that all words have a Greek origin, which is of course comic nonsense. but the sort of claim that is sometimes actually heard in real life. "Give me a word, any word," is Gus's oft-repeated boast, "And I will give you the Greek origin of that word." A friend of the bride who has heard this boast umpteen times decides to put the old man to the test. So, when asked for a word, she disingenuously offers him "*kimono*." With hardly a moment's hesitation comes Gus's reply: "*Kimono: Kimono* is come from the Greek word *cheimon*, meaning 'winter.' Because, in the wintertime you are feeling cold, so you are wearing a cloak to wrap around you." There is indeed a Classical Greek word *cheimon* meaning "winter," but it has nothing whatever to do with *kimono*, which is Japanese; and Gus's explanation is not very convincing anyway.

In fact, even Latin, Greek and Sanskrit, the oldest documented Indo-European languages, derive from a yet older Proto-Indo-European (PIE), which has left no records and has had to be reconstructed. However, the Biblical story of the Tower of Babel in which all human beings originally spoke the same language has had an enduring appeal over the ages.[15]

## False links

Some language courses suggest learning vocabulary in a foreign language through "links" with words that just happen to sound similar to English words. For example, a Spanish course that shall be nameless suggests learning Spanish *flor*, meaning "flower," by imagining a flower lying on the **floor**. Spanish *flor* and English **floor** have nothing in common except that they sound similar. You need a strong

---

[15] See Chapter 4, THE TOWER OF BABEL.

visual memory for this, otherwise, instead of picturing a flower on the floor you might picture a rabbit sitting on the floor instead and therefore believe that Spanish *flor* means "rabbit." There is, after all, no earthly reason why a floor should remind you of a flower rather than of a rabbit. It is surely far easier and more enjoyable to learn the meaning of Spanish *flor* from English words that are actually connected with it in both origin and meaning, such as **floral**, **florid** and **florist**, all of which have meanings related to "flower." From these true links you are able to improve your English vocabulary and also learn other languages: French *fleur*, Catalan *flor*, Portuguese *flor*, Italian *fiore*, Romanian *floare*, and Maltese *fjura*. All these words, including Spanish *flor*, derive from Latin *flos*, *floris*, from which they have morphed each in their own specific but regular and predictable way.

## "Memory palaces"

Another mnemonic device peddled by some language programs is to picture each new word in a specific location in a house or a town with which you are familiar. This method is closely related to the one known as "the method of *loci*", which literally means "the method of places," *loci* being the plural of Latin *locus* meaning "place." It has a certain limited usefulness as a memorization technique for recalling a shopping list, a laundry list or list of names, concepts, dates, numbers, or playing cards, especially when they have to be remembered in a particular order.

I remember as a schoolboy going with my father to an advertised free lecture demonstrating the memory technique of Dr Buno Furst, who, I discovered much later on, had written a number of books on his technique, including one titled *You Can Remember* – a home study course in 12 volumes! The whole basis of the Bruno Furst method was a series of key words in a fixed order, the first three of which were Tea, Noah, May. These words were also ways of remembering the numbers 1, 2 and 3, because the letter T has one downstroke, N two downstrokes and M three. Suppose you have to remember a laundry list containing the following items in a fixed order: socks, underpants, shirts. You have to picture, first, socks floating in a cup of tea, then Noah dressed only in his underwear, and thirdly perhaps a maypole with a shirt attached to it and fluttering in the wind. Of course, Tea, Noah and May were only the first three of a list of ten or more key words to which items to be memorized had to be attached in your mind's eye. The free lecture was a come-on for signing up to the Bruno Furst memory course. But my father and I were not greatly impressed and did not sign up. The technique was fine for the first list that you had to memorize, and maybe for the second and third as well. But how did you disentangle all the "Teas" from one another when you had to remember even ten lists? Because the TEA-NOAH-MAY combo was the *only* 1-2-3 key provided by this technique, applicable to every single list you would ever have to commit to memory.

This does not detract from the respectable ancestry of the "method of *loci*" applied more flexibly to general non-vocabulary uses. It is discussed by the Roman writer and statesman Marcus Tullius Cicero (106–43 BCE) in his *De Oratore* ("On the Orator") and other Roman writers on rhetoric, and it can be ultimately traced back to the Greek poet and polymath Simonides of Ceos (c. 556–468 BCE) and his "collapsed banqueting hall" technique. After being himself miraculously saved from death when the building collapsed into rubble during a victory banquet, Simonides was able to identify the unrecognizable bodies of the guests crushed to death by calling to mind the seating arrangement at the dinner.

Limited as this technique is even for laundry lists, it is practically useless for learning vocabulary in a foreign language. And the same applies to the "method of *loci*" and "memory palaces." The trouble is that you need thousands of these *loci* or "palaces" to learn a new language.

Rather than for his mnemonic technique, Simonides is perhaps better remembered for his haunting and evocative epitaph for the Spartans who died at the Battle of Thermopylae in 480 BCE:

> "O xein', aggellein Lacedaimoniois hoti teide keimetha, tois keinon rhemasi peithomenoi."

("O stranger, report to the Spartans that we lie here in obedience to their orders.")

## Word proximity method

A different, but essentially similar, method of learning vocabulary has been put forward by Tim Doner, who claims to have been able to speak over 20 languages since the age of 16. Citing the three unrelated Indonesian words *kepala* ("head"), *kabar* ("news") and *kantor* ("office"), Tim Doner says that thinking of one of these words reminds him of the others because of their similar initial sounds. The three words are not related to one another in either meaning or origin. (Tim Doner "Breaking the Language Barrier," TED X Teen – independently organized TED event, YouTube, 2014.) This would appear to be a variant of the *loci* or "word palaces" mnemonic techniques, because words are remembered by their physical proximity to other words in an alphabetical list. It relies on visual and audial memory, but does not seem too different from simply memorizing a list of words in time-honoured fashion. If it works for Tim Doner, it is probably because he clearly has a prodigious natural memory.

These three Indonesian words were singled out by Tim Doner, not selected by myself. It is true that they are not related to one another in any way, yet, as it happens, two of them, *kepala* and *kantor*, are loanwords from other languages with links to English:

❖ *Kantor* ("office") is borrowed directly from the Dutch *kantoor*, which means the same. As Indonesia was under Dutch control for about three centuries until 1949, it is hardly surprising that the Indonesian language should contain Dutch loanwords, especially vocabulary associated with government, administration or commerce. Dutch and Afrikaans *kantoor* come from French *comptoir*, meaning "a counter" as in "a reception desk, a store counter, shop counter," which in turn is from Latin *computo, computare, computatum*, ("to count, tot up, reckon"), from which of course come English **compute, computer, computation**, and, via the French, even the word **count** and all its compounds, including: **account, accountant, accountancy, discount, recount** ("to relate a story").

❖ *Kepala* ("head") comes ultimately from Sanskrit *kapala* ("head, skull"). Though Indonesian is not an Indo-European language, Indonesia was intermittently under the rule of various Indian dynasties from the 2nd to the 12th century. The earliest known inscriptions found in Java, near modern Jakarta, the capital of Indonesia, include one written in Sanskrit celebrating the power of King Purnavarman (reigned c. 395–434 CE), described as "the heroic conqueror of the world" and incorporating an imprint of the royal footprints together with those of his elephants! In view of this historical background, we can't be surprised at the "borrowing" of a Sanskrit word even for so basic an anatomical feature as "head." Sanskrit is of course one of the three oldest recorded Indo-European languages, the others being Latin and Greek. And the Sankrit word *kapala* is cognate with Latin *caput, capitis*, which also means "head," which has given rise to a large number of English words, including **capital, capitation, capitulate, recapitulate** (colloquially abbreviated to **recap**, lit. "to restate the headings" hence "to summarize"), **recapitulation, decapitation, precipice** ("headlong fall"), **precipitate** ("headlong", hence "hurried"), **precipitation** (lit. "hurling down," hence in chemistry: "separation of a solid from a liquid"), **captain**; and from the French: **chapter, chef** (French: "person in charge," hence "head of the kitchen"), **chief, achieve, mischief** (lit. "something brought to a head badly"), **mischievous, chattel** ("property other than land," from Medieval Latin capitale, lit. "principal thing," hence "property"), **cattle**.[16] Also, from Late Latin *capitellum* ("little head") and Spanish *Caudillo* ("head man, leader" – the title assumed by Spanish dictator Francisco Franco as equivalent to Italian *Duce* and German *Führer*). By Grimm's Law, English **head**

---

[16] See Chapter 20, MONEY MAKES THE WORLD GO ROUND.

(from Anglo-Saxon *heafod*, "leader") and all compounds, including **headlong** (lit. "head first"), **headache**, **headlight**, **behead**, **heading**. Also German *Haupt* ("head", literal and figurative – but German *Kopf* ("head") does not have the same origin); "head" both literal and figurative in Dutch: *hoofd*, Danish: *hoved*, Norwegian: *hode*, Swedish: *huvud*.

Though I don't actually know any Indonesian,[17] I doubt that I will ever forget the two words *kepala* and *kantor*! I have gone into a lot of byways and alleyways connected with these words here – a lot more than you would need to remember them! But you now have a way of remembering them through genuine links with English words. In the process, you can pick up words in other languages as well – and enhance your English vocabulary to boot. This natural method is really the best type of mnemonic.

## "Don't sleep, there are snakes."

Comparative linguistics owes a debt of gratitude to the Anglo-Welsh judge stationed in India, Sir William Jones (1746–94), who recognized that Latin, Greek and Sanskrit were cognate languages with a common ancestor. In 1786 he wrote:

"The Sanscrit language" bears to both Latin and Greek "a stronger affinity ... than could possibly have been produced by accident; so strong indeed that no philologer could examine them all three without believing them to have sprung from some common source, which perhaps no longer exists; there is a similar reason ... for supposing that both the Gothic and the Celtic, though blended with a very different idiom, had the same origin with the Sanscrit, and the old Persian might be added to the same family."

Jones had identified what is now called the Indo-European family of languages (although he erroneously also included in it "Egyptian,"

---

[17] But see Chapter 12, LOAN OR THEFT?

Chinese and Japanese), though he was not actually the first to hit on this idea, which can be traced back to the Dutch scholar Marcus van Boxhorn (1612–53), who held, quite correctly, that Greek, Latin, Persian, German, Dutch, and the Slavic, Baltic and Celtic languages all had a common ancestor which he called "Scythian."

The work of Sir William Jones gave birth to the science of comparative philology, which had its heyday in the nineteenth century, with the writings, among others, of Jacob and Wilhelm Grimm, (yes, the very same Brothers Grimm who produced Grimm's Fairy Tales). Grimm's Law, the work of Jacob Grimm (1785–1863), remains of towering significance to this day, though it was refined by later scholars.[18]

The influential textbook titled *Language* (1933) by the American scholar Leonard Bloomfield (1887–1949), following Ferdinand de Saussure's *Course in General Linguistics* (1916), established the dominance of "structural linguistics," which replaced diachronic (historical) with synchronic (static, non-historical) analysis.

Since the mid-1950s, the field of linguistics has been dominated by Noam Chomsky (born 1928), with his so-called "generativist" approach to linguistics. The focus in this approach is on grammar, and particularly syntax, with very little attention to vocabulary, which has done a major disservice to language learning.

In Chomsky's "Deep Structure/Surface Structure" analysis, now abandoned, vocabulary issues could potentially raise their head, e.g. A. "John is eager to please'" B. "John is easy to please." Chomsky's analysis is that the "surface structure" of the two sentences is the same, but the "deep structure" is different.[19] This analysis is not terribly helpful. The difference between the two sentences is that in A. John wishes to please somebody else, whereas in B. the position is

---

[18] For more on this, see Chapter 8, A GRIMM TALE.
[19] John Maher & Judy Groves, *Introducing Chomsky*, 1999, p. 76.

reversed; In the first sentence other unnamed persons are the prospective beneficiaries, while in the second sentence John is the prospective beneficiary. The real difference is between the adjectives "eager" and "easy." **Eager** is an ordinary adjective describing John, but **easy** has almost a passive sense. In both sentences John is the grammatical subject, but in B. John is effectively the object, because the act of pleasing is not being done by John but to him. The sense of **easy**, meaning "not difficult," is the key. What is not difficult? Not John, but the act of pleasing him. So B. could be rephrased: "Pleasing John is easy."

Chomsky's approach has undergone several revisions, starting with "transformational grammar," moving on to "universal grammar" and, most recently, the so-called "minimalist program." Here's an early quote from Chomsky, showing the strong emphasis on grammar: "The fundamental aim in the linguistic analysis of a language L is to separate the grammatical sequences which are the sentences of L from the ungrammatical sequences which are not sentences of L and to study the structure of the grammatical sequences." (*Syntactic structures*, 1957, p. 13). Despite some major shifts in Chomsky's position over the years, the emphasis on grammar and syntax remains.

The basic objection to this whole approach is that poor grammar will not usually prevent you from making yourself understood in a foreign language, while lack of vocabulary is very likely to have that effect, e.g. "Have you book on music modern?" is not too difficult to understand as meaning: "Do you have a book on modern music?" But wrong vocabulary, albeit with perfect grammar, would prevent communication, e.g. "Do you like a cook on modern sick?"

Chomsky is not actually interested in *languages* from a practical point of view, but only in *language* in a theoretical sense. This can be seen from some of the disputes that Chomsky has been involved in. One particularly acrimonious dispute was with Daniel Everett over the question of "recursion." In Chomsky's theory there was an assumption – almost an article of faith – that all languages shared the same grammatical characteristics, including "recursion," meaning the ability to create one sentence inside another, as in subordinate clauses, e.g. "Did you know that Chomsky says that all languages have recursion?" That is an example of recursion. Without recursion, one would have to say something like this: "All languages have recursion. Chomsky says so. Did you know that?" Daniel Everett (born 1951), who had spent years in the field with the tiny Pirahã tribe in the Amazon jungle of Brazil, and who had mastered their extremely complex language, found that this language lacked recursion. The language also lacked many other features present in most other languages, and the Pirahã way of saying goodnight was "Don't sleep, there are snakes" – which there apparently were, in abundance. Everett used this phrase as the title of a book published in 2008.

Although Chomsky had no knowledge of the Pirahã language, he was unable to accept what he took to be an attack on his theory, because if even one language lacked recursion, this invalidated Chomsky's universal theory, which he was not prepared to contemplate. Instead, he went on the attack, dismissing Everett as a "charlatan," one of Chomsky's favourite terms of opprobrium. Chomsky even went so far as to assert categorically: "There is no question that the language is built on a recursive process."[20] When Everett, "the little flycatcher," as he was sympathetically described in Tom Wolfe's wonderfully barbed *Kingdom of Speech* (2016), would not back down, recursion suddenly mysteriously disappeared from Chomsky's theory.

But why had Chomsky been so adamant that every language had to have recursion? This could possibly be connected with his egalitarian political position. Although, as far as I know, he has never actually said so, it may well be that he believes that all languages are equal, and that by denying that the Pirahã language possessed this feature, Daniel Everett was branding that language and its speakers as

---

[20] Daniel Everett, "Chomsky, Wolfe and me," – aeon.co/why-language-is-not-everything-that-noam-chomsky-said-it-is.

inferior. At one point the Brazilian government apparently did try to accuse Everett of racism, but nothing could be further from the truth. He certainly did not believe that the Pirahã language's lack of recursion and other supposedly "essential" characteristics of a language made the language or its speakers inferior to any other language or people.

A 2003 broadside against Chomsky's whole approach by Professor Larry Trask (1944–2004) of Sussex University is quoted by Tom Wolfe: "I have no time for Chomskyan theorizing and its associated dogmas of 'universal grammar.' This stuff is so much half-baked twaddle, more akin to a religious movement than to a scholarly enterprise. I am confident that our successors will look back on UG (universal grammar) as a huge waste of time." Trask also referred to Chomsky's theory as "this sludge."[21]

Underlying all the vagaries of Chomsky's theory is the belief that language is innate, which explains why most children as young as two years of age can converse in full grammatical sentences and have the capacity to create an unlimited number of new sentences. On the basis of differences between languages, Daniel Everett has countered Chomsky's view of language as innate with the argument that language is a cultural tool created by man like the bow and arrow. This position, argued in Everett's book titled *Language: The Cultural Tool* (2012), was followed up by *How Language Began: The Story of Humanity's Greatest Invention*, published in 2017.

In a 2014 article titled "How Could Language Have Evolved?" Chomsky, together with three collaborators, made the apparent admission: "The evolution of the faculty of language largely remains an enigma." Does this mean that Chomsky has now finally renounced the "innate language" theory? Not at all. The key word in this article is the word "evolved." The article asserts that "The faculty of language is likely to have emerged quite recently in evolutionary terms, some

---

[21] Tom Wolfe, *The Kingdom of Speech*, p. 143.

70,000–100,000 years ago, and does not seem to have undergone modification since then..."[22]

After more than half a century, Chomsky's views are now under heavy attack. In a 2016 article in *Scientific American,* under the online headline reading "Evidence Rebuts Chomsky's Theory of Language Learning," Paul Ibbotson and Michael Tomasello point out that "cognitive scientists and linguists have abandoned Chomsky's 'universal grammar' theory in droves because of new research examining many different languages – and the way young children learn to understand and speak the tongues of their communities. That work fails to support Chomsky's assertions. ... Much of Noam Chomsky's revolution in linguistics, including its account of the way we learn languages, is being overturned. ... Children acquire language via general cognitive abilities and the reading of other people's intentions."[23]

Regardless whether Chomsky's theories are true or false, in largely ignoring vocabulary and also in maintaining that language is "innate," they are less than helpful in regard to language learning.

---

[22] Bolhuis JJ, Tattersall I, Chomsky N, Berwick RC (2014) How Could Language Have Evolved? PLoS Biol 12(8): e1001934. https://doi.org/10.1371.journal.pbio.1001934.

[23] Paul Ibbotson and Michael Tomasello, "Language in a New Key," *Scientific American* 315(5), pp.70-75, October 2016.

## CHAPTER 4

# THE TOWER OF BABEL

ACCORDING TO THE Bible, everybody on earth originally spoke the same language. The image of the Tower of Babel is one of the most evocative in the Bible:

"And the whole earth was of one language, and of one speech. ... And they said, Go to, let us build a city and a tower, whose top may reach unto heaven. ... And the LORD came down to see the city and the tower, which the children of men builded. And the LORD said, Behold, the people is one, and they have all one language and this they begin to do. And now nothing will be restrained from them, which they have imagined to do. Go to, let us go down, and there confound their language, that they may not understand one another's speech. So the Lord scattered them abroad from thence upon the face of the earth: and they left off to build the city. Therefore is the name of it called Babel; because the LORD did there confound the language of all the earth: and from thence did the LORD scatter them abroad upon the face of all the earth."[24]

This memorable passage actually contradicts a brief earlier reference to a diversity of languages among the descendants of the three sons of Noah, Shem, Ham and Japheth: "Every one after his tongue, after their families, in their nations."[25] This may possibly derive from a different source from that of the Tower of Babel.

---

[24] Gen. 11:1-9 KJV.
[25] Gen. 10:5 KJV.

## THE TOWER OF BABEL

The story of the Tower of Babel combines three significant elements:

1) The claim of initial universal linguistic unity;
2) God's jealousy, resulting in a diversity of languages and a geographical scattering of the population;
3) A purported explanation of the name "Babel," probably a false etymology for the name Babylon, which was actually from *Bab-ilani*, meaning "gate of the gods," but which lent itself to an onomatopoeic etymology related to the Hebrew word *balal*, meaning "confused, confounded."[26] It is similar in sound to Greek *barbaros* and Latin *barbarus*, a common childish attempt to reproduce the sounds of unintelligible foreign speech, and hence a label applied to the speakers of such languages and their customs, from which we get English **barbarian**, **barbaric**, **barbarism**, **barbarous**.

Is there any truth to the Tower of Babel story? Was there originally a single language and, if so, what was it, or how did it come into existence? Or did separate languages arise independently in different parts of the world? This is related to the question of whether homo sapiens originated in one place and spread from there or in several places independently of one another.

### Chomsky's theories

The controversial linguistic theorist Noam Chomsky has suggested that a single chance mutation in a single individual produced the "language faculty" in "perfect" or "near-perfect" form about 100,000 years ago.[27] Needless to say, there is no proof of any such occurrence. In response to criticism of the suddenness of the emergence of speech in Chomsky's theory, he came out with a slightly more nuanced version in 2016, written in collaboration with computer scientist Robert C. Berwick, which allows for the emergence of language a

---

[26] Isaac Asimov, *Asimov's Guide to the Bible, vol 1: The Old Testament*. Avon Books, p. 55f.
[27] *Reflections on Human Nature and the Social Order*, London, Pluto Press, 1996, p. 30.

window between 200,000 to 60,000 years ago, based on the estimated period between the arrival of modern man in southern Africa and the latest date for his exodus from there. "That leaves us," say Chomsky and Berwick, "with about 130,000 years [curious arithmetic!], or approximately 5,000–6,000 generations of time for evolutionary change. This is not 'overnight in one generation' as some have (incorrectly) inferred – but neither is it on the scale of geological eons."[28] This revised theory is just as speculative as Chomsky's original one, despite the addition of the mystique of computer science!

## Darwin

A more plausible explanation of the origin of language is that it developed gradually, either from apes or from humans alone. In his *Descent of Man*, published in 1871, Charles Darwin opined: "I cannot doubt that language owes its origin to the imitation and modification, aided by signs and gestures, of various natural sounds, the voices of other animals, and man's own instinctive cries."[29]

## The bow-wow theory

Darwin may have been thinking of the so-called "bow-wow" or "cuckoo" theory, according to which human speech originated in imitation of animal cries, and certain monkeys and apes certainly do seem to have the ability to communicate with one another by sound. Vervet monkeys, for example, have different warning calls, including a "leopard call," a "snake call" and an "eagle call," each of which elicits a different reaction among members of the group hearing these signals. Chimpanzees in captivity appear to have different "words" for

---

[28] *Why Only Us: Language and Evolution.* Cambridge, Mass: MIT Press.
[29] *The Descent of Man, and Selection in Relation to Sex*, 2vols. London: Murray, p.56.

different foods, such as carrots, apples, grapes and presumably bananas.[30]

But to generate the sounds of speech a specifically shaped vocal tract and a lower-positioned larynx is needed. Recent research suggests that Neanderthal man, who lived in Eurasia for many thousands of years until they died out about 28,000 years ago, may have been anatomically equipped to speak, though it is not known whether they actually did so – nor of course what language(s) they would have spoken had they done so.

## The original language?

For a long time there was a preoccupation with what the earliest language was – usually on the assumption that there must have been a single language to begin with. According to the Greek historian Herodotus (*Histories* 2:2), the Egyptian Pharaoh Psammetichus isolated two new-born children with strict orders that nobody should speak to them. After two years was announced by the shepherd who was rearing them that "both children ran to him stretching out their hands and calling 'bekos'," which turned out to be the Phrygian word for bread. This convinced the Pharaoh that the Phrygians were the oldest people on earth and that their language was the original language. If there is any truth to the story at all, it may well be that the shepherd was himself Phrygian and had been talking to the children in his language. Another possibility, as my friend Tom Malnati suggests, is that what sounded like "bekos" was the children's imitation of the bleating of sheep with which they were raised.

King James IV of Scots (reigned 1488–1513) is reported to have conducted a similar experiment, entrusting the care of two young children to a "dumb woman" to see what language they spoke "when

---

[30] Christopher M. Gibbons, (2007). The referentiality of chimpanzee vocal signalling: behavioural and acoustic analysis of food barks (Ph.D. Thesis) Ohio State University.

they came of the age of perfect speech." It was announced that they spoke "good Hebrew," which served to validate the story of the Tower of Babel, but the truth of this announcement was challenged even at the time and is obviously highly improbable, not to say impossible.[31] The Mughal Emperor Akbar (reigned 1556–1605) conducted a similar experiment, from which he came to the correct conclusion, which was that children raised without hearing speech would be dumb. His experiment appears to have been quite rigorously controlled. Newly born children were placed in a secure house to which only "tongue-tied" (i.e. dumb) wetnurses were admitted. Four years later, when the Emperor himself inspected the facility, "No cry came from that house of silence, nor was any speech heard there. In spite of their four years, they had no part of the talisman of speech, and nothing came out except the noise of the dumb."[32] This logical conclusion, that a child brought up from birth without being exposed to language would be unable to speak, is confirmed by the few actual cases on record.[33]

## Humboldt's parrot

Another linguistic puzzle surrounds the claim made by the German naturalist, explorer and polymath Alexander von Humboldt (1769–1859) of discovering fragments of the long-lost Maypore language from the Amazon basin in South America – through some pet parrots. Humboldt claimed that in his travels along the Orinoco River in modern Venezuela he made contact with the Carib tribe, whose pet parrots spoke a different language. The Caribs explained that the parrots had previously belonged to a rival tribe, the Maypore, Maypure or Maipure, which the Caribs had wiped out in battle leaving the parrots to the Caribs as spoils of war. Humboldt identified about 40 words spoken by the parrot and recorded them phonetically in his

---

[31] Robert Lindsay, *The Cronicles (sic) of Scotland*, vol I, Edinburgh, 1814, p. 249f.
[32] Abul Fazal, *The Akbar NAmA of Abu-l-Fazl*, transl. H. Beveridge, reprinted 1993.
[33] See Wikipedia article on "Language deprivation."

journal. The curious story was given a new lease of life when in 1997 Rachel Berwick of Yale School of Art and Sue Farlow, a parrot fancier, teamed up to stage a parrot-centred art exhibition based on Humboldt's legend. They trained two Amazon parrots to repeat each of the 40-odd words by repeatedly pointing to an object associated with that word. The experiment and the show based on it was pronounced a great success.[34] However, a pinch of salt is undoubtedly called for. Though Humboldt wrote down the way the 40 words sounded to him phonetically, that could hardly replicate their precise pronunciation. Moreover, there is no way Humboldt – or the Carib for that matter – could possibly have known the meaning of the 40 words. So, it is a bit of a stretch to suggest that the 1997 experiment revived or reconstructed the lost Maypore language in any way at all. The most that can be claimed for it is that it showed that it is possible to train Amazon parrots (who are known to be amongst the most adept at speech imitation) to repeat 40 words on the basis of arbitrary meanings assigned to those words by the trainers. The significance of the story is that it demonstrates an endless and uncritical fascination with anything to do with language.

## Monogenesis

But we divert from our theme, the origin of language, which continues to exert endless fascination on the human mind. A leading supporter of monogenesis, or the idea that all languages derive from a single ancestor – ultimately traceable to the Tower of Babel legend – was Morris Swadesh (1909–67), the American linguist, who specialized in comparative and historical linguistics and who pioneered the techniques of lexicostatistics and glottochronology. Lexicostatistics is a method of comparative linguistics comparing cognate words between languages to determine their relationship. On this basis Swadesh generated a list of 200 words, later pared down to 100. Isidore Dyen,

---

[34] See rachelberwick.com/Maypore.php.

Joseph B. Kruskal and Paul Black produced a list of 200 meanings for 84 Indo-European languages in digital form in *An Indo-European Classification: A Lexicostatistical Experiment,* Transactions of the American Philosophical Society 1992.

Glottochronology (from Greek *glotta* "tongue" + *chronos* "time") is the aspect of lexicostatistics dealing with the relationship between languages over time. This is based on a presumption of a "core vocabulary" common to all languages which changes only very slowly over time. On the basis of Swadesh's 200-word or later 100-word list, the percentage of cognates is then measured. The larger the percentage of cognates, the more recently the two languages in question are presumed to have separated and the closer they are. Various mathematical formulae have been devised to verify this theory. It has however been rejected by many Indo-European linguists of the traditional comparative method. The mumbo-jumbo of glottochronology is an attempt to convert into a scientific theory linguistic changes that are well documented without being reduced to a pseudo-scientific formula. For example, it does not take much analysis to recognize that Italian diverged from Latin much later than, say, French, and that Italian is a lot closer to Latin than French is. It is hard to see what purpose is served by trying to turn that into some sort of mathematical formula. What is important is to know the "rules" governing the change from Latin or Vulgar Latin into Italian, compared with the "rules" governing the equivalent changes into the other Romance languages. So, for example, Latin *clamo, clamare, clamatum* "to call" becomes *chiamare* in Italian, *llamar* in Spanish, *chamar* in Portuguese, and *clamer in* French, the meaning being "to call" in all the languages except French, where it means "to proclaim", as in: *clamer son innocence* "to proclaim his innocence." The Latin word is itself a derivative of an unrecorded Proto-Indo-European (PIE) word, whose root has been reconstructed as *$kelh_1$- and which has given rise to derivatives in Greek and the Germanic, Baltic and Slavonic families, all of which are cognates with one another and with the Latin word.

Merritt Ruhlen has identified the following roots for the Proto-Human or the Mother Tongue, the Ancestor of all the languages in the world:[35]

- *Ku* = "who"
- *Ma* = "what"
- *Pal* = "two"
- *Akʷa* = "water"
- *Tik* = "finger"
- *kanV* = "arm"
- *boko* = "arm"
- *bunjku* = "knee"
- *sum* = "hair"
- *putV* = "vulva" (The symbol V stands for "a vowel whose precise character is unknown.")[36]
- *čuna* = "nose, smell"

This list is supposedly derived from a comparison of 12 language families across the globe, one of which is "Eurasiatic" including all the Indo-European languages! The validity of this list is pretty low in my view and its usefulness is zero. I can only find two words here that relate in any way to the Indo-European family:

- *\*ku* "who" – which can be linked to Latin *quis*, French *qui*, Italian *chi*, Spanish *quien* and Portuguese *quem*;
- and *\*akwa* "water" – which is obviously similar to Latin *aqua* "water" and all its derivatives.

*\*Ma* is Hebrew for "what?" but is not etymologically related to *\*ku* "who?" – though in most languages the words for "who" and "what" are related to each other, as in the two English words themselves, Latin *quis* and *quid*, German *wer* and *was*, and also Hebrew *mi* and *ma*.

---

[35] *The Origin of Language: Tracing the Evolution of the Mother Tongue*, New York: John Wiley & Sons, p. 105.
[36] Ruhlen, Ibid., p. 105.

Attractive though the idea is that all languages have a common origin, this seems unlikely. There are a number of unrelated language families, each containing numerous branches, most of which are made up of hundreds of languages. How this reflects on the equally vexed question of the origin of man – whether from one place (probably Africa) and spreading out from there, or independently from a number of places at the same time – remains a mystery.

The language family that we are interested in is the Indo-European family, whose speakers account for about 45% of the world population. The main branches of this family include: the Germanic, the Romance (or Italic), the Hellenic, the Celtic, the Balto-Slavic and the Indo-Iranian groups of languages. Though these languages are very diverse, they undoubtedly all have a common origin in an unrecorded language known as Proto-Indo-European, (PIE), the reconstruction of which is highly problematical, but much less important than current scholarship would lead one to believe, because PIE has to be reconstructed from its daughter languages, not the other way around.

### Are your thoughts shaped by your language?

Finally, let me turn to another vexed problem associated with the unity and diversity of language – namely the Sapir-Whorf hypothesis, or Whorfianism, (named after Benjamin Lee Whorf and Edward Sapir, who never actually collaborated) which is the belief in "linguistic relativity," which claims that a person's thought processes are *determined*, or at least *influenced*, by their native language. So, according to this theory, the way you think is shaped to a greater or lesser degree, not only by language, but also by the specific language that you speak.

The *Economist* magazine held a debate in 2010 on the motion: "This house believes that the language we speak shapes how we think." Of those who voted on the result, no fewer than 78% agreed with the motion and 22% disagreed. Linguistic relativity, perhaps better described as linguistic relativism, is based on observations such as the fact revealed by Whorf that "Hopi had no words for time (like days and months), and therefore perceived time far differently than European-language speakers do ... In the dominant school of post-war linguistics, such 'Whorfian' thinking has traditionally had a bad reputation. (This is not least because Whorf's knowledge of Hopi proved to be hopelessly incomplete.)"[37]

This kind of thinking is nevertheless still common, generally based on what Greene terms the "no word for X trope," like US President Ronald Reagan's remark that the Russian language has no word for "freedom" when it actually does: *svoboda*. Or the unintentionally comical and equally wrong remark by President George W. Bush that the French have no word for **entrepreneur** – which of course is a French word itself! Assistant Professor Lera Boroditsky, proposing the motion, made the point that "speakers of languages with gendered nouns tend to think even of abstract nouns as feminine or masculine." So, do Germans think of a table as male because their word *Tisch* is masculine, while French people think of it as female because their word, *table*, is feminine? The only evidence that Ms Boroditsky cites is anecdotal: "German artists paint death as a man (masculine in German) while Russians paint her as a woman (feminine in Russian)" – adding gratuitously "and non-artists are no less affected." Really? How does she know? And, even if all this is true, why does it matter? Do Russians fear death less because it is perceived as female? Do they look forward to its motherly embrace? And does their reaction differ according to whether they themselves are male or female?

Another example cited in favour of the "language-shapes-thought" proposition is to do with colour: "Languages divide up the world of colour differently, and as a result speakers of English, Korean, Himba, Tarahumara and Greek differ in their ability to perceptually discriminate colours. Such differences can be seen in the brain a mere 100 milliseconds (one-tenth of a second) after a colour appears in

---

[37] Robert Lee Greene, moderator of the debate – http:/www.economist.com/debate/days/view/626.

view. This demonstrates that language per se plays a causal role, meddling in basic perceptual decisions as they happen." Whatever the truth may be about different perceptions of colour, the last quoted sentence is a logical *non sequitur*: even if different languages have different perceptions of colour – which is by no means certain – it certainly does not follow that language "meddles" with "basic perceptual decisions" – whatever that means.

The debate about colour perception is far from new. As long ago as 1858 the British Prime Minister William Gladstone, who was also a Homeric scholar, wrote in his *Studies on Homer and the Homeric Age* that the ancient Greeks could not see colour the way it is now seen and that "the organ of colour and its impressions were but partially developed among the Greeks of the heroic age." Gladstone remarks on the "paucity" of Homer's colours, identifying only eight words "which can with certainty be described as adjectives of colour properly so called."[38] This can be explained by the fact that Homer was blind, as he is traditionally said to have been – assuming that the Homeric epics were composed by a single person at all, which is by no means certain. Gladstone laments the fact that Homer has no words to represent the colours orange, green and violet and Homer's generally vague uses of colour words, often applying the same colour label to a variety of disparate objects. What Gladstone fails to appreciate is that the Homeric epics are *poetry*, not a hardware store catalogue, and they make full use of poetic licence – which is what gives the *Iliad* and the *Odyssey* a good deal of their charm and grace. Besides using the same colour description for a number of different things, Homer also has some stock epithets, most famously perhaps *oinops pontos*, which is generally rendered in English as "the wine-dark sea."

Most of the arguments in favour of the "language-shapes-thought" proposition are based on differences between Western languages and

---

[38] Ibid., p. 459.

languages spoken by what would once have been termed "primitive" peoples. So there is a latent ranking of languages involved, which is a gratuitous insult to the speakers of the languages with lower rankings. Is the Hopi language inferior because, as has been suggested, it has the same word for "insect," "airplane" and "aviator"? Not at all. It is simply a reflection of the Hopi experience of the world. Once they established a Hopi International Airport to compete with Phoenix Sky Harbor International Airport, they would no doubt have a separate word not only for "airplane" but also for every type of aircraft as well!

**CHAPTER**

# SEMANTIC DRIFT

HOW DO WE know whether languages are related to one another? And why does it matter? Words have a natural tendency to morph over time in both form and meaning. Recognizing these changes for what they are is a useful way of building your English vocabulary and unlocking other related languages.

English is generally taught in the same way to Turkish or Chinese students as to those whose first language is Spanish or German. Yet Spanish and German are both related to English, while Turkish and Chinese are not. So, wouldn't it make sense to use the links between related languages to help in the learning process? Of course, but when I suggest this, the objection I get is this: If two languages are related, how come they are mutually incomprehensible? The answer is that you need to know how words have changed in form and meaning over time in order to use family relationships between languages as a learning tool.

Superficial similarities between words are not a reliable guide and can actually be dangerous. An online Spanish course that is based on this fallacious method (referred to in Chapter 2) suggests, for example, that to learn the Spanish word *flor*, meaning a "flower," you should picture a **floor** with a flower on it. The English word **floor** is not of course related in any way to Spanish *flor* either in origin or meaning. It just happens to sound similar. So why should your mental picture of a floor conjure up a flower? Could it not equally well conjure up a mental picture of a mouse on a floor – in which case your memory would tell you that Spanish *flor* means "mouse"? It's a lot easier and more interesting to remember *flor* meaning "flower" through genuine links with English words like **flora**, **floral** and **florid**, all of which have meanings related to "flower" and which, like Spanish *flor*, all derive from the Latin word *flos, floris*, meaning "flower." In fact, the English word **flower** itself is also related as well as having the same meaning.

This chapter deals with semantic drift, that is changes in **meaning**. Later chapters deal with changes in **form**.

## Horse sense

Why does English have the word **horse** for what is called in German *Pferd*, French *cheval*, Latin *equus*, Vulgar Latin *caballus*, and Greek *hippos*, even though all these languages are related to one another? *Hippos* and *equus* are actually cognate (that is, they have the same origin)[39] and English has derivatives from or relatives of all but one of these words.

From Greek *hippos* we have:

- ❖ **Hippodrome**, from *hippos* plus *dromos* (lit. a "horse race course") originally applied to a stadium for horse and chariot races and in modern times a name given to a number of large venues for popular entertainment. **Drome-** itself (not to be confused with **drone**) comes from Greek *dromos*, literally "a running, a course," from which we also get such words as **aerodrome** or **airdrome**, "a landing field with buildings and equipment for aircraft," now largely replaced by **airport**; **palindrome**, "a word or phrase that reads the same backward and forward" (lit. "a running back"), such as "Madam, I'm Adam" and "Able was I ere I saw Elba" (a reference to Napoleon); **dromedary**, "single-humped camel," so called because traditionally used for riding, racing and carrying.

---

[39] See Chapter 14, SOUND MOVES.

- **Hippopotamus** (lit. "river horse"), affectionately abbreviated to **hippo**, a large, rather comical-looking water mammal. In German and Dutch the two components of the word are translated into authentic Germanic equivalents meaning "Nile + horse": German *Nilpferd*, Dutch *nijlpaard*. Most of the other Germanic languages similarly convert it to "river horse": Danish *flodhest*, Norwegian *flodhest*, Swedish *flodhäst*, Icelandic *flóthhestur*. Afrikaans uniquely renders it as "sea cow," *seekoei*, and the female of the species, amusingly, as *seekoeikoei* ("sea cow cow").

- In Classical Greece the aristocracy was associated with horses, as horse-breeding was expensive. So the aristocracy and those with aristocratic pretensions often bore names incorporating the word *hippos*. Examples abound, including *Hippias, Hipparchus, Hippomenes,* and of course the "Father of Medicine," *Hippocrates,* who gave his name to the **Hippocratic Oath**, which still forms the basis of the oath taken in many countries by newly qualified physicians. But the most important of all these horsey names is *Philippos* (lit. "horse-lover", from *philos*, "loving" plus *hippos*, "horse"), which survives in the popular English name, **Philip**. The ancient Olympic Games were very horsey affairs, and, true to his name, Philip II of Macedon, father of Alexander the Great, celebrated the Olympic victories of his horses on his coinage.

From Latin *equus* we have:

- **Equine**, "of or like a horse," parallel to **bovine** ("of or like an ox," from Latin *bos, bovis*), **ovine** ("of or like a sheep," from Latin *ovis*), and **porcine** ("of or like a pig," from Latin *porcus*).
- **Equestrian** ("of or relating to horse-riding or horsemanship").

From Vulgar Latin *caballus* we have:

- **Cavalry**, **cavalier** and **cavalcade**. Vulgar Latin *caballus* originally denoted "a nag or pack-horse" but later displaced *equus* as the ordinary Latin word for "horse" as Vulgar Latin eventually turned into the Romance languages.
- **Cavalry** denotes "mounted soldiers, troops mounted on horseback," or, now that horses are no longer used in warfare, "a tank regiment, or troops in armoured vehicles." **Cavalier** originally referred to a **cavalryman**, but, as horses were associated with the aristocracy, or upper

classes, **cavalier** came to refer to "an upper class gentleman," and hence one of the supporters of King Charles I in the English Civil War, distinguished by their long hair from their opponents, the **Roundheads**. By extension, the phrase **cavalier attitude** refers to a "haughty, disdainful, or laid-back disposition." **Cavalcade**, which originally meant "a horseback procession," can now be applied to any kind of "procession," and has given rise to other words ending in **-cade**, notably **motorcade**, "a procession of motor vehicles."

- So complete was the replacement of *equus* with *caballus* after the fall of the Roman Empire in the West that the word for "horse" in the Romance languages is *cavallo* (Italian), *caballo* (Spanish), *cavall* (Catalan), *cavalo* (Portuguese), and *cheval* (French), each with derivatives of its own. *Cheval* looks a little different from the rest, but it conforms to the special rules by which French developed from Latin. After the fall of the Roman Empire in the West, Latin gradually morphed into the various Romance languages: chiefly French, Italian, Spanish, Catalan, Portuguese, and Romanian. As Italy was the original center of the Roman Empire, Italian is the closest of the Romance languages to Latin. French and Romanian are outliers: Romanian because it's influenced by the Slavic languages by which it is surrounded. And French because it developed in one of the latest areas to be Romanized, namely northern Gaul (as it was called by the Romans), inhabited by Celts, who had trouble getting their tongues around the Latin language. So, for example, Latin *cantare* ("to sing") has become *cantare* in Italian, *cantar* in Spanish, *cantar* in Catalan, *cantar* in Portuguese – but in French *chanter*, from which we get English **chant**.

So let's look at English derivatives from French *cheval*:

- **Chivalry**, meaning "the qualities associated with knighthood," and
- **Chivalrous**, meaning "having the qualities of chivalry, courteous, gallant."

The normal German word for "horse," *Pferd* is the odd one out. There is no English word closely related to it.

- But German also has the word *Ross* (originally *hros*), meaning "a spirited horse, a steed," which is cognate (that is, sharing a common origin) with English **horse**.

- *Hengst*, "stallion," is another German word with an English connection, namely henchman, from Old English *hengest* + man, referring to a servant whose job it was to look after the horses. **Henchman** has now taken on the disparaging sense of a "sidekick, or trusted subordinate, to a criminal or gang-leader." Other Germanic languages have words related either to German *Pferd* or *Hengst*: *paard* (Dutch), *perd* (Afrikaans), *hest* (Danish), *hest* (Norwegian), *häst* (Swedish), *hestur* (Icelandic).

- Another horsey word that has undergone major shifts of meaning is **marshal**, originally denoting a stable hand (lit. "horse-servant"), the first part of which comes from an early form of what is now mare, "a female horse," related to German *Mähre*. Marshal was steadily promoted, becoming an officer of the royal court, federal marshal, a judicial officer in the US, and field-marshal , or sometimes just marshal, the highest military rank in a number of countries, including the UK and France, also a favorite rank for self-promoted dictators like Joseph Stalin of the Soviet Union and Tito of Yugoslavia.

## The world of work

Work is another common concept which is represented by apparently unrelated words in the different European languages: **Work** in English, *labor* and *opus, operis* in Latin, *ergon* in Greek, *travail* and *oeuvre* in French, *Arbeit* in German, and *rabota* in Russian. In fact, English has words derived from or related to all of these.

From Latin *labor* we have:

- The English word **labor** (Amerian) or **labour** (British), meaning "work," particularly in formal use, such as in **labor unions** or the **American Federation of Labor**, which merged with the Congress of Industrial Organizations to form the AFL-CIO. Also, in terms such as **a labor of love, labor-intensive**, and to **labor the point**, this last phrase meaning to "emphasize, over-emphasize, hammer home, or reiterate" a particular issue. Another common use of **labor** is in reference to the "physical exertion of childbirth." A **laborious** task is one that is "difficult, arduous or onerous."

Latin also has another word for "work," meaning "to produce in abundance," *opus, operis*, often referring particularly to the finished product of work, "a literary or musical work," which is used in the same sense in English, as in: "Have you read Donald Trump's latest **opus**?" Hence English **opera**, which is actually the plural of Latin *opus, operis*, referring to a musical drama made up of a number of arias interspersed with dialogue. Hence: "It ain't over till the fat lady sings." According to one story, this phrase, which is now of general application, originated when the opera-loving mobster Al Capone ordered his goons not to leave until the last aria had been sung (typically, by a large soprano).

- Latin *opus, operis* is related to Latin *ops, opis*, meaning "abundance, plenty." *Ops* was also the name of the Roman goddess of plenty. Hence the traditional British schoolboy slang exclamation **ops!**, a request for some "tuck" (sandwiches or some food delicacy) addressed by one schoolboy to another more fortunate than himself, the implication being: "The goddess of Plenty has smiled on you: let me share your bounty." Hence **opulent**, **opulence** ("wealth, riches, abundance").

- **Operate**, **operator**, **operation**, **operational**, **operative**, **cooperate**, **cooperative**, which all refer to "work" in various senses, as in: **operating** a machine, a telephone switchboard **operator**, a surgical **operation**, black **operation** or black **ops** ("covert governmental or military activity").

- French *oeuvre* "work" is used in much the same way as Latin and English **opus** and is also a slightly pretentious way of referring in English (in its unchanged French form) to the work of a writer or artist. English **maneuver**, from French *manoeuvre* (Latin *manus* + French *oeuvre*, literally, "hand-work," and hence "a clever, crafty move," originally in a military sense but now of general application. A surprising near-doublet to **maneuver** in terms of origin is **manure**, which started out meaning "hand-work" in the sense of "cultivating, working the soil," but now refers only to "fertilizer on the soil."

- Latin and English **optimum** ("best") and all the words derived from it are probably from the same root: **optimal**, **optimism** ("tendency to look on the bright side of any situation"), **optimist**.

- English **office** also comes from the same Latin root: from *op-* + *facere,* literally, "work-do," hence "duty, function, service." Hence **official** and **officiate**. **Officious** is interesting, as it now means "carrying out one's duties in an excessively punctilious, bossy and overbearing manner." French actually has an even more clear-cut distinction between *officiel,* meaning "official" and *officieux,* meaning "unofficial, informal, behind the scenes."

- Less obviously from the same root: Latin *copia*, from *com* (lit. "with" but often just an intensive + *ops*) meaning "a plentiful supply, abundance," from which we get English **copious**, "abundant, plentiful" and **copy**, lit. "to write in plenty," hence "to duplicate, reproduce."

Greek *ergon* is a surprisingly rich source of English derivatives and related words:

- It is important to note that *ergon* not only means the same as English **work** but is actually cognate with it as well. In other words, the two words share a common origin. This becomes clearer when you realize that *ergon* started out as *Wergon*, with a /w/ sound at the beginning, originally represented by the digamma ("double gamma"), which was usually written as an F.

- The extremely common English word **energy**, meaning "power, force, strength, vigor," which also has more technical applications, as in **solar energy** and **nuclear energy**, is probably the most important derivative (by way of Latin and Old French) from *ergon*. **Energetic**, meaning "active, lively, vigorous," also has a wide range of meanings. Another really common derivative (coined by an Austrian physician in 1906) is **allergy** (lit. "other work, different activity"), referring to "a negative immune response by the body to any food or other substance to which it is sensitive or hypersensitive," and by extension, "an aversion or hostility" to anything, as in: "He is **allergic** to hard work."

- Some fashionable business terms, notably **synergy** (lit. "working together"), based on the idea that "the whole is greater than the sum of its parts," and **ergonomics**, (lit. "work + law"), "the study of people's working conditions and environment."

- Some less obvious indirect derivatives in which the /e/ has morphed to an /o/ sound or a /u/ sound, as in: **organ** (lit. "something with which one works, a tool, an implement"), hence "an organ of the body," or, by extension, "the instrument by which something is done," as in "an organ of government," from which come **organism** ("a living entity, or a system analogous to a living entity"), **organize/organise** ("to systematize"), **organization/organisation** ("something that is organized, a group of people organized for some work or purpose").

❖ **Orgy** ("wild revelry involving group sexual activity") seems remote from the idea of work. But it is a good example of semantic drift, coming as it does from *ergon* via Greek *orgia*, referring to "wild rites in the service of a god, especially Dionysus," presumably by extension from the general idea of "service, worship."

❖ **Surgery** comes, via Latin *(chirurgia)* and Old French, from Greek *cheir* + *ergon*, literally "hand-work," and hence "medical treatment performed by manual operative procedures." In the UK the standard medical qualification is the joint "Bachelor of Medicine, Bachelor of Surgery" degree, or, in Latin, *Medicinae Baccalaureus, Chirurgiae Baccalaureus*, commonly abbreviated "MB ChB."

❖ **Liturgy** ("religious service") comes, via Latin and Middle French, from Greek *leito-* ("public") + *ergon* ("work, service"). **Metallurgy** similarly means, literally "metal work," hence the "scientific study of metals."

In French *travail* is the ordinary word for "work," while English **travail** refers to "an unpleasant situation or experience, usually involving a lot of effort," as in: "The travails of the Trump administration over Russia." The origin of the word is Late Latin *trepalium*, "an instrument of torture with three stakes" – reflecting a somewhat negative attitude to work! Despite (or maybe, because of) this unpromising beginning, the word has given rise to the usual term for "work" in several Romance languages: *trabajo* (Spanish), *trabalho* (Portuguese), *treball* (Catalan). Italian has stuck more closely to Classical Latin with *lavoro* ("work"), from Latin *labor*, while Romanian, often an outlier, uses *munca*, borrowed from neighboring (non-Indo-European) Hungarian *munka*.

The ordinary German word for "work" is *Arbeit*, though German also has the word *Werk*, referring to the end-product of work rather than the activity, so (in the plural) the finished works of a writer or composer. The relationship between German *Arbeit* and *Werk* is similar to that between *labor* and *opus* in Latin and between *travail* and *oeuvre* in French. German *Werke* in the plural can also have the same connotation as English **works** in industry, as in *BMW*, the abbreviation for a well-known German automobile manufacturer: *Bayerischer Motoren Werke*, "Bavarian Motor Works," their blue and white logo reflecting the Bavarian coat of arms.

In Dutch and Afrikaans the regular word for "work" is *werk* – cognate with Greek *ergon* – but most of the other Germanic languages have a word related to German *Arbeit*: Danish *arbejde*, Norwegian *arbeid* and Swedish *arbete*. But English does actually have a word related to *Arbeit* as well: **robot**, "an automaton, an android, a human-like machine that performs mechanical tasks on command." The computer term **bot** is actually short for **robot** and refers to "an automated computer program that performs online searches and other (sometimes malicious) tasks."

**Robot** entered the English language in a rather unusual way: through a 1920s science fiction play by Czech writer Karel Capek about artificial people called *roboti*, a made-up word modeled on the Czech word *robota*, meaning "forced labor, drudgery," which in turn comes from the Czech word *rab*, meaning "slave." In several other Slavic languages *robota* (Ukrainian) or *rabota* (Russian, Bulgarian, Macedonian) is the ordinary word for "work."

These words are all cousins of German *Arbeit* and have the same meaning as well. The origin of this group of words is a root meaning "to be deprived," represented by Latin *orbus* ("orphaned, deprived, destitute") and Greek *orphanos* ("orphaned, fatherless") – from which, via Late Latin *orphanus*, we get English **orphan**. The jump from the concept of "deprivation" to that of "slavery" and thence to "work" is not as much of a leap as might at first have been expected. What about German *Erbe*, meaning "an heir"? This is part of the same group of words, too, the concept of inheritance not being a million miles from that of being orphaned. There are related words in the other Germanic languages: Dutch *erven* and Afrikaans *erf* mean "to inherit," and, by extension, in both those languages *erf* as a noun refers to property, especially land – the most traditional type of inheritance of all. The words for "heir" in the other Germanic languages are also related: Danish *arving*, Norwegian *arving*, Swedish *arvinge*, Icelandic *erfingi*.

# CHAPTER 6

# THE FRENCH CONNECTION

IT IS COMMONLY suggested (by *Wikipedia*, for example) that 29% of English words come from French and a further 29% from Latin. This is misleading, as many of the words of Latin origin entered English via French. A computerized tally published by Andreas Simon in 2017 indicates that, after the 1,875 most frequently used English words (which are very largely of Germanic origin), words of French and Latin origin together represent 56% of the core vocabulary of 5,000 words.[40] Henriette Walter has suggested that "words of French origin represent more than two thirds of English vocabulary."[41]

The French incursion into the English language happened in several waves, starting with the Norman Conquest of 1066, which remains probably *the* most memorable date in the whole of English history. It is estimated that about 10,000 French words, mostly derived from Latin, crossed the channel in the wake of the Conquest, around 7,000 of which survive in modern English.[42]

The language brought by the Normans to England is known as Anglo-Norman or Anglo-Norman French. This was overlaid on top of a bedrock of Old English or Anglo-Saxon, a Germanic language, which continued to be spoken by the great majority of the population. French vocabulary gradually began to percolate down in the period of

---

[40] Andreas Simons, "The English language is a lot more French than we thought, here's why" – medium.com/@andreas_simons.
[41] "influence of French on English" – Wikipedia.
[42] medium.com/English-language-faq.

Middle English, conventionally dated by the OED to between 1150 and 1500. Early Modern English, roughly covering the period from the accession of Henry VII in 1485 until the Restoration in 1660, covering what is sometimes called the English Renaissance, saw a further influx of French words into English together with Latin and, on a smaller scale, Greek "borrowings." Late Modern English or just Modern English, as it is sometimes called, takes the story down to the present day. The Industrial Revolution, the development of technology, British colonization, and the rise of American English, all added to the richness of the language with words chiefly from Latin, largely "borrowed" directly, but many still via French as well.

## 1066 and all that

William the Conqueror defeated the luckless King Harold at the Battle of Hastings in 1066. Harold may or may not have been killed by an arrow to the eye. The near-contemporary Bayeux Tapestry is not quite clear on the point, though there is little doubt that Harold was killed in battle. His mother's offer to pay William the weight of Harold's dismembered body in order to retrieve it was curtly denied. Instead, William ordered Harold's body to be thrown into the sea, but several competing versions of Harold's end kept swirling around for quite some time, including the charming legend that he did not die at Hastings at all, but escaped and became a hermit in Chester.

Although William claimed the English throne through his relationship with the childless Edward the Confessor, his first cousin once removed, who appears to have chosen William as his successor, the Anglo-Saxon to Norman transfer of power was far from seamless, even after being cemented by battle. Indeed, after the Battle of Hastings the Witenagemot (a precursor of Parliament) elected Edgar Aetheling, a nephew of Edward the Confessor, as king.

The Norman Conquest of England had a momentous linguistic effect on the British Isles by overlaying the existing Anglo-Saxon or Old English (a pure Germanic language) with a variety of Norman French (a Romance language) now known as Anglo-Norman French or simply Anglo-Norman.

The ruling Normans would not have known any Anglo-Saxon, so their Saxon subjects had to learn Norman French. When the Norman baron, seated at table, wanted a joint of **beef**, he would clap his hands and demand *buef* (Modern French *boeuf*). The Saxon herdsman, summoned into the august presence of the Norman baron, would probably have been nonplussed – at first. But it would soon dawn on him that what his lord was calling for was what he himself knew in its live state as *oxa*. In Modern English these words are **beef** and **ox** respectively, which however are not synonyms. The Norman baron saw the animal only as meat served up at table, which remains the meaning of **beef** today, while the Germanic word **ox** refers to the animal while alive and well and walking around on all fours, as the Saxon herdsman would have experienced it. In North America, however, the word **beef** and, curiously, a now archaic plural form, **beeves**, continued to be used for livestock well into the nineteenth century.[43]

A similar near-duplication is found with other animals. A slaughtered **pig**, known to the Saxon herdsman as *swin*, which in Modern English has become **swine**, when roasted and served up at table would have been hailed by the Norman lord as *porc*, which in Modern English is of course **pork**. The origin of **pig**, according to the OED is "obscure." **Swine**, now used chiefly as an insult or term of abuse, belongs to PIE *\*su-* "pig," from which we also get **sow**, "a female pig." Cognates include Latin *sus*, "pig" and Greek *hys* "pig," not to be confused with Greek *hyios*, meaning "son." (The Roman Emperor Augustus is said to have remarked in Greek that he would rather be King Herod's pig, *hys*, than Herod's son, *hyios*, because Herod, who was Jewish, would not slaughter a pig but did have his own son put to death!) The

---

[43] See *The Natchez Court Records, 1767-1805*, Reprint, Clearfield, 2009, p. 297 and Paul I. Wellman, *The Trampling Herd*, Reprint, University of Nebraska Press, 1988, pp. 91-92.

## THE FRENCH CONNECTION

equivalence between initial Latin [s-] and Greek [h-] or rough breathing, is described elsewhere in this book.[44]

**Gammon**, "cured or smoked ham," is from Norman French *gambon* (Modern French *jambon*, "ham" from *jambe*, "leg"), from Late Latin *gamba*, "animal leg," which is found in the Italian name for the precursor to the modern cello known as the *viola da gamba*, or "viol for the leg" (a large instrument held upright between the legs as distinct from the violin or viola, known as *viola da braccio*, or "viol for the arm," which is held under the chin). Late Latin *gamba* itself is from Greek *kampe* ("a bend, a curve") from Greek *kampto, kamptein* ("to bend, to curve"). The conceptual link here is presumably the bend of the knee joint. Hence English **gambol**, "to leap about playfully." English **door jamb** ("a doorpost, side-post of a doorway") is so called from its supposed resemblance to a horse's leg. English **campus**, now used in reference to "college or university grounds," is from Latin *campus*, "an open field," which de Vaan suggests is of the same origin, though the semantic connection seems tenuous at best. However, from Latin *campus* comes French *champ* "field," as in the famous boulevard in Paris, the *Champs Élysées*, as do English **camp, camping** and **encamp**, originally with a military connotation meaning "battle, struggle," which is reflected in German *Kampf*, "battle, struggle," – an early Germanic borrowing from Latin – as in Adolf Hitler's book, *Mein Kampf*.

**Calf/veal** and **sheep/mutton** are similar doublets, the former being the Germanic word for the living animal and the latter the French-based word for it as meat served up at table. **Veal**, now *veau* in French, comes ultimately from Latin *vitellus*, "a little calf." **Sheep** is paralleled by German *Schaf*, Dutch *schaap*, Afrikaans *skaap,* while **mutton** is from Old French *moton*, now *mouton* in Modern French. **Lamb** is used in English, both for the living animal, a young sheep, and for its meat. Cognates of English **lamb**, with the same meaning,

---

[44] See Chapter 11, A GREEK DRAMA.

are found in the other Germanic languages: German *Lamm*, Dutch and Afrikaans *lam*, Danish and Norwegian *lam*, Swedish *lamm*. Interestingly, the earliest reference cited in the OED to **lamb** as meat dates only from 1620. Today "**lamb**" is regularly found on menus, while "**mutton**" hardly ever is – probably indicative of a desire on the part of restaurateurs and hoteliers to give the impression that the meat is from a younger rather than an older animal. Cf. "Mutton dressed as lamb" referring to an older woman trying to look younger. This phrase was probably also intended as a pun, as **dressed** has an alternative meaning of meat cleaned and prepared for cooking. The English word **dress** is ultimately from Latin *dirigere* "to set straight," from *dis-* "in different directions, away" or "de-" "down" + *rego, regere, rectum* "to rule, direct, guide." If taken as compounded with *dis-*, it would appear to mean "To arrange in different directions," exactly the opposite of its main meanings in Latin, namely, according to Lewis & Short, "To give a particular direction to, to set in a straight line, to send in a straight line, to direct to a place." So perhaps the correct derivation is not from *dis-* but from *de-*, which Lewis & Short describe as a different word, and the OED gives as an alternative. From the sense of "to set straight," which still survives as a military command, as in "Dress right, dress!" and the tailoring enquiry, "On which side does Sir dress?" (referring to the position of a male customer's penis), **dress** now has as its chief meaning "to decorate, adorn, put on clothes," parallel to **address**, which is **dress** compounded with Latin *ad-* "to, towards," so "to mark as the destination of a letter, speak to directly." Similarly, **direct**, meaning "to point in the right direction, guide, order."

English is exceptional in having so many different words for the living animal and for the slaughtered animal used as meat – an example of the enrichment of the language as a result of the French Connection, which continued with French loanwords long after the Norman Conquest.

The Norman barons were evidently big meat eaters – though not meat-and-potatoes people, because the potato only reached Europe from South America in the 16th century. But were the Normans not partial to **fish**? The English word **fish**, of Germanic origin, is and has always been used to represent both the living and the dead animal. The words for "fish" in other Germanic languages are German *Fisch*, Dutch and Afrikaans *vis*, and Danish, Norwegian and Swedish *fisk*.

The PIE grandaddy of all these Germanic words is *\*pisk-*, which also gave rise to Latin *piscis*, which in turn spawned Italian *pesce*, Spanish *pescado*, Portuguese *peixe*, Catalan *peix*, and (yes!) French *poisson*. From Latin *piscis* derive Italian, Spanish and Portuguese *piscina* and French *piscine*, literally "a fishpond," and hence "pool or swimming pool" – but pronounced in a way that might suggest a rather ruder meaning, though one undoubtedly reflected in reality!

The Classical Greek word for "fish," *ichthys*, supposedly comes from a completely different PIE root, variously represented by the unpronounceable *\*dguH-* [45] or the equally unpronounceable *\*dhghu-*. [46] English derivatives from *ichthys* include **ichthyology**, "the study of fish," and **ichthyologist** "someone who studies fish." Evangelical Christians can sometimes be seen sporting a brooch or badge depicting a fish, denoting the Greek letters making up the word I-CH-TH-Y-S , an acronym for the Greek words *Iesous Christos, Theou (H)Yios, Soter*, meaning "Jesus Christ, Son of God, Savior." In Modern Greek, *ichthys* has been supplanted by *psari* "fish," from Classical Greek *opsarion*, diminutive of *opson*, "side dish of meat or fish."

**Motoring and transportation**

Surprisingly, perhaps, words of French origin figure prominently in motoring and transportation:

---

[45] Beekes.
[46] EOL.

- **Automobile**, a Greek-Latin hybrid via the French, made up of: **auto-** (Greek *autos* "self") plus **mobile** (from Latin *mobilis* "movable," from Latin *moveo, movere, motum* "to move.")

- **Chauffeur**, "(professional) driver," French *chauffeur*, an early nickname for "a motorist," from French *chauffer*, "to warm up," from Latin *calefacere* "to make hot," from Latin *caleo, calere* "to be warm" + Latin *facio, facere, factum* "to make." Latin *caleo, calere*, from which we get **calorie** "unit of heat." Also, French *chauffer*, from which we get **chafe** "to inflame (feelings), vex, irritate, irritate the skin by rubbing." Latin *calidus* "warm" has derivatives Italian *caldo*, Spanish *caliente*, Portuguese *caloroso*, and *quente*, from Old Portuguese *caente* "hot, warm" all meaning "hot, warm" – and of course French *chaud*, "hot, warm." Warning: Don't assume that [C] on a tap/faucet in a hotel means "cold," In France and other Francophone areas, such as Quebec – or rather, Québec – in Canada, the chances are that [C] stands for *"chaud."* A misunderstanding could scald you!

- **Car**, from Late Latin *carra*, from Latin *carrus* "a wagon," evidently from Old Celtic *\*karros* "war chariot," which entered Anglo-French or Old Norman French as *carre*. In Modern French *car* means "a bus, coach," but an automobile is *une voiture, from Latin veho, vehere, vectum*, "bear, convey, carry," from which we get English **vehicle**, the "official" legal term for a **motor car**, whereas in ordinary English the word **car** is the most usual term, while in American English it is often called an **automobile**, from Greek *autos* "self" + Latin *mobile* "movable" from *moveo, movere, motum* "to move." In American English, **car** is used to refer to a railway carriage, and this usage carried over to the London Underground, where a carriage is still referred to "officially" as a **car**, as in "Please move to the front of the car." **Carry**, **carriage**, **career**, **charge** (via French) and **cargo** (via Spanish) are from the same origin. **Car** is ultimately derived from the major PIE root *\*kers-* "to run," giving rise to Latin *curro, currere, cursum*, and all its derivatives, such as **current, currency, cursor, cursory, cursive, occur, concur, discursive**, and, via French *cours*, meaning "stream of water, course (of events), course (of study)": **course, courier, concourse, corridor** (from Italian), **recourse**.

- **Saloon**, a type of motor car with a closed top for four persons, as against a **coupe**, a two-seater, from French *couper* "to cut (in half)," from French *coup* "a blow," as in **coup d'état**, which has been taken over bodily into English. **Coup** is from Latin *colaphus*, an early low-class borrowing from Greek *kolaphos* "a blow, punch, slap." The **saloon** or **dining saloon** on a train. Also a **saloon bar** in a pub or public house, proving greater comfort than the public bar. **Saloon** is from French *salon*, "elegant reception room," often used to describe a regular meeting place of a "high society" French lady, such as Louis XV's mistress Madame de Pompadour. **Salon** has been imported directly into English, as in **hairdressing salon**. From *salle* "hall, room for some specific purpose," as in *salle à manger* "dining room," from Old High German *Sal*, Modern German *Saal* "hall."

- ❖ **Chassis**, "the base frame of a motor car, with its mechanism, as distinguished from the body or upper part" (OED). Taken over directly from the French, from Latin *capsa* "box, case," from which comes English **case** "cover, container," as in **briefcase**, from Latin *capio, capere, cepi, captum* "to take," with its huge family of derivatives, including **capable**, **capture**, **accept**, **receive**, **deceive** – and cognate with **have** and all its Germanic cousins. Not connected with **case** from Latin *casus*, lit. "a falling" meaning "an event, legal matter," as in **case-law**, also grammatical **case**, lit. "a falling from the nominative," from Latin *cado, cadere, cecidi, casum* "to fall."

- ❖ **Cab**, abbreviated from French *cabriolet* "light horse-drawn carriage," a diminutive ultimately from Latin *caper, capri* "goat," meaning "leaping like a young goat." **Cab** has almost equal standing in both Britain and America with **taxi** (short for **taximeter**) with which it is sometimes combined as in **taxicab**. **Taxi** is from French ultimately from Medieval Latin *taxa*, "tax, charge." As a verb, to **taxi** refers to an aircraft's slow movement on the ground possibly "in allusion to the way a taxi driver slowly cruises when looking for fares" (Barnhart).

- ❖ **Engine**, from French *engin* "instrument, machine," from Latin *ingenium* "innate ability," from Latin *in-* ("in") + *gigno, gignere, genitum*, "to give birth, beget," from one of the most important PIE roots, *\*gen-* "to give birth, beget."[47]

---

[47] See the section on IT'S ALL IN YOUR GENES.

## False friends – faux amis

Many French words that have entered English in either the same or altered form are "false friends" or faux amis, because their meanings are different – sometimes hilariously or embarrassingly so.[48]

- **Assist/attend**: The meaning of these words is very different in English and French – almost opposites, in fact. Though French *assister* can mean "to help, assist," its most usual meaning is "to attend." French *attendre*, on the other hand, means "to wait, await."

- **Genial**: This word is part of the major Indo-European word family based on the PIE root *\*gen-*, meaning "to give birth, beget, produce, generate," on which see the section titled IT'S ALL IN YOUR GENES. English **genial** itself, ultimately from Latin *gigno, gignere, genitum* "to beget, procreate," originally indicated some connection with the marital bed, but now means simply "cheerful, pleasant." In French, however, *génial* means "genius" and is now used in colloquial speech as an exclamation equivalent to "Super!" indicating excited approval. English **genius** is of course also related, indicating "inborn nature, natural spirit" and hence "a person of high natural intelligence" and also "distinctive spirit, character," as in "Rasputin was considered by many to be the **evil genius** of the Russian imperial family."

- **Sensible**: From Latin *sentio, sentire, sensum* "to feel, perceive," English **sensible**, "rational, endowed with common sense," used to mean "aware," as in "He is **sensible** of his mistake." Cf. the title of Jane Austen's novel *Sense and Sensibility* (1811), a tale of two sisters, one of whom epitomized **sense**, meaning "good judgment, prudence," while the other represented **sensibility**, or "sensitivity, sympathy or emotion." Thomas Paine popularized the term **Common Sense** in his pamphlet of that name published in 1776, but it was already well-established by then, being defined in 1535 as "the plain wisdom that everyone possesses," though it may well be doubted that **common sense** is as common or widespread as that implies. The meaning of French *sensible* is more akin to Jane Austen's understanding of the term, namely "sensitive," but it can also mean "perceptible." To

---

[48] See Saul H. Rosenthal, French Faux Amis: The Combined Book, Tucson: Wheatmark, 2009.

## THE FRENCH CONNECTION

translate English **sensible** French would say *sensé* or *raisonnable*, from which of course we get English **reasonable**. In English law there has been a certain amount of confusion between "*Wednesbury* **unreasonableness**" and "**irrationality**," both of which derive ultimately from Latin *ratio, rationis* "reason, reasoning, understanding."[49]

❖ **Preservative**: From Latin *prae-* "beforehand, in advance, ahead" + *servo, servare, servatum* "to keep, keep safe, save, guard," as in "**artificial preservatives**." However, French *préservatif* has a completely different meaning, namely "a condom," presumably from the sense of "prevention" rather than "preservation." Note: Latin *servo, servare, servatum* and its derivatives **conserve, conservation, conservative, reserve, reservation** are unconnected with Latin *servio, servire, servitum* "to serve" and its derivatives **serve, service, servile, serf, servant, deserve, subservient. Desert** meaning "what one deserves," as in "getting your just deserts," is also from Latin *servio*. **Dessert** "pudding sweets, fruit (after meal)" is from *dis-* lit. "in different directions," or with a general negative connotation, + *servio, servire*, so literally "to un-serve," hence "to clear the table (after the meal)." But **desert** meaning "a wasteland" and the verb **desert** meaning "to run away" have a different origin altogether, from Latin *desero, deserere, desertum*, from *de-* "down from," or with a general negative connotation + *sero, serere* "to join together," so "to abandon, quit (without permission)."

❖ **Sympathetic**: What is the difference in meaning between the English words **sympathetic**, **simpatico**, **empathetic** and **pathetic**? They all come from Greek *pathos* "suffering, feeling, emotion," which has entered English directly as **pathos**, referring to a work of art or play "evoking pity or compassion" (MW), cf. **bathos** "ludicrous anticlimax, a descent from the sublime to the ridiculous" (EOL), from Greek *bathos* "depth." Two famous classical compositions are known by the French sobriquet "*Pathétique*," meaning "moving, emotive" – Beethoven's Piano Sonata No. 8 and Tchaikovsky's Symphony No. 6 – the latter evidently a mistranslation of a Russian word meaning "passionate." But

---

[49] A decision so unreasonable that no reasonable person could have made it. The expression stems from a celebrated case in English law (Associated Provincial Picture Houses v Wednesbury Corporation (1948). See M. Arnheim, *Anglo-American Law: A Comparison*, 2019.

English **pathetic** has a completely different meaning, "pitiful," often used in colloquial speech as an exclamation of opprobrium: "What a **pathetic** excuse!" English **sympathetic**, from Greek *syn-* "together" + *pathos* "suffering" means "well-disposed, favourably inclined," as in "Though the jury was sympathetic to his plight, they still found him guilty." Cf. **simpatico**, borrowed directly from Spanish and Italian, meaning "easy to get on with." English **empathy** and **empathetic**, a 19th century German coinage from Greek *en-* "in" + *pathos* "feeling," refers to the ability of an observer "being sensitive to and vicariously experiencing the feelings ... of another." (MW) French "*sympathique* doesn't mean sympathetic, it means likeable, warm, agreeable, nice or pleasant" (*Faux Amis*) – similar therefore to *simpatico*.

- **Actual**: From Latin *actus*, "a doing," from *ago, agree, actum*, "to do, drive," hence "real, as against imagined or planned," hence **actually**, which has become one of the commonest "filler" words in colloquial English: "Are you coming to the party tomorrow?" "I don't think so, because I wasn't actually invited." French *actuel,* by contrast, means "current, at present," hence *actualités*, meaning "news."

- **Realize/realise**: From Latin *res* "thing, matter," English has two distinct meanings: firstly, "to make real," as in "to realize your dreams," and secondly, by extension from the first meaning, "to recognize, understand, become aware." French *réalisation* has the same meaning as the first English sense, but lacks the second one altogether. However, the French verb *réaliser,* while officially frowned upon, is now used colloquially in much the same way as both English senses.

- **Envy** – From Latin *invideo, invidere, invisus*, "to look askance at, to be prejudiced against, to envy, begrudge. However, though French *envie* can also mean "envy," it generally has the far less hostile meaning of "desire, craving."

- **Officious**: From Latin *officium*, from *opificium*, made up of *opus* "work" + *facio, facere, factum* "to do, make," so "service, function, duty," hence Latin *officiosus* "obliging, courteous, dutiful," but in English *officious* has come to mean "over-zealous, bossy, bureaucratic," while French *officieux* still retains something of the flavor of the original Latin and actually means "unofficial." English **official** is *officiel* in French, and the French for **efficient**, which is effectively the opposite of **officious**, is *efficace*.

## THE FRENCH CONNECTION

- **Library**: French *librairie* and its cognates in the other Romance languages do not mean "library" but "bookshop, bookstore." For "library" the Romance languages resort to the Greek word for book, *biblion*, hence French *bibliothèque*.

- **Patron**: From Latin *pater* "father," in English, this word has come to be used to refer to a regular customer of a business or restaurant, or a supporter of a public institution such as a library or symphony orchestra, but in French it refers to the proprietor of a restaurant or other such establishment.

- **Eventual**: From Latin *e(x)-* "out, out of" + *venio, venire, ventum* "to come," so lit. "coming out of…," hence ultimate, final," but French *éventuel* means "possible" and the French for English **eventually** is *enfin* or *finalement*. However, English **eventuality** is much closer to the French, meaning as it does "a possible occurrence," as in: "In the unlikely eventuality of a storm…"

- **Forfeit**: From Latin *foris* "outside, beyond" + *factum* "deed" via French, "a misdeed, offence," and by extension "penalty for misdeed," but in French *forfait* also has the very different meaning of a fixed-price contract for rental etc., though quite why is not entirely clear.

- **Parent**: From Latin *pario, parire, partum*, "to give birth," hence parturition. But don't be surprised to be told in French: "*je n'ai que trois parents*," which does not mean "I have only three parents," but "I have only three relatives."

- **Bless**: From a Germanic root related to **blood**. French *blesser* "to wound, hurt" is from a completely different Germanic origin meaning "to discolour, bruise." It seems to have started life meaning "to bruise" in the sense of "to discolour," and thence "to wound" more generally, figuratively as well as literally.

# CHAPTER 7

# A ROMAN TRIUMPH

IN A SENSE, the Roman Empire never came to an end:

- Latin remained the language of serious discourse and academic writing for well over a thousand years after 476, the conventional date of the fall of the Roman Empire in the West. As late as the seventeenth century Thomas Hobbes (1588–1679), the great British philosopher, complained that Latin had ruined his English writing style – and he actually composed his magnum opus, *Leviathan*, in Latin before translating it himself into English. For a long time after Classical Greek was introduced into the curriculum at Oxford and Cambridge in the 1530s, Greek writings were always printed interleaved with a Latin translation. In the Dutch universities, lectures were still given in Latin until well into the 19th century. This practice was only discontinued when a professor casually remarked in Latin in the course of a lecture, "*Claudite cortinas!*" ("Close the curtains!"), and, instead of acting on this instruction, the students just wrote it down in their notebooks.
- Until the second Vatican Council of 1962–65, Latin was the language of the Roman Catholic Mass all round the world, when it was phased out in favour of the vernacular in the various countries. However, Latin remains the official language of the Church and of the Roman curia, the central administration of the Vatican, though the working language of the curia and of the synod of bishops is now Italian. The Vulgate, the translation of the Bible into Latin by St Jerome in the late fourth century was the official Bible of the Catholic Church until the publication in 1979 (and revised in 1986) of the *Nova Vulgata*, or "New Vulgate," written in a more Classical form of Latin. Until the late sixteenth century, the Catholic Church did not allow the Bible to be translated into any vernacular language. The Latin Vulgate was the only

Bible allowed, and it was chained up in churches, so nobody could read the Bible at home, even if they could understand Latin, which few of the ordinary people would have been able to do. The translation of the Bible into English by William Tyndale (1494–1536) was banned by royal proclamation in 1530. Fleeing abroad, he was eventually sentenced to death for heresy by the authorities in present-day Belgium and, after being strangled, was burnt at the stake. Yet, only three years later, with Henry VIII's switch to Protestantism for his own personal reasons, the King authorized for use in church services the so-called Great Bible, an English translation based on Tyndale's banned version!

- ❖ Latin has survived as a living spoken language by morphing into what are now known as the Romance languages, the main ones being French, Italian, Spanish, Catalan, Portuguese and Romanian.[50]

- ❖ A number of Latin expressions are used unchanged in English. So embedded have some of them become that English speakers may not even realize that they are direct imports. Here are a few examples:
  - *Ad hoc* – lit. "to this," so "for a specific temporary purpose," as in: "This arrangement is made on an *ad hoc* basis."
  - *Ante meridiem* – lit. "before noon," always abbreviated *a.m.*, as distinct from *post meridiem*, "after noon," abbreviated *p.m.* The all too common misunderstanding of these simple abbreviations is a sign of illiteracy. How often have you seen a notice or sign announcing an event as due to take place at "12 p.m."? In fact, of course, there is no such time, because 12 o'clock is either noon or midnight and is not either "before noon" or "after noon." So, what is the correct substitution for "12 p.m." or "12 a.m."? Instead of "12 p.m." you just have to say, "12 noon" or simply "noon," and replace "12 a.m." with "midnight."
  - *Alibi* – lit. "elsewhere," but it is used as a noun in English, meaning evidence given by an accused that he was not at the scene of the crime at the crucial time, as in: "Would Lee Harvey Oswald have had an *alibi* if he had been charged with the assassination of President Kennedy?"

---

[50] For more on this, see Chapter 10, LATIN ROMANCE.

- *Bona fide* – lit. "in good faith," used in English as an adjective meaning "real, genuine," as in: "Are you a *bona fide* refugee or just an economic migrant?" *Bona fide* is often pronounced to rhyme with "slide," but this is not actually correct. The final [e] should not be silent.
- *Carpe diem* – lit. "seize the day," so "grab the opportunity, don't let grass grow under your feet," an aphorism made famous by the Roman poet, Horace (65–8 BCE). Similar sentiments are expressed in the medieval student song, *Gaudeamus igitur* ("Let us rejoice therefore"), dating from 1287 and still popular today.
- *Curriculum vitae* – lit. "course of life," usually abbreviated *c.v.*, a summary of one's education, qualifications and experience prepared by an applicant for a position or employment, a résumé. **Curriculum** on its own now refers to the syllabus of study at a college or university. From Latin *curro, currere, cursum* ("to run"), from which come, directly or via French, English **current** (but not **currant**), **currency**, **course** (but not **coarse**), **recourse**, **concourse**, **discourse**, **intercourse**, **courier** and **corridor**.
- *De facto* – lit. "in fact," used in English to denote the factual as against de jure, the legal position, e.g. "Cardinal Richelieu was the de facto ruler of France during the reign of Louis XIII."
- *Ego* – lit. "I," used in English to mean "the self," as in: "To become president of America you need a big ego." The terms ego, id (lit. "it") and super-ego were appropriated by Sigmund Freud (1856–1939) for use in psychoanalysis: "In its relation to the id, [the ego] is like a man on horseback, who has to hold in check the superior strength of the horse."[51] The id acts as a conscience. In English, the [e] in ego is usually pronounced like the [e] in "serious," which is strictly incorrect, as it is short in Latin, like the [e] in "egg." From Latin *ego* we have English **egoism** and **egotism**, which are not synonyms. **Egotism** is "an exaggerated sense of self importance or conceit," whereas **egoism** means simply "undue concern for oneself."

---

[51] Quoted Wikipedia, "Id, ego and super-ego."

- *Ergo* – "therefore," and used in the same sense in English, chiefly in a formal context, with pompous overtones. The Latin phrase *Cogito ergo sum* ("I think, therefore I am") is a fundamental philosophical argument propounded by the French philosopher René Descartes (1596–1650).
- *Et cetera* – lit. "and the rest," meaning "and other similar things," generally abbreviated "etc." or sometimes "&c," greatly overused in English as a filler, e.g. "I like apples, oranges, duck, etc."
- *Ex post facto* – lit. "from something done afterwards," so "retroactive," as in: "The UK War Crimes Act 1991 gave the courts ex post facto jurisdiction over crimes committed half a century earlier."
- *Exempli gratia* – lit. "For the sake of example," simply "for example." Always abbreviated "e.g."
- *Festina lente* – A favourite expression of the Emperor Augustus – lit. "make haste slowly," similar to the English phrase "more haste, less speed."
- *Id est* – lit. "it is," always abbreviated "i.e.," meaning "that is, in other words." Often misused instead of *videlicet* (lit. "it is permitted to see," "it may be seen," so "namely, to wit"), strangely abbreviated to "viz.," a manuscript shorthand from the days before the invention of printing. Viz., which is largely confined to scholarly references, is not an exact synonym of i.e., and neither should be confused with e.g. For example: (a) "King Kong has four children, viz. Eenie, Meenie, Minie and Mo." It would be wrong to use i.e. here, just as it would be wrong to say, "King Kong has four children, that is Eenie, Meenie, Minie and Mo." (b) But i.e. is correct in this sentence: "King Kong does not wear clothes, i.e. he is naked." The test is to replace i.e. with, "that is" or "in other words." So, "King Kong does not wear clothes; in other words, he is naked." (c) Viz. and i.e. are almost interchangeable, but it is a real solecism to mistake either for e.g. The test here is whether you can replace e.g. with "for example." So: "King Kong likes fruit, e.g. bananas." This is correct, as you can restate the sentence as: "King Kong likes fruit, for example bananas."
- *Impromptu* – A contraction of Latin *in promptu*, lit. "in readiness," though its meaning is seemingly the opposite of this: "extempore" (from Latin, lit. "out of time"), extemporaneous,

unrehearsed, improvised (from Latin *in* + *provisus*, lit. "unforeseen"), e.g. "The student made an impromptu speech about why he had failed to prepare his presentation."

- *Per se* – lit. "by itself" or "by themselves," much overused, but correct as in: "Belief in the Big Bang per se is not enough to explain evolution."

- *Pro bono (publico)* – lit. "for the public good," meaning legal representation without charge. "*Publico*" is usually omitted. Alternatively referred to in certain jurisdictions (e.g. the Netherlands) as *Pro Deo*, lit. "for God."

- *Quid pro quo* – lit. "what for what," so "something in return for something else," e.g. "President Trump was accused of demanding a *quid pro quo* in return for military aid to Ukraine." **Quid** meaning a pound sterling may possibly have the same origin.

- *Re* – Short for Latin *in re*, "in the matter of" Originally in the title of a lawsuit but now commonly used in the sense of "about," "concerning" as in the subject of an email reading: "Re: Moon Travel."

- *Status quo (ante)* – Short for *status quo ante bellum*, lit. "the situation before the war," a term originating in the language of diplomacy, then shorted with a more general meaning to *status quo ante* and just *status quo*, meaning "the existing state of affairs."

- *Verbatim* – lit. "word-for-word," a literal transcription of the original. From Latin *verbum*, "word."

- *Versus* – lit. "against," and used in the same sense in English, abbreviated either to "vs." or just "v." especially in the title of a lawsuit, as in "Hogg v. Frogg," or a sports match, as in "New York Yankees vs. Boston Red Sox."

- *Vice versa* – lit. "with position turned," so, "conversely, the other way round," e.g. "The earth revolves around the sun, not vice versa."

- *Felicior Augusto, melior Traiano* – lit. "(May you be) more fortunate than Augustus (and) better than Trajan," an invocation on the inauguration of a new Roman Emperor.

❖ Though the bedrock of English is Germanic, from Anglo-Saxon or Old English, about 60% of modern English vocabulary derives from Latin, either directly or via French.

## Roman Britain

Britannia, as the Romans called it, comprising England, Wales and, for a time, even the Lowlands of Scotland, formed part of the Roman Empire for about four hundred years, from the conquest by the Emperor Claudius in the year 743 until about 410, yet the Latin language never took hold. Yet there was considerable migration, both from within Britain and from the rest of the Roman Empire, to the cities established by the Romans, notably Camulodunum (Colchester), the first Roman city in Britain, Verulamium (St Albans), Eboracum (York), Mamucium (Manchester) and the capital, Londinium, now London, At its height at the end of the fourth century the population of Roman Britain probably numbered around 3.6 million, but the urban population was only about 240,000. The Roman settlements were abandoned not long after the Romans left in the early fifth century. The extensive network of Roman roads, aqueducts and conduits survived much longer than the Latin language. The majority language both before and after the Roman occupation was a form of Celtic and the only sign of Roman rule was about 800 words borrowed from Latin.

The Germanic tribes who dominated Britain after the Romans left spoke a variety of dialects that eventually coalesced into what is now called Anglo-Saxon or Old English. A descendant of this language remains the bedrock of Modern English, overlayed after the Norman Conquest of 1066 by Norman-French or Anglo-Norman, which was largely Latin-based. So, ironically, the first dollop of Latin was deposited not by the Romans during their 400-year rule, but much later by the Normans.

## Double-dipping

The chief reason for the richness of English vocabulary is its double-dipping into Latin: first via Norman-French and later by direct borrowing from Latin during the so-called Enlightenment and beyond. Taking both these sources together, words of Latin origin account for about 60% of the words in modern English. French, a Romance language, itself draws over 80% of its vocabulary from Latin. For example, the Latin word *rex, regis* ("king") has given rise in English to both **royal** (from Old French *roy*, Modern French *roi*) and **regal** (directly from Latin). Similarly, English **legal** is from Latin *legalis*, which in turn is from Latin *lex, legis* ("law"), which has also given rise to English **loyal** via Middle French *loyal*, from Middle French *loy*, Modern French *loi* ("law"). Latin *ligo, ligare, ligatum* ("to bind") has likewise given rise both to English **league** (from French *ligue*) **liable**, and **ally, alliance, lien** and **liaison** (all from the French) as well as to such English words as **ligament** and **ligature** directly from the Latin. The underlying concept common to all the words related to *ligo, ligare* is the idea of binding, whether literal or figurative. The sound shifts from Latin to French and the other Romance languages are discussed elsewhere in this book.[52]

Latin comes into its own in English particularly in more formal speech and writing, as for example in the oath of office of the President of the United States as laid down by the US Constitution:

"I do **solemnly** swear (or **affirm**) that I will **faithfully execute** the **Office** of **President** of the **United States** and will to the best of my **Ability, preserve, protect** and **defend** the **Constitution** of the **United States**."

All the words printed in bold are from Latin, either directly or via the French:

---

[52] See Chapter 10, A LATIN ROMANCE.

- **Solemnly**: From **solemn**, meaning "serious, earnest, formal, accompanied by religious sanctions," from Latin *sollemnis* "formal, ceremonial, religious," possibly related to Latin *sollus* "whole," from PIE root *\*sol-* "whole, entire, intact," from which via Latin and French come English **solicitous, solicitor, solid, solidarity, consolidate, solder, insouciant** and via Latin *salvus* ("safe") via French come English **save, safe, salute, salutary, salubrious, salvage**. **Soldier** is worth a mention, referring to "one who serves in an army for pay" (OED), from Latin (via French) *solidus*, a Roman gold coin. Cf. the phrase "the King's shilling" in reference to army pay. PIE *\*sol-* also gave rise to Greek *holos* "whole, entire," from which English **hologram, holocaust, catholic** (lit. "general, universal").

- **Affirm**: Literally "to make firm," so "to confirm, assert," from English **firm**, meaning "strong, steadfast, stable," from Latin *firmus* with the same meaning, giving us **confirm, infirm, infirmary, firmament, terra firma, farm** (from the idea of a fixed payment or lease, French *ferme*, meaning a farm, also French *fermer*, "to close").

- **Faithfully**: From **faithful**, meaning "loyal, honest, devout," from Latin *fides* ("faith, trust, belief") via French. Directly or indirectly from Latin *fides* come English **fidelity, hi-fi** (abbreviation of "high fidelity" implying sound quality "highly faithful" to the original), **Wi-Fi** (wireless internet capability, term modelled on hi-fi), **confide, confidence, con** ("confidence trick"), as in **con man** ("confidence trickster"), **confidant, diffident, diffidence, infidel, perfidy, fiduciary, affidavit, fiancé, faith**.

- **Execute**: Needless to say, this has nothing to do with capital punishment! Coming from Latin *ex* ("out") plus *sequor, sequi, secutus* ("follow"), English **execute** essentially means "to follow through, carry out." It can be used in a general sense or in a specific sense. Here it refers to the "carrying out" of the office of president. In a related sense, Article II of the US Constitution declares: "The **executive** Power shall be vested in a President of the United States." The government of the US (and of many other countries) is divided between the **executive**, the legislature (i.e. the lawmaking branch; in the US, this is the Congress), and the judiciary (i.e. the law courts.) The word **executive** can also refer to people in a company or business who have managerial responsibility. The connection of **execute** and **execution** with capital punishment is simply an application of the general sense of "carrying out" to carrying out a judicial death sentence. That is why in its earliest uses **execute** or **execution** needed some further explanatory word or phrase to indicate that it related to the death sentence. The OED quotes a 1577 source with the phrase "**executed to death.**" Incidentally, the term **capital punishment** is so called because it involves the head, from Latin *caput, capitis*, either literally, as in a **decapitation** (from the same origin) or **beheading**, or in a figurative sense, as in death by hanging, electrocution (by means of the "electric chair"), firing squad, or lethal injection. What all these different forms of punishment have in common is that they all cause death, and therefore, in a sense remove the "head."

- ❖ **Office**: Meaning "post, government position, official employment," from Latin *officium*, from which directly or indirectly come **officer, official, officious, forfeit**.

- ❖ **President**: From Latin *prae* ("in front") + *sedeo, sedere, sessum* ("to sit"), literally meaning "person sitting in front," hence "person in charge, head of state, institution or corporation." Not to be confused with **precedent**.

- ❖ **United**: From Latin *unus*, "one," from which come **unity, union, unison, unique, universe, university, universal, unanimous**. The name "United States" is actually misleading, as the country is not a **union** but a **federation**, a much looser type of association. Hence the **Federal Government**, the **Federal Bureau of Investigation** (**FBI**), the **Federal Reserve**, and the slang term "**the feds**." But at the same time there is the **State of the Union** address by the President, and, for example, the **Union Army** (in the Civil War).

- ❖ **States**: From Latin *status* ("standing, situation, position, arrangement") from *sto, stare, statum* ("to stand"). The transition from this general concept to the meaning of state as "country, province, domain" can be seen in this description of Sir Thomas More's *Utopia* (1551) as quoted by the OED: "A fruitful and pleasant work of the best **state** of a public weal." (Spelling modernized).

- ❖ **Ability**: From English **able**, which in turn is from Latin *habilis* ("manageable, fit, apt, expert") from Latin *habeo, habere, habitum* ("to have, hold"). The initial [h-] dropped off because it came via French *habile* ("skilful, deft, clever"), in which the [h-] is silent (as usual with initial [h-] in French.) The [h-] is preserved in related English words such as **habit, habitat, habitation, exhibit, inhibit, prohibit, prohibition**.

- **Preserve**: From Latin *prae-* ("before") + *servo, servare, servatum* ("to save, protect, keep safe"), related to English **conserve, conservative, observe, observatory, reserve, reservoir, reservation** (both in the literal sense of an area set aside, e.g. for Native Americans, and figuratively, as in "I have reservations about his proposal to fly to Mars"). But beware: French *préservatif* means "a condom," from the concept of protection. It is important to note that English **serve** and all its derivatives are from a different root altogether, Latin *servio, servire, servitum* ("to serve"), giving us **serve, service, servant, desert** (usually in plural, as in "just deserts"), but not **desert** (meaning "to leave, abandon"), **desert** ("wasteland"). However, **dessert**, traditionally used to refer to fresh fruit served after a meal but now more usually to pudding or "sweets" served after the main course of a meal, comes from the same root as **serve**, from Latin *dis-* (negative connotation) + *servio, servire, servitum* ("to serve"), so to "un-serve," as it were, "to clear the table." Cambridge students invited by their tutor to **dessert** (as used to be done) were surprised to find themselves offered fresh fruit, possibly with some cheese, instead of the puddings and pastries that they were expecting.

- **Protect**: From Latin *pro-* ("in front") + *tego, tegere, tectum* ("cover"), from which we get English **detect** (lit. "to uncover"), **detection, detective, integument**. From the Germanic cognate come English **deck, thatch, tile**. From the same origin come German *decken,* Dutch *dekken* ("to cover").

- **Defend**: From **Latin** *defendo, defendere, defensum* (lit. "to ward off, repel, avert, keep off") from *de-* ("down from, away") + *-fendo* ("to ward off" – does not exist on its own), from which come English **defence** (British spelling), **defense** (American spelling), **forfend** ("prevent"), archaic or jocular, as in **"Heaven forfend!"** ("God forbid!"). Cf. French *défense* ("prohibited"), as in *défense d'entrer* ("no entry").

- **Constitution**: From Latin *constitutio* ("order, ordinance, edict"), as in the *Constitutio Antoniniana*, an edict issued by the Roman Emperor Caracalla in the year 212 giving citizenship to all free men in the Roman Empire. From Latin *con-* (intensive) + *statuo, statuere, statutum* ("to set, place, arrange"), causative of Latin *sto, stare, statum* ("to stand").

The legal sense of **constitution** is a figurative extension of its literal meaning, "the way something is made up, composed," often as applied to health, e.g. "He has the constitution of a horse," "I go for a constitutional (run) every morning." English derivatives from Latin *sto, stare, statum* include **status, station, statue, statute, static, statistic, constitute, constituent, constituency, substitute, restitution, institute, institution, prostitute, prostitution, constable, obstacle, obstinate, circumstance, substance, estate, establish**. From Latin *sisto, sistere,* ("to place"), another causative of *sto, stare, statum* come ("stand") come English **consist, consistency, resist, resistance, subsist, subsistence**. From Greek cognate *histanai* ("to place, set") come **ecstasy, prostate** (but not **prostrate**, which is from *prosterno, prosternere, prostratum*, "to spread out in front"). Germanic words from the same root include English **stand, withstand, standard** and the following words all meaning "to stand": German *stehen*, Dutch and Afrikaans *staan* (as in the old Afrikaans song, *Brandewyn, laat my staan*, "brandy, leave me alone"), Danish, Norwegian and Swedish *stå*.

## CHAPTER 8

# A GRIMM TALE

ALMOST ALL THE languages of Europe are related to one another, the main exceptions being:

- Basque
- Finnish
- Estonian
- Sami
- Hungarian

Finnish, Estonian and the Sami languages (previously known as Lapp or Lappish, labels that are often now considered pejorative) are closely related to one another and, very much more distantly, to Hungarian, and belong to the Finno-Ugric family of languages, which, together with the so-called Samoyedic (or Samodeic) languages, forms the Uralic family.

Basque, or *Euskara* as it is called by its speakers, is spoken in an area straddling France and Spain in northern Spain and southwestern France. It is unrelated to any other known language, and so is technically a "language isolate." It is a highly complex language, with no fewer than 12 cases for nouns and adjectives. There has been a good deal of speculation about the origins of the Basque language and people. Detailed analysis of DNA samples found that Basque genetic patterns differed from those of the neighbouring non-Basque populations, pointing to the conclusion that the Basque presence in the area goes back to the Stone Age, predating the arrival on the scene of the Indo-Europeans.[53]

The overwhelming majority of the languages of Europe, including English, together with a number of languages spoken in Asia, belong to the vast Indo-European family. With the above major exceptions, all the remaining languages of Europe are spoken by about 45% of the world's population. All the IE languages derive ultimately from a common ancestor known as Proto-Indo-European (PIE), which is extinct, was never written down and which has had to be reconstructed from its daughter languages, chiefly Latin, Greek and Sanskrit.

The main sub-groups within the IE family are:

- **Latin and the Romance languages**: The Romance languages, including French, Italian, Spanish, Portuguese, Catalan and Romanian, are all daughter languages of Latin.
- **The Germanic languages**: English, German, Dutch, Afrikaans, Danish, Norwegian (Bokmål and Nynorsk), Swedish and all the other Germanic languages (see table below) derive from a reconstructed dead Proto-Germanic language.
- **Greek**: Greek has had a number of dialects and has undergone some major changes over the centuries but has never given rise to any daughter languages as such.
- **The Celtic languages**: The living Celtic languages include Welsh, Breton, Irish and Scottish (or Scots) Gaelic, with Manx and Cornish being recently revived languages.
- **The Slavic (or Slavonic) languages**: This large group of languages includes Russian, Ukrainian, Bulgarian Serbo-Croat (now treated separately as Serbian and Croatian), Slovenian, Polish, Czech and Slovak.

---

[53] These findings were published in 2012 by the Genographic Project of the National Geographic Society.

- **The Baltic languages**: The main surviving languages in this group are Latvian and Lithuanian, the latter being among the most archaic of all living Indo-European languages.
- **The Indo-Aryan or Indic languages**: This group of languages is dominant in the Indian subcontinent. The most ancient language of the group is Sanskrit, now extinct, and among the largest modern members of the group are Hindi, Urdu, Bengali, Punjabi, Marathi and Gujarati. The Indo-Aryan group is itself a branch of the Indo-Iranian group of languages, the other main component of which is the Iranian group of languages.
- **The Iranian languages**: Old Persian and the Zoroastrian sacred language, Avestan, both extinct, belong to this group, which is now represented chiefly by Persian (Farsi), Pashto, Kurdish and Balochi.

*Table A: A partial family tree of the Indo-European family of languages*

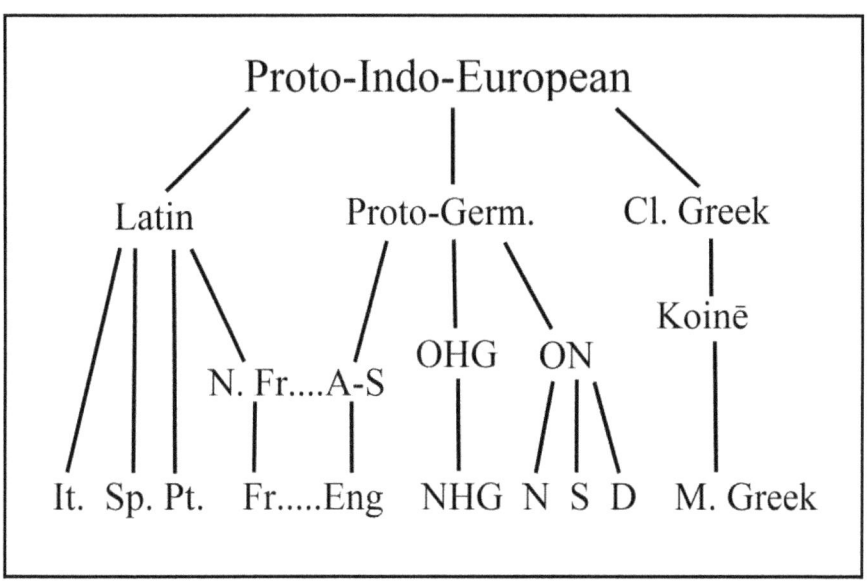

Key: Cl. Greek = Classical Greek/ M. Greek = Modern Greek/ N. Fr = Norman French/ A-S = Anglo-Saxon/ OHG = Old High German / ON = Old Norse / NHG = New High German/ N = Norwegian/ S = Swedish / D = Danish

Is English really related not only to German, Swedish and French, but also to Russian, Punjabi and Kurdish? The answer is Yes. But it has to be remembered that, as in all families, some relationships are closer than others, and even in the best of families it is not uncommon for some members not to be on speaking terms with others! So, the amount that English has in common with Punjabi, for example, is not very great. But there is no doubt that both languages belong to the same extended Indo-European family.

## Where did the Indo-Europeans come from?

The leading "steppe" or "kurgan" theory (named from a particular type of burial mound) is that the Indo-European peoples and languages originated in the steppes of Russia and Ukraine north of the Black Sea about 6,000 years ago and gradually fanned out from there to cover the whole vast area that they now occupy in Europe, Asia and then in the Americas, Africa and Oceania. The chief rival theory is that of Professor Colin Renfrew of Cambridge, which places the Indo-Europeans in Anatolia (modern Turkey) as long ago as 8,000 or even 9,000 years ago, spreading out from there to the East and West. There are also several other "fringe" theories.

However, there is no real proof of any of these theories, nor of the form or pronunciation of any words in the original Indo-European language, or Proto-Indo-European (PIE), which is of course extinct, of which no written records exist and which has had to be reconstructed from its daughter languages, chiefly Latin, (Ancient) Greek and Sanskrit, and to a lesser extent from Hittite, Luwian, Lycian and Tocharian (Tokharian).

## "Laryngeal theory"

The so-called "laryngeal theory" – of which there are several competing varieties – posits three or four mystery phonemes (sounds) in PIE, designated $h_1$, $h_2$, $h_3$, and $h_4$, the pronunciation of which is unknown. There were already several different reconstructions for many PIE roots, and the laryngeal theory has created even more confusion together with the suggestion that our ancestors spoke a language containing a large number of unpronounceable words, or at least words requiring a good deal of facial contortions and oral gymnastics, e.g. the PIE root for "wind" is reconstructed as *$h_2wéh_1$-ṇt-;[54] alternatively simply as *we-, (with *$h_2wéh_1$- "blow" described as the "oldest form").[55] First, why are there so many different forms for supposedly the same thing? Why was so unpronounceable a reconstruction posited in the first place, considering that actual recorded Indo-European words for "wind" are really quite simple and easily pronounceable: Hittite *huwantes* "winds," Latin *ventus* "wind," Greek *a(w)ent-* "blowing," Sanskrit *vata-* "wind," and the following words for "wind": German, Dutch and Afrikaans **Wind**, Danish, Norwegian and Swedish *vind*, Lithuanian *vėjas*, Latvian *vējš*, Russian *veter*, Polish *wiatr*, Welsh *gwynt* – not to mention English **wind** itself together with some words with related meanings, such as **weather**, **window** and Latin derivatives **ventilate**, **ventilation** and **vent**, which, besides a physical meaning, as in "air-vent" and a "side vent" in a jacket, since Shakespeare's time has also had a figurative meaning of "to give free expression to," as in "to vent one's spleen."

Professor James Clackson of Cambridge claims that: "The reconstruction of three laryngeals is now firmly accepted in IE linguistics, and there is much agreement on where laryngeals should be reconstructed and which laryngeal to reconstruct."[56] Really? Can the "laryngeals" be said to have been reconstructed at all, considering that their pronunciation is unknown. But Clackson at least admits that "some questions still remain. Particularly puzzling is the paradox that laryngeals are lost nearly everywhere, in ways that are strikingly similar, yet apparently unique to each language branch."[57] A much more puzzling question is simply why there is such emphasis among

---

[54] Clackson, J. *Indo-European Linguistics: An Introduction*. Cambridge: CUP, 2007, p. 56.
[55] AHDIER.
[56] Clackson, location 1549 (Kindle edition).
[57] Ibid.

"Indo-Europeanists" on the highly speculative reconstructions of Proto-Indo-European (PIE) at all. The point is that, as there is no written record whatsoever of PIE, it has to be reconstructed from its daughter languages.

## How important is Proto-Indo-European?

The Indo-European family is fortunate enough to contain two extremely well preserved and well recorded ancient languages, Latin and Sanskrit, each with many living descendants, namely the Romance and Indo-Aryan languages respectively, plus Greek, which is demonstrably cognate with both Latin and Sanskrit and is still spoken in a slightly changed modern form. In addition, the Indo-European family of languages contains a number of other obviously related groups, such as the Germanic, Celtic, Balto-Slavic and Iranian languages. There is actually no need to reconstruct the great-granddaddy of all these languages, though there clearly must have been one. Far too much emphasis is placed on this will-o'-the-wisp by "Indo-Europeanist" academics. It is the sound equivalents between the known languages that are of practical importance, not the sound equivalents or sound shifts between known languages and some hypothetical reconstructed language. There have even been attempts to write whole stories in PIE, originally in 1868 by German linguist August Schleicher and more recently by Andrew Byrd of Kentucky University based on work done by H. Craig Melchert. The reconstruction of two short "fables," "The Sheep and the Horses" and "The King and the God" is a text bristling with "laryngeals," and Andrew Byrd's recording of the two fables as he imagines they would have sounded five thousand years ago sounds unlike any language that I have ever heard.[58]

---

[58] See archaeology.org/exclusives/articles/1302-proto-indo-european-schleichers-fable.

## History of Indo-European linguistics

The similarities between Latin and Greek were well recognized in ancient times. When westerners travelled to India similarities between Sanskrit and western languages started to be noticed, and the picture of an Indo-European family of languages gradually came to be recognized, for example by Filippo Sassetti, a Florentine merchant, in 1585. In 1647 the Dutch scholar Marcus van Boxhorn suggested that Greek, Latin, German and Dutch were related to one another and that the Slavic, Celtic and Baltic languages and Persian also formed part of the same family of languages, with a lost common ancestor which he called "Scythian." Later writers on the subject include Turkish traveller Evilya Çelebi in 1665, the Russian polymath Mikhail Lomonosov in 1755, and in 1767 the French Jesuit missionary Gaston-Laurent Coeurdoux, later hailed as the father of comparative philology. However, it is the Anglo-Welsh polyglot Sir William Jones (1746–94) who is more often given credit for recognizing the existence of an Indo-European family of languages, especially the relationship between Latin, Greek and Sanskrit. Similar observations were made by the British scientist Thomas Young in 1813 and the German linguist Franz Bopp in 1816.

In 1806, the German philologist Friedrich Schlegel noted the correspondence between Latin [p] and Germanic [f], and in 1818, the Danish linguist and philologist Rasmus Rask (1787–1832) extended the correspondences to the full range of consonants involved. In 1822, in his Deutsche Grammatik, Jacob Grimm (1785–1863) used Rask's work, which he formulated into what is now known as Grimm's Law. This is a sound shift rule or "law" of correspondences between Proto-Indo-European (PIE) or, more accurately, between Latin, Greek and Sanskrit and the Germanic family of languages.

## The Brothers Grimm

It is no accident that Jacob Grimm, together with his brother Wilhelm (1786–1859), commonly referred to as "the Brothers Grimm," are associated with what are known in English as *Grimms' Fairy Tales*. In fact, they are more accurately described as folk tales, because they were not invented by the brothers, but collected by them from people all around Germany. In so doing the brothers were seeking the common cultural heritage of Germany and of the Germanic peoples in general, and Grimms' *Fairy Tales*, or *Kinder- und Hausmärchen* ("Children's and Household Tales"), as they were originally titled, were a compilation of traditional tales. First published in 1812, the book struck a chord with the German people and went through numerous editions. It was said that it was one of two books found in every German household, the other being Luther's Bible (at least for Protestants).

It was the same interest that impelled Jacob Grimm to write his monumental three-volume *Deutsche Grammatik* (German Grammar), which embraced not only the German language itself, but also other Germanic languages, including English. It was in this book that Grimm's Law was first enunciated based on the recognition of an Indo-European family of languages derived from a common ancestor, known as Proto-Indo-European (PIE) or Aryan.[59]

The brothers were prolific writers, and their list of publications includes the mammoth dictionary of the German language, the *Deutsches Wörterbuch*, (DWB) the initial volumes of which were published in 1854, but which was only finally completed by a succession of later scholars and institutions and published in 32 volumes more than a century later in 1961, with a supplementary volume appearing in 1971, and revision of the earlier volumes starting in 2004 and still ongoing at the time of writing.

As no records of PIE survive, it had to be reconstructed. Grimm's Law concentrates on three sets of sounds, which Grimm posited were the same in Latin, Greek and Sanskrit as in PIE. So, the sound shift from

---

[59] The term "Aryan" was abandoned after it had come to be used by nationalistic politicians as a racial rather than as a purely linguistic label.

PIE to the Germanic languages can be traced through Latin, Greek and Sanskrit, without having to rely on reconstructed (and therefore hypothetical) words in PIE. In fact, Grimm's Law can be used simply to figure out the correspondences in sound between Latin, Greek and Sanskrit on the one hand and the Germanic group of languages on the other. There is no need to bring PIE into the formula at all – and PIE is really redundant anyway, because it has no independent verifiable existence of its own but has to be reconstructed from its daughter languages, particularly Latin, Greek and Sanskrit. And it is this that makes Grimm's Law such a useful practical language-learning tool – by enabling you to move from a Latin, Greek or Sanskrit word to a word in a Germanic language without concerning yourself with some unpronounceable hypothetical "reconstruction."

## Grimm's Law

This grid represents the basis of Grimm's Law. It is important to note that what are shown here are not letters but *sounds*.

*Table B: Grimm's Law*

| (voiceless or unvoiced) | /p/ | /t/ | /k/ |
|---|---|---|---|
| (voiced) | /b/ | /d/ | /g/ |
| (aspirated) | /f/ | /th/ | /h/ or /ch/ |

Concentrating on the niceties of unvoiced, voiced and aspirated sounds makes this practical tool unduly complicated. In brief, however, "voiceless" or "unvoiced" refers to a sound made without vibrating the vocal chords, as against a "voiced" sound, which entails vibrating the vocal chords, and an "aspirated" one, which is immediately followed by a little puff of air.

This table is not just a party game. Simple though it is, it contains the key that unlocks remarkable relationships between words in different languages.

- **From Latin, Greek or Sanskrit to Germanic**: To find the Germanic equivalent of a sound in Latin, Greek or Sanskrit, move **two down** from the first row, or **one up** from the lower rows.
- **From Germanic to Latin, Greek or Sanskrit**: To find the Latin, Greek or Sanskrit equivalent to a Germanic sound, move **one down** from the first row, **one down** from the second row and **two up** from the bottom row.

Caution: "Germanic" here excludes Modern German, which underwent a second sound shift (*zweite Lautverschiebung*), as discussed below.

In more detail:

- A /p/ sound in Latin, Greek or Sanskrit is represented by an /f/ sound in Germanic, e.g. Latin *pes, pedis*, Greek *pous, podos* "foot" == English (Germanic) **foot**.
- A /b/ sound in Latin, Greek or Sanskrit is represented by a /p/ sound in Germanic (no known examples).
- An /f/ sound in Latin, Greek or Sanskrit is represented by a /b/ sound in Germanic, e.g. Latin *fero, ferre* "to carry," Greek *phero, pherein* "to carry" == English (Germanic) **bear**; Latin *frater* "brother," Greek *phrater/phreter* lit. "brother," but in Classical times supplanted in that sense by *adelphos* and used in the sense of "fellow clansman, fellow tribesman" cf. *phratria* "clan" == Proto-Germanic *brothar*, English (Germanic) **brother**.
- A /t/ sound in Latin, Greek or Sanskrit is represented by a /th/ sound in Germanic, e.g. Latin *tenuis* "thin" == English (Germanic) **thin**. Also *frater* == **brother** (see above).
- A /d/ sound in Latin, Greek or Sanskrit is represented by a /t/ sound in Germanic, e.g. Latin *pes, pedis*, Greek *pous, podos* "foot" == English

Germanic **foot**. Latin *cor, cordis*, Greek *kardia* "heart" == English (Germanic) **heart**. See below for fuller discussion.

- A /th/ sound in Latin, Greek or Sanskrit is represented by a /d/ sound in Germanic. Greek *thyra* "door," Latin *fores* "folding doors" (Latin had no /th/ sound, so the sound was represented by /f/ == Old English (Germanic) *duru*, English **door**, Dutch and Afrikaans *deur*, Danish and Norwegian *dør*, Swedish *dörr*.

- A /k/ sound in Latin, Greek or Sanskrit is represented by an /h/ or /ch/ sound in Germanic. Latin *cor, cordis*, Greek *kardia* "heart" == English (Germanic) **heart**. See below for fuller discussion.

- A /g/ sound in Latin, Greek or Sanskrit is represented by a /k/ sound in Germanic. Latin *genu*, Greek *gonu* "knee" == German *Knie*, English **knee**. For the important Latin and Greek root *gen-*, see Chapter 16, IT'S ALL IN YOUR GENES.

- An /h/ or /ch/ sound in Latin, Greek or Sanskrit is represented by a /g/ sound in Germanic. Latin hostis, originally "stranger, foreigner," in Classical Latin "enemy" == Old English (Germanic) *gæst* English **guest**, German *Gast*. Guest-friendship in the ancient world was a reciprocal relationship of guest and host, with English **host** coming via the French from Latin *hospes, hospitis, (from hostis + potis* "able, powerful")[60] meaning both "guest" and "host." A stranger could become your guest-friend or an enemy – hence the change of meaning in Classical Latin of *hostis* to refer to an enemy, from which comes English **hostile**.

And the same equivalents apply in reverse.

## Examples of the Grimm network

Here are two fuller examples of the how Grimm's Law can be applied:

- **Heart**: The English word **heart**, which is purely Germanic, not only means the same as the Latin word *cor, cordis* (stem: *cord-*) and the Greek word *kardia*, but is also cognate with them, or, in other words, has the same origin as them. Though at first sight these words do not

---

[60] See de Vaan.

appear very similar, Grimm's Law reveals their close relationship. The initial /k/ sound in Latin and Greek is represented in Germanic by an aspirated /h/ sound – precisely in accordance with Grimm's Law. Similarly, the /d/ sound in Latin and Greek is represented by a /t/ sound in English and other Germanic languages, such as Dutch, where the word is *hart*. In Modern German the word is *Herz*, because that language has undergone a **second sound shift**, which is discussed below. The *heart-cor-kardia* word-family is a huge extended family. English **heart** itself is of Germanic origin, giving rise to **hearty, heartfelt, hearten, heartening, dishearten** and cognate with Dutch and Afrikaans *hart*, Danish and Norwegian *hjerte*, Swedish *hjärta* – all meaning "heart." From Latin *cor, cordis* come English **cordial, concord, record, discord**, where the concept of "heart" is used in a figurative sense, e.g. **concord**, literally "hearts together," so "agreement, harmony, friendship." Hence the name of several American cities, also **concordat**. Cognate with French *cœur*, Italian *cuore*, Spanish *corazón*, Portuguese *coração* – all meaning "heart." From Greek *kardia* come a number of technical medical terms, including **cardiac, pericardium, pericarditis, tachycardia**, and **EKG** or **ECG** standing for **electrocardiogram**, "a recording of the electrical activity of the heart."

- **Foot**: The English word **foot**, another good Germanic word, has a similar pedigree to that of **heart**. Here the Latin cognate is *pes, pedis* (stem: *ped-*), the Greek cognate is *pous, podos* (stem: *pod-*) and the Sanskrit cognate is *pad-*. And here again, these words are not only cognate with **foot** but have the same meaning as well. Other Germanic equivalents are Swedish *fot* and Dutch *voet*. Once again, Modern German shows a divergent form, *Fuss*, as a result of the **second sound shift**. *Foot-pes-pous* is a large word-family. English has a **foot** (pun intended) in all three camps: Germanic, Latin derivatives and Greek derivatives. It is this multilateral relationship that gives English vocabulary its great richness. The basic English word **foot** is Germanic, cognate with Dutch and Afrikaans *voet* (pronounced the same as English foot), Danish *fod*, Norwegian *fot*, Swedish *fot* – all meaning "foot." English **foot** can denote a measure of length as well a part of the body, and there are many compounds and phrases from it as well, e.g. **footing, footfall, footsy**, "feet first," "foot in mouth." From the Latin *pes, pedis* we have English **pedal, pedestrian, impede, expedite**,

**expedition, expeditious, expedient** – the last four used in a figurative sense. "The Latin word etymologically means 'to free (a person's feet from fetters)' ... hence, to free from difficulties, to help forward,"[61] e.g. "too fond of the right to pursue the expedient."[62] A particularly strange derivative from the Latin is English **pedigree**, via French *pied de grue* "crane's foot," "so called from a three-line mark (like a broad arrow) used in denoting succession to **pedigrees**."[63] Romance derivatives from Latin *pes, pedis* include French *pied*, Italian *piede*, Spanish *pie*, Portuguese *pé* – all meaning "foot." From Greek *pous, podos* come English **tripod**, **octopus**, **podiatry**, **podium** (from Greek podion, "foot of a vase").

It is important to remember that Grimm's Law represents sounds, not spellings.

Another caveat is to realize that the sounds did not actually change from Latin and Greek to the Germanic languages: they represent equivalents rather than sound shifts as between Latin and Greek on the one hand and the Germanic languages on the other. The reason they are termed sound shifts or sound changes is that the sounds in Latin, Greek and Sanskrit are posited to be the same as the original sounds in PIE, so when we say that the [p] in Latin *pes, pedis*, Greek *pous, podos* and Sanskrit *pada*, all meaning "foot," *changed* to an [f] in German *Fuss*, Dutch and Afrikaans *voet* (with the [v] pronounced as /f/), Danish *fod*, Norwegian and Swedish *fot* and English **foot**, what we really mean is that the /p/ sound in the Latin, Greek and Sanskrit words corresponds to or is equivalent to the /f/ sound in the Germanic languages – because the Germanic languages do not derive from Latin, Greek or Sanskrit, but are cognate with them. In other words, the Germanic languages are sisters, not daughters, of Latin, Greek and Sanskrit. So, why do we refer to Grimm's Law as being about sound shift or sound change? Because, as I just said, it is posited that the Latin, Greek and Sanskrit sounds are the same as in

---

[61] OED.

[62] Goldsmith 1774, quoted by OED.

[63] Skeat.

the original Proto-Indo-European language. Since that language does not exist in any verifiable recorded form but is all reconstructed and quite often conjectural, speculative or hypothetical at best, I prefer not even to mention PIE in dealing with Grimm's Law. Involvement of PIE reconstructions, as in all books on the subject, including etymological dictionaries, only complicates matters unnecessarily. To put it simply, reconstructed PIE words (or, as is often the case, just roots) are irrelevant to an understanding – and practical applications – of Grimm's Law.

## Verner's Law

Grimm's Law created a great sensation, but it soon became apparent that it did not work all the time. There were some exceptions, of which Jacob Grimm himself was aware, but for which he could find no explanation. This was left to the Danish linguist and philologist Karl Verner, who cracked the problem in 1875 by what came to be called Verner's Law. He was apparently taking a nap at the time, dreamt the solution, woke up with a start and then remembered it – for the benefit of posterity!

The main problem solved by Verner was already present in the prime example of Grimm's Law, the Latin and Greek word *pater* "father" and Sanskrit equivalent *pitar*. According to Grimm's Law the initial /p/ sound in Latin, Greek and Sanskrit should be represented by an /f/ sound in Germanic – and it is. The word for "father" is English **father**, German *Vater*, Dutch and Afrikaans *vader*, Danish, Norwegian and Swedish *far*, contracted form of *fader*. All the Germanic words for "father" have an initial /f/ sound. The initial [v] in the German, Dutch and Afrikaans versions are not exceptions, because they are pronounced /f/ as well. So far (no pun intended), so good.

But it is in the /t/ sound in the Latin, Greek and Sanskrit words where the problem lurks. According to Grimm's Law, this /t/ sound should be represented in Germanic by a /th/ sound. Well, you might say, is this not the case with English **father**? Actually not, because the /th/

pronunciation only came in around the 15th century, prior to which the word was *fader*, with the [d] pronounced /d/, as indeed is the case in all the other Germanic languages cited above except for Modern German (*Neuhochdeutsch*), which has undergone a second sound shift (*zweite Lautverschiebung*) – see below. The reason for this exception, as Verner's Law makes clear, is to do with stress. Both Latin/Greek *pater* and Sanskrit *pitar* have the stress on the second syllable.

The fact that English **father** and the other Germanic words with the same meaning all have the stress on the first syllable is irrelevant. It is only the stress on the Latin, Greek and Sanskrit words that counts as far as Verner's Law is concerned. By contrast with the words cognate with English **father**, those cognate with English **brother**, namely Latin *frater* and Classical Greek *phrétêr/phratêr,* have their stress on the first syllable. So here Grimm's Law operates without any modification and the /t/ sound in the Latin and Greek words has its Proto-Germanic equivalent in a /th/ sound – *\*brothar*. But, it may be objected, if that is correct, why then do none of the Germanic words for brother except English **brother** itself (and the unprintable Icelandic equivalent) have that /th/ sound? Instead we have German *Bruder*, Dutch *broeder*, Afrikaans *broer*, short for *broeder* and Danish, Norwegian and Swedish *broder* or *bror*. Though Proto-Germanic *\*brothar* (or *\*brother*) is reconstructed, documented Old Dutch is *bruother* and Gothic, Old Norse and Old Swedish also exhibit that /th/ sound. So, what happened? In Dutch and the Scandinavian languages (except Icelandic) the pronunciation changed and the /th/ sound slipped into a /d/ sound.

**The second sound shift**

After the sound shift from Proto-Indo-European to Proto-Germanic, High German underwent a sound shift that differentiated it from the Low German languages. The terms "high" and "low" do not represent any form of rating, and they are actually misleading in terms of the map, because High German is south of Low German! The terms "high" and "low" actually refer to altitude – "High German" being the language spoken in the mountainous southern part of the Germanic *Sprachraum* (Germanic-speaking area) and the "Low" Germanic languages being those spoken primarily in the Netherlands (the name indicating the altitude or lack of it!), Belgium and also Scandinavia and of course Britain. High German is today represented chiefly by Modern Standard German, or *Neuhochdeutsch* ("New High German"), the official language of Germany, Austria, Switzerland (17 cantons) and Liechtenstein. The second sound shift refers to consonantal changes that took place in stages probably between the years 600 and 800, from Proto-Germanic to High German, which did not affect the Low Germanic languages of English, Dutch (and Afrikaans), Danish, Norwegian (both main varieties), Swedish and Icelandic.

Here are a few examples.

Note: Where all the words have the same meaning, it is shown only once, at the end.

>    p >> pf   Dutch *paard*, Afrikaans *perd*, German *Pferd* ("horse")
>    Not to be confused with PIE *perd-*, Greek *perdomai*, *perdesthai*, Latin *pedo, pedere*, which, in accordance with Grimm's Law together with Verner's Law, gives rise to English **fart**. In accordance with the second sound shift the /t/ sound changes to /z/ in German *Furz* (noun), *furzen* (verb). The meaning of all the words is "flatulence" (noun), "to break wind loudly" (verb).
>
>    p >> ff   English **open**, Dutch *open*, Afrikaans *oop*, Danish *åben*, Norwegian *apen*, Swedish *öppen*, German *offen* ("open")
>
>    Note: Initial /p/ goes to /pf/, but intervocalic /p/ (i.e. between vowels) goes to /ff/.
>
>    t >> ss   English **eat**, Dutch *eten*, Afrikaans *eet*, Swedish *äta*, German *essen* ("to eat")

t >> ss   English **water**, Dutch/Afrikaans *water*, Danish *vand*, Norwegian *vann*, Swedish *vatten*, German *Wasse*r ("water")

t >> z   English **timber**, Dutch/Afrikaans *timmerman* ("carpenter"), Danish and Norwegian *tømmer*, Swedish *timmer* ("timber"), German *Zimme*r ("room")

t >> z   English **tide**, Dutch *tijd*, Afrikaans *tyd*, Danish, Norwegian and Swedish *tid*, ("time"), German *Zeit* ("time") (English **tide** originally referred to a point of time. Hence the phrase "Time and tide wait for no man." Its current sense relating to the rise and fall of the sea can be traced back to the 14th century. The relationship between the concepts of time and tide is probably that the time could be calculated and predicted from the tide.)

k >> ch   English **make**, Dutch *maken*, Afrikaans *maak*, German *machen* ("to make")

d >> t   English **daughter**, Dutch *dochter*, Afrikaans *dogter*, Danish and Norwegian *datter*, Swedish *dotter*, Icelandic *dóttir*, German *Tochter* ("daughter")

d >> t   English **devil**, Dutch *duivel*, Afrikaans *duiwel*, Danish *djævel*, Norwegian *djevel*, Swedish *djävel*, German *Teufel* ("devil")
(This is actually an early borrowing from Latin *diabolus* (from which come English **diabolical**, French *diable*, Italian *diavolo,* Spanish *diablo),* which in turn is from Greek *diabolos.* Ol0d English already had the form *deofol.*)

# CHAPTER 9

# THE GERMANIC COUSINHOOD

ONLY ABOUT A quarter of English words are of Germanic origin, but these words form the bedrock of the English language, which is why English is classified as a Germanic language. This Germanic bedrock goes back to Anglo-Saxon or Old English, which has provided the language with much of its most basic vocabulary, including **head, heart, father, mother, brother, tree, fire, work, new, young, eat, water**. All these words have cognates (i.e. words sharing a common origin) in other branches of the Indo-European family. There is also a common stock of Germanic words which can be used to learn other Germanic languages.[64]

Although not mutually intelligible (except for the Scandinavian group Danish-Norwegian-Swedish and separately, the Dutch-Flemish-Afrikaans group), the Germanic languages are quite close to one another, as can be seen, for example, from the opening words of the Bible in four Germanic languages:

> **English**: In the beginning God created the heaven and the earth.
> **Dutch**: *In den beginne schiep God den hemel en de aarde.*
> **Danish**: *I Begyndelsen skabte Gud Himmelen og Jorden.*
> **German**: *Am Anfang schuf Gott Himmel und Erde.*

The only non-Germanic feature of the English version is the word **create**, which is of Latin origin. All the other Germanic languages use

---

[64] For the sake of clarity, I am including some examples already discussed in Chapter 2, NOT ANGLES BUT ANGELS.

*schaffen* (German) or a related word. The English words **shape** and **shave** are related to these but have developed divergent meanings. The Latin words *scabo, scabere* ("to scratch, scrape") and *scabies* ("itch, mange"), the latter of which is also now found as a medical term in English, are probably cognate with **shave**.

## The second Germanic consonant shift

The common ancestor of all Germanic languages is Proto-Germanic. The only written records of this language are some runic inscriptions and a few isolated words recorded in Roman writings, such as Tacitus's *Germania*. It has been reconstructed from its daughter languages by what is known as the comparative method. Proto-Germanic (PGmc) itself descended from Proto-Indo-European (PIE), which is an entirely unattested and entirely reconstructed language. What differentiates PGmc from PIE is the consonant shift first identified by Rasmus Rask and Jacob Grimm known as Grimm's Law and modified by Verner's Law.[65] This important development took place several centuries prior to the Christian era. Then, in the third and fifth centuries CE, or possibly about two centuries later, a second consonant sound shift took place purely within the Germanic languages. In German this is known simply as *die zweite Lautverschiebung* ("the second sound shift").

You may well be baffled by the descriptions of this sound shift that you will find in books and online, with references to "voiceless stops," "fricatives," and "affricates." In fact, the changes are really quite straightforward. The changes occurred in High German (originally in Old High German and still present in Modern German, or *Neuhochdeutsch*) which is so called not because it is superior to "Low German" in any way but simply because it was (and is) spoken in the higher altitude parts of the German-speaking area as against the low-lying areas including the Netherlands, which of course gets its name

---

[65] See Chapter 8, A GRIMM TALE.

precisely from this fact. To put it at its simplest, this second sound shift differentiates the German language itself on the one hand from Dutch, Afrikaans, Danish, Norwegian, Swedish, Icelandic and of course English on the other hand. While the German language experienced the sound shift, these other languages kept to the original sounds of Proto-Germanic. These changes did not all take place at once, but what follows is a list of changes as they exist in practice today, regardless of when they occurred:

Initial /t-/ from /d-/

- German *Teil*, English **deal**, Dutch and Afrikaans *deel*, Danish and Norwegian *del*. The basic meaning is "a part, share, portion," which is shared by all the languages except English **deal**, where the meaning has shifted to "a business arrangement among several people," hence US President Franklin Roosevelt's "**New Deal**." The verb **deal** is still used to mean "to divide up cards," and, in the phrase **to deal with**, meaning "to manage a situation." English **dole** is also cognate, meaning "a handout," British slang for government welfare payments, hence **on the dole**. The phrase to **dole out** means "to distribute, apportion," usually in reference to small handouts by way of charity. No relation to **deal** meaning a plank of pine or fir wood.

- German *Teufel*, English **devil**, Dutch *duivel*, Afrikaans *duiwel*, Danish *djævel*, Norwegian *djevel*, Swedish *djävel*. All the words mean "devil" and derive from a Late Latin loanword *diabolus*, which has also given rise to French *diable*, Italian *diavolo*, Spanish *diablo*, Portuguese *diabo*. Latin *diabolus* is itself from Greek *diabolos*, literally "obstacle, attacker," which is itself a translation of Hebrew *Satan*, literally "obstacle, adversary."

- German *treiben*, "to drive, to do," as in the slang phrase: *Was treibst du denn so den ganzen Tag?* "What do you get up to all day?" (Wiktionary). German has two nouns, *Trift* and *Drift,* the latter being a borrowing from Low German and therefore unaffected by the sound shift (both meaning "drifting, pasture"), English **drive**, Dutch *drijven*, Afrikaans *dryf,* Danish *drive*, Norwegian *drive*, Swedish *driva*. All these mean "to drive, to push, drift" with English drive having a wider range of meanings, including notably "to drive (a car)." The English noun **drift** is also cognate, as is *drift* in Dutch, Norwegian and Swedish, where it has a wide meaning including "urge, strong desire," while cognate Afrikaans *drif* refers to a "ford, river crossing" in addition to "passion, impetuosity, anger, fury."

- ❖ German *Tisch* ("table"), English **dish, disk/disc, desk, dais, discus**. A loanword from Medieval Latin *discus*, which in turn is from Greek *diskos*, "disc, platter," no longer thought to derive from the Greek verb *dikein* ("to throw") (Beekes). **Dais**, meaning a platform, is from French *dais*, originally platform or high table. German *Tafel* has not undergone the expected sound shift – though in Old High German, the expected form, *Zabel*, is found. It is a modified loanword from Latin *tabula*, originally meaning a "board, plank, writing tablet." German *Tafel* is a blackboard, a list or panel in a book, a chocolate slab, or a table set for a festive meal. Cf. Italian *tavolo, tavola*, both from Latin *tabula*. *Tavolo* is the usual word for table, but when referring to a table set for a meal the word to use is *tavola*.[66]

Besides English, the main Germanic languages spoken today are:

- ❖ **Modern German**: Referred to in this book simply as "German," this is the language referred to in German as *Neuhochdeutsch*, literally "New High German." There are about 100 million native speakers in the world today, making it the most widely spoken native language in the European Union (EU). Before Brexit it was also the second largest language in the EU overall, and the third most commonly spoken foreign language in the EU, after English and French.
    - The so-called *Deutscher Sprachraum* ("German-speaking area") encompasses Germany, Austria, 17 cantons of Switzerland and Liechtenstein, in all of which German is the only official language. In four other Swiss cantons, Luxembourg, South Tyrol in Italy and Eastern Belgium, German is a co-official language.
    - There is no single standard of German. There are several dialects in the spoken language, though the written language is more uniform. As a medical doctor, my father used to receive German calendars and diaries every year, and I was surprised to find Saturday referred to in all these publications as *Samstag*, though

---

[66] For more on the second sound shift, see Chapter 8, A GRIMM TALE.

*we* used to refer to it as *Sonnabend*. It turns out that *Sonnabend*, literally "Sunday eve," by analogy with "Christmas Eve" or New Year's Eve," is confined to North Germany, while *Samstag*, which is found elsewhere in the German-speaking world, is from a nasalized version of Latin *sabbatum*, which in turn is from Greek *sabbaton*, from Hebrew *shabbath*, "the Sabbath," plus *Tag*, "day."

- German is essentially a phonetic (or phonemic) language, i.e. its pronunciation is regular and the same letter or combination of letters consistently represents the same sound. However, there are some regional dialects, which can be broadly characterized as belonging either to High German or Low German. The latter, generally referred to in Germany as *Plattdeutsch* (lit. "flat German"), may be regarded as dialects or even as a separate language. These Low German dialects, spoken in Northern Germany, have not undergone the second sound shift and therefore, in some respects, resemble Dutch. The High German dialects, on the other hand, have undergone the second sound shift. They include the Austro-Bavarian dialects spoken in the southern German state of Bavaria and also in Austria. Swiss German, known in German as *Schweizerdeutsch*, while technically a High German dialect or a number of dialects, is really a separate language, which most Germans cannot understand (see below). Yiddish is also a variant of High German and is also really a separate language (see below).

❖ **Swiss German**: What is known in German as *Schweizerdeutsch* ("Swiss German") and in Switzerland as *Schwizerdütsch* or *Schwitzertütsch*, is made up of a number of dialects spoken in the German-speaking parts of Switzerland, Liechtenstein and Austrian Vorarlberg. It is largely a spoken language. For written communications German-speaking Swiss would normally use Swiss Standard German (SSG), referred to in Germany as *Schweizerhochdeutsch* ("Swiss High German") and by the Swiss themselves as *Schriftdeutsch* ("written German"). This is not a dialect but simply a variety of standard German, known in German as *Standarddeutsch* or *Hochdeutsch* ("High German"). SSG is the official written language in German-speaking Switzerland, with only a few variations from the Standard German of Germany, such as the French word *velo* for "bicycle," as against *Fahrrad*; *parkieren* for "to park," as against *parken*; and *Spital* (short

## THE GERMANIC COUSINHOOD

for *Hospital*, for "hospital"), which is also used in southern Germany, Austria and Liechtenstein, as against north German *Krankenhaus* (lit. "sick house").

- SSG must not, however, be confused with the spoken language, *Schweizerdeutsch*, which, besides having considerable differences in vocabulary, is also pronounced much more gutturally and spoken much faster than Standard German as spoken in Germany and also with a good deal of slurring of the words together. Some specific Swiss words are: *gumpe* (probably related to English **jump**) instead of *springen*, *hüpfen*, "to jump"; *schaffe* (related to Dutch *scheppen*, English **shape**) instead of *arbeiten*, "to work"; *luege* (related to English **look**) instead of Standard German *schauen* or colloquial *gucken* (pronounced *kucken*), meaning "to look"; *lose* (related to English **listen** and also **loud**) instead of *hören*, meaning "to listen"; *laufe* (related to English **leap**) instead of *gehen*, for "to walk," though in German *laufen* can mean "to walk" as well as "to run." Notice the dropping of the final /-n/ of the infinitive in Swiss German. You can sometimes see these three words stencilled on Swiss pedestrian crossings: *LUEGE – LOSE – LAUFE*, meaning "look, listen, walk." Instead of the Standard High German genitive (possessive) case Swiss German uses the preposition *vo* (shortened from *von*), meaning "of" followed by the dative case, as in: *de Titel vo dem Buech*, "the title of the book." Swiss German does not have the simple German past or imperfect tense, but always uses the perfect tense. So German *Ich lebte in Zürich* ("I lived in Zurich") becomes in Swiss German: *Ich ha in Züri gläbt*. In fact, of course, in Standard German as spoken in Germany the perfect has largely supplanted the imperfect, which is now mainly relegated to writing.

❖ **Yiddish**: Though written in the Hebrew alphabet, Yiddish is essentially a High Germanic language with a number of Hebrew and Slavic loanwords. Before World War II, Yiddish was spoken by about 12 million Jews living in Eastern Europe, most of whom perished in the Holocaust. Today it is estimated that there are about two million Yiddish speakers worldwide, with 1.5 million speaking the Eastern dialect of the language. About 40% of those are in Ukraine, 15% in Israel and 10% in the US. Yiddish speakers are chiefly ultra-orthodox Ashkenazic Hasidic Jews, known in Hebrew as *Haredim*, who prefer to speak

Yiddish rather than Hebrew, which they regard as too sacred a language to be used in everyday conversation. The word *Haredim* literally means "tremblers," i.e. those who tremble in awe of the word of God, strangely similar to the nickname "Quakers" given to members of the Christian group who call themselves the Religious Society of Friends.

- The Hebrew alphabet proper is made up entirely of consonants, with vowels represented by *nekudot*, vowel points written underneath (though generally omitted altogether). The Hebrew alphabet includes two letters, the *aleph* and the *ayin*, which represent no particular sound but take on a phonetic value from the *nekudot*, written beneath them. Yiddish has adapted these letters together with some others to represent vowel sounds. So, unlike the Hebrew alphabet proper, the Yiddish alphabet represents all vowels as well as all consonants.

- Yiddish has numerous colourful words and expressions, some of which have entered English (shown in **bold**), e.g. **bagel**, "a ring-shaped doughy bread roll," from Old High German *boug* "a ring"; **chutzpah**, from Hebrew, meaning "cheek, audacity, effrontery, daring, determination," with either positive or negative connotations; *alter kacker*, purely of German origin, lit. "old crapper," equivalent to "old fart"; **dreck**, "rubbish, worthless merchandise," from German *Dreck,* "dirt, filth," connected with Greek *skatos* (OED), from which English **scat**, "dung, filth"; **goy**, a" non-Jew, gentile" from Hebrew *goy* "nation," plural *goyim*, an exact parallel to the use of English **gentile**, from Latin *gens, genti*s, "people, tribe, nation," as in the New Testament: "To the Jew first, and also to the **Gentile**," (Romans 2:10); **kibitz** or **kibbitz**, American slang "to look on at cards in an interfering manner," so "to offer unwanted advice," from German *Kiebitz*, lit. "a lapwing," not to be confused with **kibbutz**, a Hebrew word, literally meaning "a gathering," used to refer to an Israeli collective settlement; **kosher**, from Hebrew "ritually pure food, especially meat," and by extension in slang, "legitimate, in order, genuine"; **mazel tov!** "Congratulations!" from Hebrew *mazal tov*, lit. "good star," so "good luck!" used after rather than before a propitious outcome; **Mensch**, "a person of integrity," from German *Mensch*, "a person, human being"; *meshugge*, "insane, crazy," from Hebrew; *mohel*, "a ritual circumciser," from Hebrew; **naches**, from Hebrew *nachat*, "relaxation, contentment," used particularly in reference to parents' sense of pleasure or pride at the achievements of their children; *nebbish*, "an unfortunate wretch," from Eastern Yiddish *nebekh*, "unfortunately," from Slavic, as in Old Polish *niebog*, "poor, unfortunate"); **Oy vey!**, literally, "Oh, woe!, so "Oh dear," from German *Weh*, "pain," cf. English **woe**; **putz**, literally "penis," hence (chiefly American) slang, "fool, jerk." OED quotes Judith Krantz, *Scruples* (1978): *"You ... are a putz, a schmekel, a schmuck, a schlong, and a shvantz."* These words are all Yiddish for "penis," used as pejorative descriptions for a stupid man; **shtick, shtik**, American slang, "a comic act or stage routine," from German *Stück*, "piece"; **shtuck, shtook**, "trouble," as in "**in shtuck**," despite appearances, is not a Yiddish word at all, and its origin is unknown; **shtum**, "silent, quiet," especially in the phrase "to keep **shtum**," is certainly Yiddish, from German *stumm*, "dumb (unable to speak), mute, silent (not speaking, or in reference to a letter that is not pronounced)"; **tush, tushy, tushie**, American slang, "buttocks," from Yiddish *toches*, from Hebrew *tachat*, "underneath." <u>Note:</u> Yiddish follows the Ashkenazic pronunciation of a final [taf] in Hebrew as /s/. The official pronunciation in Modern Hebrew is the Sephardic pronunciation of the final [taf] as /t/.

❖ **Plattdeutsch**: *"Snackt ji Platt?"* You may be accosted with this question in parts of Northern Germany if you look as though you might be a local. It sounds nothing like its equivalent in High German: *"Sprechen Sie Plattdeutsch?"* ("Do you speak Plattdeutsch?"). *Snacken*, or *schnacken* is Plattdeutsch for "to speak, to chat," apparently originating from "to snap" in reference to a dog and from there to engaging in idle chatter, boasting, or (in Swedish) to revealing secrets (under interrogation). But it is now the ordinary word for "speak" in a number of Low German languages, with slight variations: Danish *snake*, Norwegian Bokmål *snake*, Norwegian Nynorsk *snakka*, Swedish *snacka*. In Dutch *snacken* just means "to snack," the same as English **snack**, which effectively retains the original association with eating as against speaking. The normal Plattdeutsch greeting at all times of day, and meaning both "Hello" and "Goodbye" is *Moin* or *Moin Moin*, which is explained as being either a version of the High German greeting *(Guten) Morgen*, often reduced simply to *Morgen* ("good morning") or else as deriving from Dutch *mooi* ("beautiful, good"), as in *Mooien Dag*, though the equivalent greeting in Dutch is actually *Goedemorgen "good morning."* You will notice that, as a Low German language, Plattdeutsch has not undergone the second sound shift. So, *drinken* instead of High German *trinken* (English meaning and cognate **drink**); *eten* instead of High German *essen* (English meaning and cognate **eat**); *höpen* as against High German *hoffen* (English meaning and cognate **hope**); *Ik weet ("I know")* for High German *Ich weiss; dat* for High German *dass* (English cognate and meaning **that**); *wat* for High German *was* (English cognate and meaning **what**); *kort* for High German *kurz* (English meaning and cognate **short**, which is also cognate with **curt**, **skirt** and **shirt**); *groot* for High German *gross* ("big, large" – English **great** and also perhaps **grit** are cognate, **gross** not cognate but influenced by it ); *laten* for High German *lassen* ("to allow, leave"), *maken* for High German *machen* (English meaning and cognate **make**).

❖ **Dutch**: The language of the Netherlands and one of the three official languages of Belgium (the other two being French and German) as well as being spoken in Suriname and the Dutch possessions in the Caribbean. The language known as "Dutch" in English is called by its speakers *Nederlands*. The English word **Dutch** is related to **Teuton/Teutonic** and to the German word *Deutsch*, which is what the Germans call themselves. All these words appear to derive from reconstructed Proto-Germanic *\*theudo*, which in Old English became *theod* ("people, tribe, nation"). This in turn seems to have come from a reconstructed PIE root variously represented as *\*teutā-* or *\*tewtéh₂*. The word **Teutonic**, which first appears in English in the 17th century, was actually borrowed from Latin *Teutones*, the name given by various Roman writers to a particular Germanic tribe. Some modern writers have disputed this, claiming that the Teutones were actually a Celtic tribe. However, as the word **Teutonic** itself is clearly linked to Old English *theod* and Modern German *Deutsch*, denying the Germanic identity of the Teutones would seem to be futile as well as irrelevant.

  – **Double Dutch**: The term "Double Dutch" means "nonsense, gibberish," or an incomprehensible language. But why should Dutch be thought of by the English as difficult to understand, considering how closely related the two languages are? The term "Dutch" did not just mean what we now call Dutch, as spoken in the Netherlands, or "Holland," as it is still commonly called, though Holland is strictly just one part (formerly a province) of the Netherlands, but the term "Dutch" would have included all varieties of German as well. This is reflected in the changes in meaning of the English word **Dutch**, especially in America, where the language of the Amish and other "Pennsylvania Dutch," who are still so called, is actually a West Franconian dialect of High German.

- **Flemish**: The Dutch spoken in Belgium used to be referred to as Flemish, from "Flanders," the principal region in Belgium where it is found and where it is the only official language. It is now generally referred to simply as "Dutch," or as "Flemish Dutch" to distinguish it from "Netherlands Dutch," as its various dialects differ from the Standard Dutch of the Netherlands in several ways, most obviously in pronunciation, Flemish having a much softer sound and lacking the rasping guttural consonants of Dutch. A colloquial *Tussentaal* (lit. "in-between language") has recently grown up, fostered by entertainment programmes on television, which bridges the gap between local Belgian dialects and Standard Dutch. Some differences between Standard Dutch and Flemish are the result of the influence on Flemish of French, the other main language of Belgium. So in Dutch, English **jam** is called just that, *jam*, while in Flemish it is referred to by the French word *confiture*. Similarly, if you want to order toasted cheese, in the Netherlands call for a *tosti*, but in Belgium ask for a *croque monsieur*. Other differences cannot be explained in the same way, e.g. in Belgium the word *lopen* means "to run," while in the Netherlands it just means "to walk," with *rennen* being used for running. In Belgium, "to walk" is *stappen,* which in the Netherlands means "to go out." This is a common area of confusion among Germanic languages. Afrikaans uses *loop* for "walk" and *hardloop* for "run," but also has *stap* for walk. In German itself, *laufen* can mean "to walk" or "to run," or something in between. For "to walk" Germans normally just say "gehen," whose basic meaning is simply "to go," which in Dutch and Afrikaans is *gaan*. If you want to indicate fast running or racing, the word to use in German is *"rennen."* All these words have English cognates: **run**, **lope** (meaning "to run with long strides"), **elope**, **leap**, **go**. English **walk** is from a root meaning "to turn, to roll," cognate with Latin *volvo, volvere, volvi, volutum* ("to roll, turn around, revolve," and Greek *elyo, elyein* (to wrap"), from Greek root *Fel-* (the initial letter being a digamma, pronounced like English /w/), which is the origin of English **helix** and **helicopter**, lit. "spiral, twisted wing."

- Dutch loanwords are embedded in some other languages, notably Indonesian, as I discovered when giving a series of lectures on English Law to a group of Indonesian bankers.[67]

- Dutch is sometimes said to fall midway between English and German, and there is a certain amount of truth in this. Dutch has ditched a lot of the grammatical forms that learners of German have to grapple with. Strangely, though Dutch still officially has three genders, masculine, feminine and neuter, as in German, in practice in most areas there is no practical grammatical distinction between masculine and feminine, which tend to blend into a single "common" gender. The dialects spoken in the Southern Netherlands and Belgium are generally more conservative in this as in other respects.

❖ **Afrikaans:** This is one of the newest and most streamlined of all European languages. It is spoken chiefly in South Africa and Namibia and is the home language of over 60% of White South Africans and over 75% of "Coloured" (i.e. mixed race) South Africans. It is a daughter language of Dutch and has sometimes been described as a Dutch-based creole, though this label has not been widely accepted. Between 90% and 95% of Afrikaans vocabulary is Dutch. The Cape of Good Hope at the southern tip of South Africa was first colonized by the Dutch, starting with the landing of Jan van Riebeeck in 1652. The number of Dutch speakers was swelled by an influx of French Huguenots, Protestants escaping from Catholic persecution, who arrived in 1689, and by German settlers coming in during the 18th and 19th centuries. Slaves imported particularly from Madagascar and the Dutch East Indies (modern Indonesia), who intermarried with the indigenous Hottentot population, also greatly increased the number of people at the Cape speaking Dutch and changing it in the process. The publication of the first Afrikaans-language newspaper, *Die Afrikaanse Patriot*, in 1876 marked the beginning of the language as a literary medium. In the

---

[67] See Chapter 12, LOAN OR THEFT?

words of the first edition of this publication: *"Ons wil nou met ons 'Patriot' an die wereld wys, dat ons wel de'entlik een taal het waarin ons kan sê net wat ons wil."* ("We will now show the world with our 'Patriot' that we really have a language in which we can say just what we like.") Even at this early date the language already displays its hallmark characteristics: the jettisoning of gender, the absence of inflection in nouns and verbs alike, the loss of the simple past tense leaving only the perfect tense for all past statements, and the dropping of endings like the [en] indicating in Dutch the infinitive of a verb, together with the shortening of certain words. For example, here is the conjugation (or non-conjugation) of the verb "to be" in Dutch, Afrikaans and English compared:

| ***Dutch*** | ***Afrikaans*** | ***English*** |
|---|---|---|
| ik ben | ek is | I am |
| jij/u bent | jy/u is | you are |
| hij/zij/het is | hy/sy/dit is | he/she/it is |
| wij zijn | ons is | we are |
| jullie zijn | julle is | you (plural) are |
| zij zijn | hulle is | they are |

Notice that, while Dutch has four different forms for the verb and even English has three, Afrikaans has just one: *"is"* for all persons, singular and plural alike.

- The South Africa Act 1909, the constitution of the new Union of South Africa, which would come into existence in the following year, did not mention Afrikaans at all. Instead, the country was designated as bilingual, with English and Dutch as the two official languages of the new state. In 1925, Afrikaans was finally recognized as an official language together with English. The wording of the 1925 amendment is rather curious, however. Dutch was not removed as an official language but was "declared to include Afrikaans." In practice, however, to all intents and purposes Afrikaans replaced Dutch, which was usually referred to in South Africa as "High Dutch." After being one of only two official languages for nearly 70 years, resulting in a high degree of bilingualism, in 1994 Afrikaans became one of eleven official languages of South Africa, the other ten being English and nine Bantu languages.

❖ **Danish**: Danish, in common with the other Scandinavian languages (which do not include Finnish, a non-Indo-European language), all have a common ancestor in Old Norse, a Low Germanic language unaffected by the Germanic second sound shift. According to the Icelandic so-called Gray Goose *(Grágás)* Laws of the 12th century, Swedes, Norwegians, Icelanders and Danes all spoke the same language, called the "Danish tongue." Danish, Norwegian and Swedish are still quite largely mutually intelligible today, though Swedes and Danes tend to understand Norwegian better than each other's languages. Standard Danish, or *Rigsdansk* (lit. "national Danish"), is based on dialects spoken in and around the nation's capital, Copenhagen, where more than one fourth of the Danish population reside. Though Danish is fairly uniform, there are some dialects as well. Danish is notoriously difficult to learn, partly because of its highly unphonetic spelling and partly because its pronunciation is often found difficult to master, leading to the common rather unkind description of Danish as a throat disease.

❖ **Norwegian**: Like Afrikaans, Norwegian is a new language – or, to be precise, two languages. While Norway was under Danish rule, from 1536 to 1814, upper class Norwegians spoke *dansk-norsk*, or "Dano-Norwegian," which was actually Danish with a Norwegian pronunciation, while the rest of the population spoke a variety of local dialects. In 1814, in the settlement after the Napoleonic War, Norway was placed under Swedish rule, which lasted until 1905, when a new independent kingdom of Norway came into existence, with a Danish king. Until 1885 *dansk-norsk* remained the sole official language of Norway, and in that year two forms of written Norwegian were recognized as official: one, now called *Bokmål* or "book language" (previously known as *Riksmål*, or "national language"), which was based on Danish, and the other, based on Norwegian dialects, now called *Nynorsk*, or "new Norwegian." Efforts to unite the two types of Norwegian, though supported by 79% of Norwegians in 1946, were finally officially abandoned in 2002. Note: In this book, all references to "Norwegian," unless otherwise indicated, are to *Bokmål*.

❖ **Swedish**: A law passed in Sweden in 2009 made Swedish the official "main language" of the country, with several other languages, including

Finnish and Yiddish, being granted "national minority" status. Swedish is also an official language of Finland side by side with Finnish, and street signs in Helsinki and elsewhere in Finland are bilingual. After centuries of stiff formality in forms of address, the so-called *du-reformen*, or "you-reform" was introduced in the 1960s, resulting in *du*, the familiar form of "you," being used even in formal and official contexts. Swedish has recently seen a move to encourage the use of *hen*, a newly coined gender-neutral pronoun, to replace *han* ("he") and *hon* ("she"), but this has not yet caught on among the general population. It appears to have been modelled on *hän*, a gender-neutral personal pronoun in Finnish, which lacks grammatical gender altogether.

❖ **Icelandic**: This is by far the most conservative of all the Scandinavian languages, so much so that present-day Icelandic speakers can read and understand Old Norse texts written up to a thousand years ago. Icelandic grammar also retains high levels of inflection, with four cases and plenty of irregular declensions for nouns, along with ten tenses and three voices for verbs – active, passive and also middle.

- Icelandic is also reluctant to borrow words from other languages, preferring instead to create "calques," i.e. by translating the components of foreign words back into Icelandic. For example, the Icelandic word for electricity is *rafmagn*, which literally means "electron power," because the Greek word *electron*, from which "electricity" comes, actually means "amber," because (static) electricity was first generated by rubbing amber. Similarly, the Icelandic word for computer is *tölva*, from *tala* ("number, digit") plus *völva* ("a seer"), presumably because a computer is seen as having some sort of supernatural power with numbers!

- Iceland is also conservative in its use of patronymics instead of family names. So, for example, if Sven Andersson has a son called Robert, Robert is not Robert Andersson but Robert Svensson, and his son Magnus is Magnus Robertsson, and his daughter Harpa is Harpa Robertsdottir ("Robert's daughter"). Looking up a name in an Icelandic telephone directory is a nightmare! In the other Germanic countries patronymics, as it were, "froze," so that Peter the son of John is Peter Johnson, his son Edward becomes Edward Johnson, his son James is James Johnson and his daughter Elizabeth is Elizabeth Johnson. The Icelandic pattern is, however, still found in traditional Arab societies like Saudi Arabia and in Jewish names used for religious purposes, where Moses the son of David is *Moshe ben David* and Moses' son Isaac is *Yitzchak ben Moshe*. In modern Israel such patronymics became frozen into family names, so Prime Minister David Ben-Gurion's son Amos was not Amos Ben-David" in accordance with religious tradition but Amos Ben-Gurion.

## Germanic impact

The force and immediacy of the stock of Germanic words in English is well illustrated by Lewis Carroll's comical "Father William" poem from *Alice in Wonderland*:

> "You are old, Father William," the young man said,
> "And your hair has become *very* white;
> And yet you *incessantly* stand on your head –
> Do you think, at your *age*, it is right?"
>
> "In my youth," Father William *replied* to his son,
> "I feared it might *injure* the brain;
> But, now that I'm *perfectly sure* I have none,
> Why, I do it again and again."
>
> "You are old," said the youth," as I *mentioned* before,
> And have grown most *uncommonly* fat;
> Yet you turned a back *somersault* in at the door –
> *Pray*, what is the *reason* of that?"
>
> "In my youth," said the *sage*, as he shook his grey locks,
> "I kept all my limbs very *supple*
> By the use of this *ointment* – one shilling the box –
> Allow me to sell you a *couple*?"
>
> "You are old," said the youth, "and your jaws are too weak
> For anything tougher than *suet*;
> Yet you *finished* the goose, with the bones and the beak –
> *Pray*, how did you *manage* to do it?"
>
> "In my youth," said his father, "I took to the *law*,
> And *argued* each *case* with my wife;
> And the *muscular* strength, which it gave to my jaw,
> Has lasted the rest of my life."

"You are old," said the youth, "one would hardly *suppose*
That your eye was steady as ever;
Yet, you balanced an eel on the end of your nose –
What made you so awfully clever?"

"I have answered three *questions*, and that is enough,"
Said his father. "Don't give yourself airs!
Do you think I can listen all day to such stuff?
Be off, or I'll kick you downstairs!"

All words of non-Germanic origin are printed in *italics*. All the rest are Germanic. Lewis Carroll, a master wordsmith, obviously chose the words best suited to his purpose without regard to origin. Though the language of the poem is fairly down-to-earth, it certainly does contain a lot of Latin-based words. Yet it would probably be possible to replace most of the non-Germanic words with good old-fashioned Germanic ones. Let us give it a go:

- ❖ **Very**: From Latin *verus* "true." Hence the Biblical phrase, **"Verily, verily**, I say unto thee..." Germanic synonym: **greatly**.
- ❖ **Incessantly**: From Latin *cesso, cessare, cessatum* "to cease, stop," related to **cease**. Germanic near-synonyms: **endlessly, non-stop** – though **stop** may possibly be a borrowing from Vulgar Latin *\*stuppare* "to stop or stuff with tow" (OED). In my opinion this origin is unlikely. The English sense of **stop** meaning "coming to a standstill" has been adopted by many other languages.
- ❖ **Age**: Ultimately, via Old French, from an expanded form of Latin *aetas, aetatis* "age," from which also come French *âge*, Italian *eta*, Spanish *edad*, Portuguese *idade*, all meaning "age."
- ❖ **Replied**: From Latin *replico, replicare, replicavi, replicatum* (lit. "to fold back") via French. Germanic synonym: **answer**, related to **swear**.
- ❖ **Injure**: From Latin *iniuria*, lit. "a legal wrong." Germanic synonyms: **harm, scathe** (now restricted to the present participle, **scathing**, and the negative, **unscathed**). English **hurt** is from Old French *hurter* "to strike, ram" (Modern French *heurter* "to strike, hit"), though, unusually, this is not of Latin but of Germanic origin.
- ❖ **Perfectly**: From Latin *perfectus* "completed, accomplished." Germanic near-synonyms: **thoroughly, wholly, utterly, altogether**.

- **Thorough**: Related to English **through**, German *durch*, Dutch *door*, Afrikaans *deur*.
- **Whole**: Word of Germanic origin related to English **heal, health, hale, holy**, and to German *heilen* ("to heal") and *heil* ("whole, safe," as in the Nazi greeting *"Heil Hitler!"*). The potential ambiguity of German *heil/heilen* is illustrated by the joke about the two German psychiatrist acquaintances who bump into each other on the street during the Nazi period. The one raises his hand in the Nazi salute with the words, *"Heil, Hitler!"* To which the other replies: *"Heil du ihn!"* ("You heal him!"). The [wh-] spelling of English **whole** appeared only in the 15th century. In Old English it was *hal*. All these Germanic words are cognate with Greek *holos* ("whole, entire, complete"), whence English **holocaust, hologram, holograph**. These are all also cognate with Latin *salus* ("health"), *saluto, salutare, salutavi, salutatum* ("to keep safe, greet"), *salvus* ("safe"), *solidus* ("solid") and all English derivatives from these. For the [h]/[s] equivalence between Greek and Latin.[68]
- **Utterly**: From English "out."
- **Altogether**: From English **all** + **together**, the latter word being related to **gather**, also German *Gatte* "husband."

❖ **Sure**: From Latin *securus* ("safe, untroubled") via French.

❖ **Uncommonly**: From Latin *communis* ("public, shared"), from which we get English **commune, community, communism, communicate**. In English **common** can refer either to something found generally, as in a "common noun" (e.g. table, chair, book, mouse) as against a "proper noun" (i.e. a name), or to a person looked down upon as low class, "the common people." It is **commonly** said that "common sense is not very common." The phrase "uncommonly fat" could be replaced by Germanic "greatly overweight."

❖ **Somersault**: From Middle French *sombresault*, ultimately from Latin *supra* ("over") + *saltus* ("jump"), the latter from Latin *salio, salire, salui, saltum* ("to leap, jump"), from which comes English **salient** (lit. "jumping (out)," hence "important, relevant," as in "salient point.")

---

[68] See Chapter 14, SOUND MOVES.

Germanic near-synonyms: **head-over-heels leap, back-flip, cartwheel**.

- **Reason**: From Latin *ratio, rationis* "reason." Germanic near-synonym: **goal**.
- **Sage**: Ultimately from Latin *sapio, sapere* "to taste, be wise," as in **homo sapiens** "wise man," the flattering name mankind has arrogated to itself; cognate with Greek *sophos* "wise," as in English **philosophy, sophistry, sophisticated**.
- **Supple**: From Latin *supplex* "submissive, beseeching," whence English **suppliant, supplicate**. An unusual example of a word developing a physical meaning, "pliant, bending," after a more figurative use.
- **Ointment**: From Latin *unguentum*, via French. Germanic near-synonym: **drug**.
- **Couple**: From Latin *copula* "tie, connection" via French. Germanic near-synonyms: **few, two**.
- **Suet**: Probably ultimately, via French, from Latin *sebum* "tallow, grease," from which comes **sebaceous** (glands). Latin *sebum* is cognate with English **soap**, Dutch *zeep*, Afrikaans *seep*, Danish *sæbe*, Norwegian *såpe*, German *Seife* (by second sound shift).
- **Finished**: From Latin *finio, finire, finitum* ("to finish, end, limit"). Germanic near-synonyms: **ate** (from **eat**), **swallowed**.
- **Pray**: From Latin *precor, precari, precatus* ("to beg, entreat"), via French. Germanic synonym: **ask, beg** (which, however, the OED traces from French *Beguine*, a medieval women's mendicant order, as "perhaps the most likely derivation").
- **Manage**: Ultimately from Latin *manus* "hand." Germanic near-synonyms: **handle, take over, take care of, see to it**.
- **Law**: From Latin *lex, legis* ("law") via French. Germanic near-synonyms: **bidding, behest**.
- **Argued**: From Latin *arguo, arguer, argutum*, "to prove, make clear, demonstrate," related to Latin *argentum* (the shiny substance, hence "silver"). Germanic synonym: **fought** (from **fight**), **squabbled, bandied words**.
- **Case**: From Latin *casus* (lit. "a falling," so "an event, occasion, accident"), cf. similar concept in English **befall**.

- **Muscular**: From Latin *musculus* ("muscle"). Germanic near-synonyms: **brawny**, **sinewy**.

- **Suppose**: From Latin *suppono, supponere, suppositum* ("to subordinate"), from *sub* + *ponere* ("to place under"). Germanic near-synonyms: **deem**, **daresay**.

- **Question**: From Latin *quaestio* ("query, inquiry, investigation"). Germanic near-synonym: **ask**.

# CHAPTER 10

# A LATIN ROMANCE

THOUGH THE BEDROCK of English is Germanic, huge dollops of French and Latin have been superimposed on that foundation. It is estimated that about 29% of the words in modern English are of French origin and a further 29% come from Latin, but this estimate is misleading. It is based on research published in 1975 by Professor Joseph M. Williams of the University of Chicago, who claimed to have examined the 10,000 most frequently used words in English. However, Williams's selection was based on a sample of corporate letters, not on everyday speech, and so might have been expected to exaggerate the proportion of French and Latin derivatives as against Anglo-Saxon words, because written English, and even more so, English in commercial use, tends to be more formal than colloquial speech. Nevertheless, Williams's estimates are supported by the research carried out by Andreas Simons on what he termed the "core vocabulary" of English – "the 5,000 most frequently used words in English, representing the top 2% of distinct vocabulary and making up 85% of all words in any English source." Simons concluded that "French and Latin make up the largest portion of English core vocabulary. After the 1,875 most frequently used words out of the 250,000 words in distinct English vocabulary, French and Latin dominate the English language, achieving a share of 56% at the core vocabulary level, 5,000 words."[69]

---

[69] medium.com@andreas simons/the-english-language-is-a-lot-more-French-than-we-thought-heres-why-4db2db3842b3.

## Vulgar Latin

There is an observable affinity between English and the Romance languages generally – not just French, but also, to greater or lesser extent, the other Romance languages. Before we go any further, let us be quite sure what we mean by the "Romance languages," formerly labeled "Romanic languages," "Latin languages" or "Neo-Latin languages." These are, to put it as its simplest, modern forms of Latin – what Latin eventually turned into, particularly French, Italian, Spanish, Portuguese, Catalan, Occitan and Romanian. But it is important to note that the Latin that developed into the Romance languages was not Classical Latin, the literary Latin of Livy, Vergil, Horace and Tacitus. No, it was what we call Vulgar Latin, the Latin as spoken by the ordinary people. And it is also important to understand that it is not as if Classical Latin first morphed into Vulgar Latin, which then changed into the Romance languages. Vulgar Latin was there all the time, or at least from an early date, as a substratum beneath the polished literary language of the poets, orators, historians and philosophers.

Being non-literary, Vulgar Latin is not as well documented as Classical Latin. But it is already in evidence to some extent as early as in the dialogue particularly of the slave characters in the comedies of Plautus (c. 254–184 BCE), two hundred years before the time of Julius Caesar and Augustus. However, we get glimpses of Vulgar Latin popping up even in some of the writings of that paragon of Classical Latin, Marcus Tullius Cicero (106–43 BCE), a contemporary of Julius Caesar and a leading politician, orator, jurist and philosopher, and a prolific author in all these fields, whose writings were taken as setting the gold standard for Latin prose. There is no sign of Vulgar Latin in these writings, but Cicero let his hair down in the numerous Letters that he wrote to his friend Atticus and others and which were preserved for posterity thanks to the diligence of his secretary, Tiro, a freed slave, who published Cicero's writings in his long life (he is reputed to have lived to the age of 99) after his master's grisly death. Cicero's Letters give us occasional glimpses of words from the substratum of colloquial or Vulgar Latin that would not have been deemed worthy of house-room in his more formal writings.

A rich source of Vulgar Latin is the wonderful comical sketch known as "Trimalchio's Dinner" (*Cena Trimalchionis*), part of a satirical novel titled the *Satyricon* attributed to Gaius Petronius Arbiter (c. 27–66 CE), adviser to the Emperor Nero. Trimalchio is a freedman (ex-slave) who has amassed great wealth, which he is determined to display in the most extravagant, pretentious and vulgar way possible. But he and his dinner guests, mostly freedmen like himself, are unable to shake off their humble origins, which are betrayed in their use of language peppered with words and phrases that are decidedly not Classical Latin, but belong to the Vulgar Latin substratum.

The writings of St Jerome (c. 347–420) provide later examples of Vulgar Latin. His Latin translation of the Bible was to become the official version of the Bible of the Catholic Church for many centuries to come. Its title, the Vulgate, derives not from the type of Latin in which it was written but from the fact that it was the *versio vulgata*, "the commonly used version," from Latin *vulgus* meaning "the common people, the masses." The language in which it is couched is tinged with Vulgar Latin, but not nearly as much as Jerome's Commentaries.

Three points need to be emphasized:

1) Vulgar Latin was not a separate language from Classical Latin, though it differed in certain respects in grammar, syntax and vocabulary.

2) What written evidence we have of Vulgar Latin is probably only an approximation to what Vulgar Latin, as spoken, was really like.

3) Contrary to a popular scholarly view, Vulgar Latin is unlikely to have been uniform throughout the Western Roman Empire. Different parts of the Empire were Romanized at different times, and the conquered nations and tribes in the different provinces had different pre-existing linguistic identities, which would have impacted on the way they spoke Latin – their degree of Romanization, their command of the language and their "accent," if you like.

## Saying "yes"

Dante Alighieri (c. 1265–1321), author of *La Divina Commedia* ("The Divine Comedy") and creator of Italian as an independent literary language, had a deep interest in language and wrote a treatise (in Latin) titled *De Vulgari Eloquentia* ("Eloquence in the Vernacular"), in which he classified the developing Romance vernaculars under three heads according to how they said "yes" : *alii oc, alii si, alii vero dicunt oil.* ("Some say *oc*, others *si*, and yet others *oil*.") In Classical Latin the most usual way of expressing agreement is by repeating the verb, as in the following example:

Question: *Coniuras contra Caesarem?* ("Are you conspiring against Caesar?") Answer: *Coniuro* ("I am conspiring.") *Si* (lit. "thus, so") is a rare colloquial alternative for "yes" in Classical Latin, found, for example, in the comedies of Terence, and so is really Vulgar Latin. *Si* is the normal way of saying "yes" in Italian (*sì*), Spanish (*sí*), Portuguese (*sim*, a nasalized version of the same), and Catalan (*sí*). French also uses *si* for "yes" or "but yes" as a strong contradiction to a negative question, e.g. *Vous n'avez pas de voiture? Si, j'en ai trois.* ("You don't have a car? But yes, I have three.") But the normal way of saying "yes" in French is of course *oui*, now often pronounced *ouais*, with *mouais* indicating reluctant agreement. *Oui* is represented by Dante as *oil*, because it was a contraction of Latin *hoc illud* (lit. "this that"). The dialects of Old French, as spoken in Northern France in Dante's time, came to be collectively known as the *langue d'oïl*, by contrast with the *langue d'oc* of the south of France now known again as Occitan. *Oc*, the third form of "yes" identified by Dante, is from Vulgar Latin *hoc* ("this"), and is still the word for "yes" in Occitan, whose name is based on it, as is the geographical name Languedoc (lit. "the language of oc"). Another name by which the *langue d'oc* was known is Provencal, which is particularly associated with medieval troubadour poetry and songs. Closely related to Occitan, though separate from it, is Catalan, spoken primarily in northeastern Spain.

## Italian

As the home of the Latin language, the inhabitants of Italy obviously spoke the "best" Latin, including the "best" Vulgar Latin. Although from the fifth century onward Italy had its fair share of Germanic rulers, it took much longer for that Roman heartland than for the other areas of the former Western Roman Empire to develop a separate identity from Latin. For centuries Italians assumed that the language that they were speaking was Latin, even though it was gradually diverging more and more from any Latin standard. Except for a few isolated examples, it is not until the late twelfth century that we encounter a substantial body of literature in an identifiably Italo-Romance vernacular, and Italian as a separate language really only came into its own with the publication of The Divine Comedy (*La Divina Commedia*) by Dante Alighieri in 1320.

Dante labelled the language of his masterpiece, largely based on the dialect of his native Tuscany, as "Italian" and who first gave Italian the status of an independent literary language. As a result, the Tuscan dialect became the Italian gold standard, which is still the case today. "*Lingua Romana in bocca Toscana,*" as the saying goes, "the Roman tongue in the Tuscan mouth," or in other words the Latin language as spoken in Tuscany. To get some idea of how far Italian had moved away from Latin, we need just quote the famous words that Dante placed at the entrance of *L'Inferno* ("Hell"): *Lasciate ogni speranza, voi ch'entrate* ("Abandon all hope, ye who enter").

❖ *Lasciate*: "Abandon, leave," from Latiin, *laxate*, from *laxo, laxare, laxatum*, which however has a different meaning, "to extend, expand, undo, loosen, lighten, relieve." For "abandon" Latin would prefer *relinquite*, from *relinquo, relinquere, relictum* "leave, abandon." English has links with both. From Latin *laxo*, English has **lax**, **laxative**, **relax**; and from Latin *relinquo*, English has **relinquish**, **delinquent**, **delict**, **relic**. English also uses directly the French phrase *laissez faire*, as in *laissez-faire* economics, and also "*laissez faire, laissez passer,*" a form of libertarian economic policy, lit. "leave alone, let pass." A common notice in France reads: *Les chiens en laisse* ("Dogs on a leash").

English **leash**, **lease**, **release** are all related to French *laisser*. Latin *laxo, laxare* ultimately derives from PIE *\*sleg-* or *\*leg-*, meaning "to be slack, languid," and English **languid**, **slack** and also **slacks** ("trousers") and even **sleep** come from the same origin.

❖ *Ogni*: "every, all," from Latin *omnem*, accusative singular of *omnis* ("every, all"). **Omni-** is frequently used as a prefix in English words such as **omnipotent** ("all-powerful"), **omniscient** ("all-knowing"), **omnivorous** ("eating everything indiscriminately"). The dative plural of Latin *omnis*, **omnibus**, meaning "for all," was first used by George Shillibeer in 1829 to describe his horse-drawn carriage for public transportation – the first **bus** in Britain. It had the word **OMNIBUS** emblazoned on its side. **Bus**, an abbreviation of **omnibus**, quickly entered the English language – and many other languages adopted either *bus* or *autobus* to describe this popular form of public transport, which, however, was (and still is) looked down on by snobs. David Lloyd George (British Prime Minister 1916–22) is reputed to have taunted the rather arrogant Conservative statesman, Lord Curzon, as they were walking together in Central London: Lloyd George: "You could never be Prime Minister." Curzon: "Why not?" Lloyd George: "Because I'm sure you have never travelled in an omnibus in your life." To prove him wrong, Curzon flagged down a bus and, on boarding, called out to the driver, "Carlton House Terrace, please, driver!"

❖ *Speranza*: "hope," formed from Latin *spero, sperare, speratum* ("to hope"). Latin would have used the noun *spem* here, the accusative singular of *spes, spei* "hope." The Latin saying *Nil desperandum* (lit. "nothing should be despaired of," so "Never despair") is often cited. From the Latin we have English **desperate**, now often used colloquially in the sense of "extreme," as in "I am in desperate need of a loo." From the French we have English **despair**. Words for "hope" in the Romance languages are all closely related: Besides Italian *speranza*, "hope" (as a noun) there is: French: *Espoir*, Spanish: *esperanza*, Portuguese and Catalan: *esperança*. <u>Note</u>: With the exception of Italian, all these Romance words for "hope" have added an [e-] before the [sp-]. This is a common feature of the change from Latin to Romance.

❖ *Voi*: "You" (plural) for Latin *vos* "you" (plural). *Voi* used to be used in Italian as the polite form of "you" (singular), though it conjugated the same as second person plural whether used to refer to one person or more than one. However, under Spanish influence, the third person *lei* came to be used as the polite way of saying "you" (singular), though in Naples and other parts of southern Italy *voi* has survived as the polite form of "you." Like *Usted* in Spanish, *lei* takes a third person verb, the problem with that being that Italian *lei* also means "she." So the sentence, *"Da dove viene lei?"* can mean either "Where do you come from?" or "Where does she come from?" Note that the form of the verb is the same for both. So, how can you tell which it is? Only by the context. In German, by contrast, which also uses the same word, *Sie,* for "she" and as the polite way of saying "you," the verb form differs. So, in German: "Where does she come from?" is *Woher kommt sie?* But the polite form of "Where do you come from?" is: *Woher kommen Sie?* In sum: (a) German *Sie* meaning "you" (polite form) has a verb with a third person plural ending – whereas Italian *Lei* meaning "you" has a verb with a third-person singular ending. (b) In German *Sie* is used as the polite way of saying "you" in both singular and plural – whereas in Italian *Lei* is used only in the singular; "you" (plural) is *voi* in both polite and familiar speech. (c) German *Sie* "you" is always capitalized to distinguish it from *sie* "she." In Italian *Lei* "you" is sometimes capitalized to distinguish it from *lei* "she," but only in formal communications (and textbooks!). (d) Unlike German, Italian (technically classified as a "pro-drop" language) often omits the subject of the verb altogether. So you can simply say: *"Da dove viene?"* This can mean either: "Where do you come from?" or: "Where does she come from?" or: "Where does he come from?" It all depends on the context.

❖ *Che*: *ch'entrate* is short for *che entrate* ("who enter"). *Che* is from Latin *qui* "who." In Latin relative and interrogative pronouns (i.e. words for who, what, which where, when) all begin with [qu-], which in the Romance languages became either [qu-] or [ch-] (but in either case is pronounced like a [k-]). By contrast, the signature initial sound for the same concepts in Germanic languages is [w-] or, as in English, [wh-], e.g. who, what, which, where, when, why.

❖ *Entrate*: "you (plural) enter," from Latin *intratis*, from *intro, intrare, intratum* "enter," from Latin *intra* "within," which in turn is from Latin *inter* "between, among." All the Romance languages (except Romanian) have changed the initial [i-] in Latin *intrare* to [e-]. They all mean "to enter": French: *entrer*, Italian: *entrare*; Spanish, Portuguese and Catalan: *entrar*; Romanian: *a intra*.

## Spanish

The Iberian peninsula, roughly comprising modern Spain and Portugal, experienced more than six centuries of Roman rule. The conquest of what the Romans called Hispania, begun around 200 BCE, was completed under the Emperor Augustus in 19 BCE and Roman rule, eroded in the fifth century, finally came to an end in 472 CE. When the Romans came, the peninsula was shared between speakers of various Celtic languages, Proto-Basque, an early form of present-day Basque, a non-Indo-European language, and a mysterious language described simply as "Iberian," which has never been deciphered. With the exception of Basque, these languages disappeared with Romanization, which took longer in some parts of the peninsula than others. Some members of the pre-Roman aristocracy gained early access to positions of prominence in Rome itself. This included Lucius Annaeus Seneca (c. 4 BCE–65 CE), the famous Stoic philosopher who became a Roman Senator and tutor to the Emperor Nero, by whom he was eventually ordered to commit suicide. Not much more than a century after the conquest of Hispania, a Roman Emperor from there ascended the throne: the great Emperor Trajan (reigned 98–117), who was succeeded by another emperor from Spain, his cousin Hadrian (reigned 117–138), and a later emperor, Theodosius I (reigned 379–395), was also of Spanish origin.

By the time Roman rule ended in 472, Spain was thoroughly Romanized. But most of Spain was under the rule of the Visigoths, a Germanic tribe, from 410 until the early eighth century, when it fell under Arabic-speaking Muslim invaders, formerly referred to as "Moors," who ruled a gradually shrinking kingdom, known in Arabic as al-Andalus. This shrinkage was caused by the so-called Reconquista, or the reconquest by Christians of Moorish Spain, which was finally completed with the conquest of Granada in 1492.

A distinctive Spanish vernacular is detectable in the Christian parts of Spain from the eleventh century, and with the major Castilian *Poema del Cid* ("The Poem of El Cid") from the mid-twelfth century, which is surprisingly close to modern Spanish. A couple of noteworthy features:

- The rather puzzling change from initial Latin [f-] to Spanish [h-], a major feature that distinguishes modern Spanish from the other Romance languages (except Gascon) is absent from *El Cid* and only manifests itself in the fifteenth century, e.g. *filium* > *hijo* ("son"), *facere* > *hacer* (to do"), *fabulare* > *hablar* ("to speak"). Far too much ink has been expended on the cause of this curious sound shift, with some writers suggesting a Basque influence. It is worth noting that there are some exceptions to this rule, notably when the initial Latin [f-] was followed by an accented [o], [e] or [i], e.g. *fontem* > *fuente* ("fountain"), *fortem* > *fuerte* ("strong"), *focum* ("fire-place, hearth") > *fuego* ("fire"), (Vulgar Latin) *\*festa* > *fiesta* ("holiday"), *fidem* > *fe* ("faith").

- A curious feature of Spanish that *is* already present in *El Cid* is the use of an apparent indirect object instead of a direct object with names and definite objects, e.g. *Maria ama a Pedro* ("Maria loves Pedro," lit. "Maria loves to Pedro"), *Maria ama al gato* ("Maria loves the cat," lit. "Maria loves to the cat"). This may possibly have arisen as a way of compensating for the disappearance of the Latin case-endings, which had made word-order irrelevant. Another example, Genesis 1:1:5 in Spanish: "*Y llamo Dios a la luz Dia, y a las tinieblas Noche.*" ("And God called the light Day and the darkness Night," lit. "And God called to the light Day and to the darkness Night"). Strangely enough, Hebrew (both classical and modern) has a similar construction, not in this passage, but in the very first words of the Bible: *bereshit bara elohim* **et** *hashamayim ve-**et** haaretz,* ("In the beginning God created the heaven and the earth"). The untranslatable little word "*et*," which has no independent meaning, is a marker indicating that a direct object is coming next, a construction used only where the object is a personal name or noun preceded by "the." I am not suggesting that Spanish got this idea from Hebrew, though that is a possibility, as there was quite a large Jewish population in Medieval Spain. Another language that has a similar construction, which is largely confined to personal names and pronouns, is Afrikaans, a Germanic language derived chiefly from Dutch spoken chiefly in South Africa. In Afrikaans, the construction in question is still regarded as informal or colloquial, e.g. *Het jy vir Jan* *gesien?* ("Have you seen Jan?", lit. "Have you seen for Jan?"). This feature does not exist in Dutch.

## Portuguese

While on vacation in Mozambique at the age of fourteen, I found that I was able to understand the local Portuguese-language newspapers on the basis of my schoolboy Latin. The locals all understood my spoken Portuguese, but, spotting my English accent, they would try out their English on me. As I wanted to practise my Portuguese, I had to resort to saying: *Desculpe, sou Húngaro. Não falo Ingles,* ("I'm so sorry, I'm Hungarian. I don't speak English"). That left Portuguese as the only common language between us!

Spanish and Portuguese have a number of features in common, though the close nasal pronunciation of standard European Portuguese makes it very difficult for Spanish speakers to understand it. In particular, a final [-s] in Portuguese is pronounced like English [-sh], and there is a tendency for the language to be spoken quite fast, particularly in Metropolitan Portuguese as distinct from the Brazilian dialects, which are spoken more slowly and with a more open pronunciation. Moreover, cognate words sometimes have quite different meanings in the two languages. There is the apocryphal story of the Portuguese man who, flying into Madrid airport in Spain, was unable to locate his luggage on the carousel. In desperation he stood there calling out in Portuguese, "*Estou embaraçado! Estou embaraçado!*" ("I'm in difficulties!"). To his surprise, a large throng of people gathered around him – because the cognate Spanish word, *embarazado,* means "pregnant." It is easy to see how a word literally describing a state of being heavily burdened or encumbered could come to mean pregnant. English **embarrass** and **embarrassed** have the same origin as these Spanish and Portuguese words. The underlying literal meaning is "to block, impede" from Vulgar Latin *\*barra,* meaning "a bar," giving rise to English **bar**, **barrier**, the phrase **behind bars** ("in jail") and the omnipresent commercial **bar code**. The French expression "*un embarras de richesses*" has been imported directly into English (lit. "the state of having so much wealth that it has become a burden," but usually used figuratively in the sense of being spoilt for choice).

Awkward as the relationship is between Spanish and Portuguese, that between the two main variants of Portuguese, the Portuguese of Portugal, or Metropolitan Portuguese, and that of Brazil, is hardly less so. And Brazil is so vast that it is hard to generalize about usage there. Besides the 10 million inhabitants of Portugal itself, the rest of the approximately 220 million native Portuguese speakers in the world live in Brazil, which became independent from Portugal in 1822.

Even the basic word for "girl, young woman" is different: *rapariga* in Portugal, but especially in the North and Northeast of Brazil that word usually denotes "a young lady of bad repute, a prostitute." Instead, the old word *moça* is used, which is connected either with Latin *muscus* ("moss") or *mustus* ("fresh, young"), which may be related to it (de Vaan). Latin *vinum mustum*, or just *mustum* on its own denotes "must, new wine, unfermented grape juice." The underlying concept seems to be wetness or dampness, hence newness or freshness, which is why the derivative, *moça*, came to mean a young girl in (Brazilian) Portuguese and *mozo, moza* a young boy or girl, also a waiter, in Spanish, which also has got related *muchacho, muchacha* for "boy" and "girl" respectively.

Latin *mustum* was also borrowed by Germanic languages, as in German *Most* ("must, new wine, unfermented grape juice, and, in Southern Germany and Switzerland, fruit wine), Dutch *most*, Afrikaans *mos*, hence *moskonfyt* ("grape must jam"), an old recipe from the Cape of Good Hope in South Africa. (I learnt about this from my old professor, the late Theo Haarhoff, a proud Afrikaner, who likened the Boer farmer to the Roman husbandman of old and wrote a book titled *Vergil in the Experience of South Africa*, re-edited as *Vergil the Universal*.)

By the way, Latin *muscus* is not to be confused with unconnected Latin *musca*, "a fly," – "quite possibly an onomatopoeic form *$mu$

from the humming sound made by flies" (de Vaan). The feminine gender of *musca* carried over to French *mouche* ("a fly"), as illustrated in the apocryphal story set in a French restaurant: Diner: "*Garçon, il y a un mouche dans ma soupe.*" ("Waiter, there is a fly in my soup.") Waiter: "*Une mouche, Monsieur.*" Diner: "What good eyesight you Frenchies have!" In complaining about the fly in his soup, the diner had mistakenly used the wrong grammatical gender for *mouche* – *un mouche* (masculine) instead of *une mouche* (feminine). When corrected, the diner assumed that the waiter had identified the sex of the particular fly in question as female, when in fact he was only referring to the grammatical gender of the French word *mouche*. In French all flies are feminine, though not necessarily female! The same applies in Spanish and Portuguese, which however have stuck more closely to the Latin, with *mosca* as their word for "a fly."

Some quirky words are found in Brazil but not in Portugal, like *o bonde*, meaning "tram." This was a nickname for the original São Paulo tram coupons sold in batches of five which resembled colourful government bonds. The word was then applied to the tramcars or streetcars themselves, and the label stuck. In Portugal, however, trams lacked any such colourful associations, and the word for tram was and is simply *elétrico*.

Other quirky terms include Portuguese *maple* for "chair," so called not after the wood but after the furniture store in London's Tottenham Court Road, which used to export furniture all round the world in the nineteenth century. Portuguese *cadeira* is the standard word for "chair," from Latin *cathedra* ("chair"), which in turn is from Greek *kathedra* ("seat"). English has taken over directly the phrase **ex cathedra** as in an **ex cathedra pronouncement**, which is a formal statement made in an official capacity, e.g. that of a pope. A **cathedral** is so called because it is a church which is the seat of a bishop. English **chair** actually derives from Latin *cathedra* as well, via French *chaire*, which now denotes a pulpit or throne, the sense of "chair" now being conveyed by the slightly altered *chaise*, which has been borrowed directly by English in **chaise longue**, a sofa or couch with a back support at one end.

English **chair** supplanted **stool**, which was then demoted to representing a small backless, armless seat for one person. Its cognates are still the normal word for chair in the other Germanic languages: German: *Stuhl*; Dutch and Afrikaans: *stoel*; Danish, Norwegian and Swedish: *stol*. English **stool** also came to denote the special type of seat used for defecation, "a commode, privy." Hence the medical term for "faeces." The title **groom of the stole** or **stool**, which was in use from about 1500 until 1837, was held by a male body-servant to the King of England who helped the monarch with his toilet. The word **stole** was just another spelling of **stool**. The word **stool** also has other uses, e.g. **footstool, stool-pigeon** ("police informer"), and the phrase "to fall between two stools," shortened from: "Between two stools, one falls to the ground" (used figuratively).

On a bus ride in Lisbon as a student, I asked the conductor in Portuguese how much the bus fare was. "*Dez,*" ("ten") came his reply. *Dez escudos?* I inquired incredulously, because that amount seemed excessive for a short bus ride. "*Não,*" he replied, "*dez tostões.*" The *tostão*, plural *tostões* ("testoon") was a medieval Portuguese coin which came to be used in Lisbon slang to represent ten centavos, one tenth of an escudo. So the cost of the bus ride was only one escudo, which was what might have been expected at the time. I was quite chuffed that the bus conductor evidently adjudged my Portuguese good enough to address me in the arcane argot of the Lisbon working classes! The **testoon**, incidentally, was a coin widely used in medieval Europe, including England, where it was the forerunner of the shilling, one twentieth of a pound sterling. The name **testoon** came from the Italian *testone*, so called because the coin originally bore the head of the duke of Milan, the Italian word *testone* being an augmented form of Italian *testa,* "head," from the Vulgar Latin word *testa* "pot," a colloquial term for "head" that replaced Classical Latin *caput, capitis.*

## Catalan and Occitan

At the time of this writing the political and constitutional status of Catalonia hangs in the balance. Catalonia emerged as a separate legal entity under the Crown of Aragon in the late 12th century. By that time, the Catalan language had had something of a separate existence for over a century. In Catalonia itself in northeastern Spain, the Balearic Islands and Valencia, the Catalan language shares official status with Spanish (Castilian), and it is the sole official language of the sovereign microstate of Andorra. Catalan shares certain characteristics with its neighbour on the French side of the Pyrenees, Occitan. Until the late 19th century, the two languages were commonly regarded by academics as one, and they are still largely mutually intelligible. However, existing as it has for many centuries under the shadow of Spanish, Catalan has not been able to escape the influence of that language – any more than the southern and southeastern dialects of Occitan have been able to shake off the influence of French.

## French

The opening words of Julius Caesar's *Commentarii de Bello Gallico* ("Commentaries on the Gallic War"), the self-serving, account of his subjugation of most of Gaul, which was inflicted on generations of schoolchildren because of its beautifully simple Latin, begins with the words: "*Gallia est omnis divisa in partes tres.*" ("The whole of Gaul is divided into three parts.") What Caesar was referring to by "the whole of Gaul" was actually not the whole of Gaul at all, but only the unconquered part of Gaul, known to the Romans as Gallia Comata, literally "long-haired Gaul – just think of Asterix Le Gaulois and his friends with their long, often braided, hair – as distinct from the Romanized parts of Gaul that had been conquered long before, namely Cisalpine Gaul, which is now part of Northern Italy, and Transalpine Gaul, now the South of France, which had become the first Roman "province" so called and was therefore called Provincia, a name which survives in French Provence.

Caesar divided the inhabitants of Gallia Comata into three categories: the Aquitani (probably ancestors of the Basques), the Galli (Gauls, who called themselves Celts), and the Belgae, a large Gallo-Germanic confederation. Each of these groups would have learned to speak Latin with a different "accent" depending on their native tongue. Even by the time of Julius Caesar (102–44 BCE) the inhabitants of the two established provinces of Cisalpine and Transalpine Gaul would probably have spoken "good" Latin, while the conquered tribes of Gallia Comata would quite likely have continued to speak Latin with different "foreign accents" for a long time to come. Much later there was superimposed on these inherited differences the influence of several Germanic tribes, most notably the Franks, who arrived on the scene in the fifth century and eventually gave their name to the country as a whole, changing it from Gaul to what it still is today, France.[70]

## Romanian

Romanians are very proud of their Roman heritage preserved in the name of their language, which is the official language of Romania and also of Moldova, formerly a constituent republic of the Soviet Union. Romanian is spoken as a native language by some 25 million people and by a further four million as a second language. Romanians proudly trace their ancestry and that of their language from the conquest of Thrace, or Thracia, as it was known in Latin, by the Roman Emperor Trajan, who ruled from 98 to 117. However, this remote outpost of the Roman Empire was abandoned by the Emperor Aurelian in 271. Nevertheless, the Latin language became rooted here and has survived to the present day. One explanation favoured by Romanian writers, but rejected by most non-Romanian scholars, is that under Trajan the original local population was eradicated or driven out and replaced by a huge influx of Roman settlers. Unlikely as this sounds, the fact remains that there are very few traces of any

---

[70] For more on French, see Chapter 6, THE FRENCH CONNECTION.

pre-Roman language in Romanian, but there certainly is a marked Slavonic influence.

## Romance roundup

The Romance languages all have the bulk of their vocabulary from Latin, but each developed from Latin, or Vulgar Latin, in a distinctive way. You can learn these languages easily with a knowledge of English, which has "borrowed" a vast number of Latin words in a pure form and many more via French. Here are the opening words of Genesis, the first book of the Bible, in English (King James Version), Latin and six Romance languages:

- **English**: In the beginning God created the heaven and the earth.
- **Latin**: *In principio creavit Deus caelum et terram.*
- **Italian**: *Nel principio Iddio creò i cieli e la terra.*
- **Spanish**: *En el principio creò Dios los cielos y la tierra.*
- **Portuguese**: *No principio criou Deus os céus e a terra.*
- **Catalan**: *Al principi, Déu va crear el cel i la terra.*
- **French**: *Au commencement Dieu créa le ciel et la terre.*
- **Romanian**: *La început, Dumnezeu a făcut cerurile şi pământul.*

The English version stands out like a sore thumb – even more so than the Romanian. So how could I say, as I just did, that there is an affinity between English and the Romance languages? Except for the word **created**, which is of Latin origin, all the words in the English extract are of Germanic origin, whereas all the words in the Romance extracts are of Latin origin. Yet, English *does* have words that are cognate with all these Latinate words. So why aren't these words in evidence here? Because the most basic concepts – like the ones expressed in the opening words of the Bible – are expressed in English in words of Anglo-Saxon origin. Let's look at each of the words concerned:

❖ **Beginning**: The word *principio*, which is shared by all the Romance languages quoted here except French and Romanian, comes from Latin *principium*, "beginning, inception," from which we get both English **principal**, and **principle**. The former means "chief, main, most important" or as a noun meaning "person in position of authority," as in "school principal." The latter means "a fundamental belief or tenet, "hence "first principles," e.g. **Marxist principles** (not Karl but Groucho Marx): "These are my **principles**, and if you don't like them, I have others." French *commencement*, which exists with the same meaning in English, comes from Latin *com-* ("together," or simply adding intensive force) + *initium* ("beginning") from which come English **initiate**, **initiation**. Romanian *început* ("beginning") is from Latin *inceptio, inceptionis* ("a beginning") from the Latin verb *incipio, incipere, inceptum* ("to begin"), made up of in + *capio, capere, captum* ("to take, undertake"), from which we get English **incipient** and **inception**.

- **God**: All the Romance languages have a word derived from Latin *Deus* – including the rather strange-looking Romanian, *Dumnezeu*, which is actually a combination of derivatives of Latin *Dominus* ("Lord") + *Deus*. From Latin *Deus* English has **deity**, **deify** ("to make into a god"), and also **Deism**, "belief in an impersonal God," as distinct from **Theism**, from Greek *Theos* (God). Also, via French **divine**, **divinity**. On his deathbed, the Roman Emperor Vespasian, poking fun at the concept of the divinity of deceased emperors, remarked: *"Vae, puto deus fio."* ("Gosh, I think I'm becoming a god.")

- **Created**: All the translations except the Romanian use derivatives from Latin *creo, creare, creatum* ("to make grow, to produce, beget, cause"), from which we get English **create**, **creation**, **creature**, **procreate**, **recreation** and also evidently **recruit** and even (according to de Vaan) **sincere** (lit. "of one growth," so "unmixed pure). Romanian *făcut* is from Latin *facio, facere, factum* ("to make"), from which come English **fact**, **factory**, **faction**, **feat** and many compounds, such as **efficient**, **deficient**, **deficit**, **sufficient**.

- **Heaven(s)**: Latin *caelum* ("heaven") is the basis of all the Romance words for "heaven." Latin accented [ae] regularly went to [e], which in turn is then palatalized or diphthongized, to use the technical terms, into [ie] in Italian, Spanish and sometimes in French, as in the extracts quoted above. My own term for this [ie] is "offglide vowel." It is usual in Portuguese, too, though not in the example above. But it is quite common otherwise, e.g. the [e] in Portuguese *certo* ("certain") and *terra* ("earth, land") is pronounced similarly to the [ie] in Spanish *cierto* ("certain") and *tierra* ("earth, land"). This offglide effect is never reflected in Portuguese spelling. The fact that in some of the translations the word for heaven is singular and in others plural is not a feature of the Romance languages concerned. Sometimes, as in English **heaven** and **heavens**, the term may be expressed in either the singular or the plural. This is probably a reflection of the original Biblical Hebrew, where the word for heaven, *shamayim*, is plural in form.

- **Earth**: Besides English, all except the Romanian excerpt use a derivative of Latin *terra* ("earth, land"), from which come English **terrain, terrace, terrier, territory, subterranean** and even **tureen** ("soup bowl, dish," from French *terrine*, "cooking dish, **terrine**," now applied chiefly to the **pâté** that is cooked in such a dish). Romanian *pământ* ("earth") is from Latin *pavimentum* ("hard floor, level surface"), from which comes English **pavement**, which in American English refers to the road surface, but in British English to the sidewalk.

To master any one of the Romance languages, it is necessary to know the pattern of changes from Latin into that particular language. As you can see from the quoted extracts above, there are some common features in the development from Latin to Romance, but in addition each of the Romance languages displays certain idiosyncratic changes of its own.[71]

---

[71] See Peter Boyd-Bowman, *From Latin to Romance in Sound Charts,* Georgetown University Press, 1980.

# CHAPTER 11

# A GREEK DRAMA

IN THE COMEDY film *My Big Fat Greek Wedding*, the father of the bride insists that all words have a Greek origin, which is of course comic nonsense but is based on the (not entirely uncommon) misconception that Greek is the oldest living language in the world. One of the bride's friends, *sick of hearing this repeated boast, offers the old man the word kimono*. *"Kimono?"* he replies: *"Kimono* is come from the Greek word *cheimon* meaning "winter," because in the wintertime you are feeling cold, so you wrap your robe tight around you." Needless to say, there is absolutely no basis to this exercise in homespun etymology. *Kimono* is a Japanese word and completely unconnected with Greek *cheimon,* which, however, is cognate with Latin *hiems* "winter" and *hibernus* "winter" as an adjective (for *\*hiemernus*, according to Lewis & Short), from which comes English **hibernate**. The name of the famous mountain range, the **Himalayas**, derives from Sanskrit *Himalaya,* "abode of the snow," *hima* being Sanskrit for "snow."

Greek is conventionally estimated to account for only about 6% of English words. This is misleading because, in addition to some actual Greek words that have found their way into English, there is a vast number of **neologisms** (which is itself of Greek origin), i.e. new coinages, **based** (another word of Greek origin) on Greek roots. Any **technological phenomenon** (both words of Greek origin), **clinical diagnosis** (both words are of Greek origin) or **philosophical theory** (both words are of Greek origin) is likely to have a Greek-based label attached to it.

Here are a few examples:

- **Aero-**: From Greek *aer*, from which, via Latin *aer*, comes English **air**, which is also its meaning. English has a number of neologisms based on **aero-**, including **aerobics** (from *aero* + *bios* "life," hence a type of physical exercise designed to improve fitness), **aerodrome** (now mostly supplanted by **airport**), **aerodynamics**, **aeronautics**, **aeroplane** (British for American **airplane**), **aerospace**.

- **-archy**: From Greek *archein* "to rule," as in **monarchy**, **anarchy** ("no rule, no government"), **anarchist** ("one who advocates abolition of all government"), **hierarchy** (lit. "rule of priests"). Cf. **-cracy**, below. Also, **arch-** as a prefix meaning "chief, first," as in **archaic, archaeology, archbishop, archduke, arch-enemy, arch-rival, archipelago** (lit. "chief sea," from *archi-* + *pelagos* "high sea"), "a sea containing scattered islands."

- **Bio-**: From Greek *bios* "life": **biology, biography, autobiography, biodiversity, biochemistry**.

- **Chiro-**: From Greek *cheir* or *chir* "hand," **chiropodist** (from Greek *chir* + *pous, podos* "foot," so literally "hand-foot"), in practice restricted to those who deal with such problems as corns and ingrown toenails, now largely replaced by **podiatrist**, lit. "foot doctor," from *pod-* + *iatros* "doctor." A **chiropractor** (lit. "hand manipulator") is a modern coinage to represent a member of a profession that specializes in treating ailments chiefly by manipulating the spine, as against an **osteopath** (from the Greek meaning "bone disease"), a member of a rival but very similar profession. Latin *chirurgia*, from Greek *cheir/chir* "hand" + *ergon* "work," turned into English **surgery**, with related **surgeon, surgical, microsurgery**, etc.

- **-crat/-cracy**: From Greek *kratos* "strength": **aristocrat, aristocracy, autocrat, autocracy, democrat, democracy**. English treats **-crat/-cracy** as almost synonymous with **-arch/-archy**: Cf. **aristocracy** (lit. "government of the best") with **oligarchy** ("rule of the few"). Of course, **the aristocracy** can also refer to the people making up the nobility.

- **Demo-**: From Greek *demos* "people": **democracy, demographics, demotic**.

- **Dynamo-:** From Greek *dynamis* "power, strength": **dynamo, dynamite, dynamic**.
- **Eco-:** From Greek *oikos* "house," Latinized as *oeco-* and then to *eco-*, as in: **economy** (lit. "household management"), **economist, economize, econometric, ecology**. Greek *oikos* is cognate with Latin *vicus* "neighbourhood, village," from which comes English **vicinity**. Greek *oikos* was originally *Foikos*, the [F-] being the digamma, representing a sound similar to initial English [w-], which is why it is sometimes referred to as "waw" or "wau." The digamma was part of the archaic Greek alphabet but seems to have disappeared before the Homeric epics were written down in the 7th century BCE. Probably the best-known Greek word thought to have had a digamma as its initial letter originally is the word *oinos* "wine," with which Latin *vinum* "wine" is cognate. English **wine** and German *Wein* derive from an early Germanic borrowing from the Latin. The digamma entered the Roman alphabet as [F], where it was pronounced in much the same way as English [f]. Another cognate of Greek *oikos* and Latin *vicus* is Old English *wic* "village," surviving in place names such as **Greenwich, Woolwich, Dulwich**.
- **Erg-:** From Greek *ergon* "work" has given rise (directly or via Latin) to a number of very diverse English words, including: **energy, ergonomics, synergy, allergy, lethargy, liturgy, surgeon, surgery, organ** and even **orgy**. In addition, **ergon** is cognate (i.e. shares a common origin) with as well as being synonymous with English **work** (in accordance with Grimm's Law and also loss of the initial ancient Greek digamma – see below).
- **Geo-:** From Greek *ge* "earth": **geography, geology, geophysics, geopolitical**.
- **Cyber-:** From Greek *kybernetes* "steersman, pilot of a ship": **cybernetics, cybercafé, cyberspace. Cyber** by itself now refers to anything to do with the internet, so: **cyber security**. Latin converted the initial [k] to [g] in *guberno, gubernare, gubernatum*, from which, via French, we get **govern, governor, government**. "Gov" or "gov'nor" (for **governor**) is an old-fashioned respectful form of address, still sometimes used by London taxi drivers. A taxi driver who addresses me as **gov** is always guaranteed a good tip!

- **Gymno-**: From Greek *gymnos* "naked": **gymnasium**, **gymnastic**, **gymnastics**, abbreviated to **gym**, as in **gym shoes**, **gym teacher**, or just **gym**, referring to the place of exercise or the activity. So called because the ancient Greeks exercised in the nude, though it is now often thought improper. My father attended a *Gymnasium* in Berlin, where the term refers not to a place of exercise but to a school with a strong emphasis on Classical Latin and Greek. Ironically, my father's Greek teacher, nicknamed *Willie der Waldaffe* ("Willie the forest ape, or country bumpkin" because of his signature wild beard), told his students to translate Greek *gymnos* into German by the euphemistic phrase *leicht bekleidet* ("lightly clad"). According to EOL, Greek *gymnos* is from a metathesis (i.e. a transposition of sounds) of PIE root *\*nogw-* "naked," and that both English **naked** (Germanic) and **nude** (from Latin *nudus*) also come from the same (unmetathesised – to coin a term) root.

- **Halo-**: From Greek *hals, halos* "salt," from which comes **halogen**, lit. "salt producer." Cognate with Greek *hals, halos* is Latin *sal, salis* "salt." The equivalence between initial Greek [h] or "rough breathing," and initial Latin [s] is found in a number of important words, including Greek *helios* / Latin *sol* "sun," Greek *holos* "whole"/ Latin *solidus* "firm, whole, entire," Greek *hama* "together"/ Latin *similis* "alike, similar," English **same**, and Germanic words for "together": German *zusammen*, Dutch *samen*, Afrikaans *saam*, Danish *sammen*, Norwegian *sammen*, Swedish *tillsammans*. It is important to note that Greek has an /h/ sound where most other Indo-European languages have an /s/ sound. The reason is unknown. The Greek "rough breathing" was represented by a diacritical mark [ʻ] in Greek orthography until 1982, though the sound had disappeared from the Greek language long before. In modern Greek the "rough breathing" representing the sound /h/ is neither written nor pronounced. By the way, Greek *hals, halos* has nothing to do with English **halo**, in the sense of a ring of light crowning the representation of a saint or divine figure, which is from Greek *halos*, "disk of the sun or moon."

- **Heli-**: From Greek *helix, helicos* "spiral": **helix**, "spiral," now well-known from the **double helix** representation of DNA. **Helicopter** is from Greek *helix* "spiral" + *pteron* "wing." All such words as **helipad**, **heliport** and the like are wrongly formed from **helicopter**, though one can see why this incorrect formation was preferred to the correct forms, which should have been the rather clumsy *helicopad and *helicoport. Despite appearances, none of these words has anything to do with Greek *helios* "sun," whose only English derivative in common use is **helium**. See above under *halo-* for Latin cognate *sol*.

- **Homo-**: From Greek *homos* "the same": **homophone, homograph, homonym, homogeneous** ("of the same kind," <u>not</u> *homogenous, as it is often mispronounced), **homosexual**. Also related: Greek *homoio-*, Latinized as *homeo-* "similar," from which come **homeostasis, homeopathy**, a system of alternative medicine relying on treatment by highly dilute substances similar to those causing the disease that is being treated. Some **homeopathic** treatments have become entered the mainstream, such as arnica for bruises. None of these words has anything to do with Latin *homo, hominis* "man, human being," as in **homo sapiens, homo erectus, hominid**. It is connected with Latin *humanus* "human," probably from *humus* "earth," as explained elsewhere in this book.

- **Hydro-**: From Greek *hydor, hydatos* "water": See the section titled WATER, WATER EVERYWHERE.

- **Logo-**: From Greek *logos* "word, reason," which in turn is from Greek *lego, legein* "to collect, to pick out (words), to speak," cognate with Latin *lego, legere, lectum* "to read." It is noteworthy that, while Greek uses the concept of gathering or picking out to refer to speech, the Latin cognate refers instead to reading, and by extension to law, in Latin *lex, legis* "law." English derivatives abound from both Latin and Greek: **logic, logical, logistics, geology, sociology, legible, legal, loyal** (via French), **legitimate, legislation**.

- **Pedo-**: From Greek *pais, paidos* "child, boy," Latinized as **paedo-** or, more commonly nowadays, **pedo-**: **encyclopaedia/encyclopedia** (from Greek *enkyklios* "circular, in the round, general" + *paideia* "child-rearing, education"), **Wikipedia, paediatrician/pediatrician, orthopedic** (lit. "straight child"), **paedophile/pedophile**, colloquially abbreviated to **pedo** ("child-lover, unnatural sexual attraction to children"). Not to be confused with derivatives from Latin *pes, pedis* "foot" and Greek cognate *pous, podos* "foot," as in **pedal, pedestrian, pedicure, pedology, pedometer, podiatry** and **chiropodist**.

- **Gyn-**: From Greek *gyne, gynaikos* "woman": **misogynist** "woman-hater," **gynaecology/gynecology, gynaecologist/gynecologist** "specialist in women's health." Greek *gyne* is cognate with English **queen**, Danish *kvinde*, Norwegian *kvinne*, Swedish *kvinna*, Icelandic *kona*.

The English words cited above are all modern coinages from Greek roots without being actual words found in Classical Greek However, some actual Greek words entered English via Latin, usually through French, and generally quite well disguised. Here are a few examples:

- **Butter**: From Latin *butyrum*, from Greek *boutyron*, made up of *bous* "cow" + *tyros* "cheese."
- **Chair**: Via French from Latin *cathedra* "chair," from Greek *kathedra* "seat, bench." Hence, a **cathedral** is the seat of a bishop.
- **Place**: From French *place* "square," "Latin *platea* "courtyard," from Greek *plateia* "broad (way)." Derivatives include Italian *piazza*, Spanish *plaza*, Portuguese *praça*, all meaning "square," and also German *Platz*, Dutch *plaats*, Danish *plads*, Norwegian *plass*, all meaning "place."
- **Type**: From Latin *typus* "figure, image, kind," which is from Greek *typos* "a mark, an impression, form, character," from Greek *typto, typtein* "to strike, beat." English **type** ranges in meaning from the purely physical, as in **typesetting, typist, typewriter**, to meaning "kind, sort," as in "I'm afraid you're not my type." It's a good example of the way a word with a basic physical meaning can develop a figurative or metaphorical meaning.
- **Topic**: From Greek *topos* "place," or, more particularly, Greek *topoi* ("places," plural) and hence "commonplaces," "areas of discussion, subject-matter, theme."
- **Church**: From Greek *kyriakon* "of the Lord," from *kyrios* "Lord." From which come German *Kirche*, Dutch and Afrikaans *kerk*, Danish *kirke*, Norwegian *kirke*, Swedish *kyrka*, all meaning "church." Greek *ekklesia*, from which, via Latin, comes English **ecclesiastical**, means "assembly."
- **Bishop**: From Latin *episcopus*, from Greek *episkopos*, lit. *epi-* "over" + *skopos* "watcher," hence "guardian, overseer, supervisor."

❖ **Coup**: From French *coup* "a blow, knock," from Latin *colaphus* "a blow, a punch," from Greek *kolaphos* "a blow, punch." The commonest use in English is as an abbreviation for coup d'état, but French *coup* has a very wide range of meanings, not all of which are passable in polite society, and it is also the basis of *beaucoup* "very," as in *merci beaucoup* "many thanks." Italian *colp*o, Spanish and Portuguese *golpe* "blow, knock, strike" are of the same origin.

# CHAPTER 12

# LOAN OR THEFT?

IT IS CONVENTIONALLY estimated that about 26% of English words are of Germanic origin, approximately 29% come from French and a further 29% directly from Latin, plus about 6% from Greek. So, three quarters of English vocabulary is made up of words borrowed from other languages? Technically, perhaps, but this is misleading. For one thing, there is no intention to ever give them back! More seriously, though, most borrowed words have changed either their form or their meaning, or both, so as to have become fully integrated into the English language. A few words, such as **animal**, **colloquium** and **senator** have exactly the same form in English as in Latin, and pretty much the same meaning, too. In many cases the form of the word has been modified so as to look more "English" even when the meaning is essentially the same. Examples include such words as **placid** (from Latin *placidus*), **evade** (from Latin *evado*) and **fact** (from Latin *factum*). But there is sometimes a shift of both form and meaning, as for example in: **egregious** (from Latin *egregius*, meaning "exceptional," but where the English word has taken on a negative connotation) and **superb** (from Latin *superbus*, meaning "proud" or "haughty," but where the English word means simply "excellent" or "outstanding").

When giving a course of lectures on an introduction to English law to a group of Indonesian bankers some years ago, I noticed that their eyes glazed over and that they were not really following what I was saying. Hoping that this reaction was not a sign of boredom, I asked them whether they knew any Dutch – as Indonesia was under Dutch rule until 1949. "Dutch?" they queried incredulously. "No – that was long before our time." Nevertheless, every time I came across a legal, administrative or business term I would give them the Dutch and they visibly brightened up. "Where did you learn your Indonesian?" they enquired afterwards. In fact, I don't actually know any Indonesian, but they did not realize that all the Dutch terms that I had inserted into my lecture were anything other than pukka Indonesian words!

Incidentally, the word **pukka** or **pukkah** – meaning "authentic, genuine," or by extension, in English slang usage, "cool" – is itself a good example of a loanword, taken over directly from the Indian language previously known as Hindustani, which split into Hindi (the official language of India, together with English) and Urdu (the official language of Pakistan), which are very largely the same, except that Urdu contains a number of Arabic and Persian loanwords, and the fact that Hindi is written in the ancient Sanskrit Devanagari script, while Urdu is written in the Arabic alphabet.

I just said that **pukka** is a good example of a loanword, but that is actually incorrect according to the rather prissy classification now in vogue amongst academics, which distinguishes the following categories of what may loosely be termed borrowed words:[72]

- ❖ **Foreign words**: Words taken over unchanged in form (though not always in meaning) from their original languages, e.g.
    - From Latin: **abdomen**, **per annum**, **antenna** (in Latin, originally a sail-yard on a ship and only later an insect's feelers, but in English now mostly a TV aerial); **anus**, **inferior** (in Latin, "lower," but in English generally used more figuratively); **latex** (in Latin, "liquid, fluid," but in English "rubber"); **murmur** (onomatopoeic: in Latin it tends to refer to an inanimate low hum, whereas in English it tends to refer more often to "softly spoken words," but cf. **heart murmur**); **omen**, **onus** (in Latin "burden," both literally and figuratively; in English only figuratively); **ops** (the

---

[72] See Wikipedia article on "Loanword."

Roman goddess of plenty; in British schoolboy slang of yesteryear, (as the goddess of plenty has smiled on you) "give me some" (addressed to a fellow pupil blessed with a lavish lunchbox); **penis** (in Latin, originally "tail," then "penis"); **villa** ("country house").

- From French (with the same meaning in English as in French except where otherwise indicated): **attaché, aperitif, avant-garde, baguette, ballet, beret, bon voyage, brunette, bureau, champagne, chauffeur, chic, cliché, connoisseur, dossier, elite, façade, faux pas, hotel, laissez-faire, massage, menu** (in both English and French, a list of dishes available in a restaurant, but in French also a fixed-price meal or a set menu); **parasol, regime, restaurant, ricochet, silhouette, souvenir**.

- From German (with the same meaning in English as in German except where otherwise indicated): **ersatz** ("a substitute, replacement, "in English with a pejorative connotation, but in German neutral); **kaput** ("broken," in German spelt *kaputt*); **kindergarten** (lit. "children's garden"); **kitsch** ("gaudy lowbrow popular knick-knack"); **rucksack** (in English now more usually backpack); **schadenfreude** (lit. "joy from pain," delight at someone else's misfortune"); **verboten** ("forbidden, prohibited," in English generally used for comic effect); **wanderlust, zeitgeist**.

❖ **Loanwords**: Loanwords or loan words properly so called have been taken over from another language with changes in form (sometimes reflecting an older spelling in the source language) and often also of meaning. Here again, the main sources of loanwords are Latin and French, often Latin via French, e.g. **assist, attend, genial, parent, preservative, sensible** – all of which are "false friends," with different meanings in English and French. Where the form is the same, it is hard to distinguish between these "loanwords" and "foreign" words. These categories are highly artificial and not very helpful.[73] English has loanwords from many other sources, e.g.

   - **Biltong, veld** and **aardvark** from Afrikaans.

---

[73] For more on these words, see Chapter 6, THE FRENCH CONNECTION.

- **Buckram, chiffon, satin, admiral, alcohol, algebra, lemon** and **mattress** from Arabic.
- **Angst, realpolitik, weltanschauung, frankfurter** and **hinterland** from German – all of these being "foreign words."
- **Mammoth, pogrom, vodka, soviet** and **beluga** from Russian.
- **Chutzpah, bagel, kosher, spiel** from Yiddish.

❖ **Calques**: The word **calque** itself is French, literally "a copy," ultimately from Latin *calco, calcare, calcatum*, "to tread, press down," from *calx, calcis* "heel, hoof," presumably from the idea of making a copy by pressing down (cf. the now long forgotten carbon paper), evidently unconnected with Latin *calx, calcis* "limestone." (de Vaan). A **calque** is a "loan translation," a way of avoiding "borrowing" a foreign word by translating its components into your own language. The best known examples are German *Fernsprecher*, lit. "far speaker" for English **telephone**, made up of two Greek components, *tele-* "far" + *phone* "sound, voice," and German *Fernsehen* lit. "far seeing" made up of one Greek and one Latin component, *tele-* "far" + *video, videre, visum* "to see."

# CHAPTER 13

# WORDS AS METAPHORS

LANGUAGE WAS ORIGINALLY created for a very limited range of uses. Early man might have wanted to signal danger: "Beware of the lion on the prowl." Or he may have wanted to announce an achievement: "I have just bagged a buck." And he may have invited friends and neighbours to share: "Come and join in the feast." Or he may have wanted to discipline a naughty child: "Don't do that!" And of course "he" includes "she."

To put it in a more modern context, the essential uses of language can be summarized as follows:

- **To state a fact**, e.g. "It's raining." "The cat sat on the mat." "I am Japanese." "George Washington was the first president of the United States." It is important to stress that the statement does not have to be true.
- **To warn**, e.g. "Fire alert!" "Beware of falling rocks!" But these remarks are statements of fact as well, so warnings probably do not merit a separate category.
- **To express a hope, wish, prayer, desire or command**, e.g. "Please leave!" "I would like the green chicken curry." "Company, attention!" "I hope to become an airline pilot." "Liberty, Equality, Fraternity!" Though hopes, wishes, prayers, desires and commands are not the same, they overlap and all express what the speaker would like to occur.
- **To express a feeling**, e.g. "I love you." "Does your stomach hurt?" "I feel cold."

❖ **To express an opinion**, e.g. "I believe the dangers of climate change are exaggerated"; "There will be a recession within the next 18 months"; "Free trade is preferable to protectionism." This category will cover even the most abstract poetic concepts the most abstruse philosophical theory or economic prognostication.

These categories overlap to a considerable extent, and there is room for error or deliberate dissembling, misstatement or prevarication. These same categories apply equally to statements, questions, commands and exclamations.

But the key point is that it is the prime need for **communication** that dictated the invention of language. And **communication** is still the prime function of language today, no matter how basic or how sophisticated the message being communicated might be. "The price of admission is ten pounds." "You are disgusting!" "The square on the hypotenuse in a right-angled triangle is equal to the sum of the squares on the other two sides." "I wouldn't dive into that pool if I were you." All these very different sentences are an attempt by the speaker or writer to communicate something to other human beings. The earliest uses of language all relate to the physical world in which mankind found itself. But the words invented to make sense of the world soon started to extend their meanings from the purely physical and literal to **figurative** uses.

### Metonymy and metaphor

Among these **figurative** uses are **metonymy** and **metaphor**. **Metonymy** is the replacement of a word with some attribute associated with it. An example is the use of "the Crown" to refer to the Queen or the Government. Or "the top brass" for the highest-ranking officers, originally in the army, and by further extension, in a business or corporation. Or: "The pen is mightier than the sword" – meaning that writers have more power than armies.

**Metaphors** are related to **metonyms** and much more frequent. **A metaphor** compares something to something else, though unlike a **simile**, does not use the word "like" or any similar word. So, "The Assyrian came down like the wolf on the fold," as Lord Byron famously put it in his 1815 *Hebrew Melodies*, is an example of a simile. This could have been rephrased as a **metaphor**: "The Assyrian wolf attacked the Judean sheepfold." Other examples of **metaphors** abound: "My brother is the black sheep of the family." (In fact, my brother is neither black nor a sheep.) "Once you get used to the office routine, the work will be plain sailing." (In fact, the job is not at sea nor on a ship.) "You are an early bird, but I am more of a night owl." (Neither of us is a bird, but our habits resemble different kinds of birds.)

In each of these examples, the speaker or writer is consciously adopting a **metaphor** as a **figure of speech**. All these metaphors are examples of "visual thinking," or seeing words as pictures in the speaker's mind's eye, which seems to be the way the majority of people think and learn ("visualising modality," as against "auditory modality" and "kinesthetic modality").

## Frozen metaphors

So natural is this way of thinking, that speakers and writers often use words in extended figurative or, more specifically, metaphorical senses without even realizing that they are doing so. These uses are what might be termed **frozen metaphors**. These account for a great many extended meanings of words, to the extent that they can even cause confusion.

## Fast talk

A good example of this is the English word **fast**, a Germanic word going back to Old English or Anglo-Saxon *fæst*, meaning "firm, firmly fixed in place, not easily moved or shaken, settled, stable."[74] This

---

[74] OED.

meaning survives in the word **fastness**, "a stronghold," and also in phrase **colour-fast** (British)/**color-fast** (American), referring to colours that are fixed, resistant to fading or **running** (which is itself a frozen metaphor). In the phrase **hard and fast rule**, meaning "a definite, fixed, invariable rule," the word **fast** has a meaning that has moved only slightly from its basic literal meaning, while in **fast friends**, meaning "close, inseparable friends," the meaning is more figurative. **Steadfast** "fixed or secure in position," can be used in a purely literal sense or in a figurative sense applied to a person, meaning "loyal, true," as in Chaucer's expression "and I swore ever to be steadfast and true," dating from around 1369 – showing just how early on it developed this figurative meaning.[75] German cognate *fest* has a meaning close to the original "hard, solid, fixed," with a figurative meaning, for example, in the well-known hymn composed by the German reformer Martin Luther, titled *"Eine feste Burg ist unser Gott"* ("A Mighty Fortress is Our God").

But we have only just scratched the surface (another metaphor!) of the figurative meanings of **fast**, because of course the commonest meaning it has in Modern English is "quick, swift, rapid, fleet." The OED suggests that this meaning developed from expressions like **to run hard**. As we know from phrases like **hard and fast**, there is a certain affinity between the two words. **To run hard**, meaning "to run vigorously," hence quickly. Cf. Afrikaans *hardloop,* lit. "to walk hard," hence "to run."

Another puzzling meaning of **fast** is "to abstain from food," which again is figurative, from the sense of "to hold firm," and so "to hold firmly to a pledge, to a religious obligation."

These are all examples of **frozen metaphors**, because, when you remark, for example, "This hybrid car can really go fast," there is no conscious attempt to create a **figure of speech**. Indeed, most people uttering a remark like that would have no idea that their use of the

---

[75] OED.

word **fast** was anything but literal or that the sentence had anything to do with **fast** meaning "fixed" or the verb **fast** meaning "to abstain from food."

## Other frozen metaphors

Many other words are used in a similar figurative sense as **frozen metaphors**. For example, English **refuse** comes ultimately from Latin *refundo* (*re* + *fundo*), meaning literally "pour back" and by extension "give back, restore," from which we get English **refund**. But **refuse** as a noun then came to mean "something rejected, rubbish, trash," and as a verb, "reject, decline, deny." English **reject** and **decline** are also both used in a metaphorical, as well as in a literal, sense. **Reject** comes from a Latin word literally meaning to "throw back," from which the English word came to mean to "refuse to accept."

**Decline** comes from a Latin word *declinare*, literally meaning to "bend, lean or slope down." The meaning of the English word has drifted in three different directions: firstly to "go down in value, price or condition, deteriorate," secondly, to "refuse an offer or invitation," and nowadays very commonly to "reject a credit card" and thirdly, in a grammatical sense, meaning to "inflect a noun, pronoun or adjective in various cases, such as nominative (subject form), accusative (object form), etc." Incidentally, the word **case**, which comes from Latin *casus*, meaning a "falling," is an exact parallel to **decline** in its grammatical sense. All the cases other than the nominative are referred to as **oblique** cases, so called because they are seen as "slanting" away from the nominative – another similar metaphor to **decline**, **inflect** and **case** itself. But **case** also means "what **befalls**" – another example of the same metaphor as **case** in the sense of "happening, event, situation," and from there to "court-case, lawsuit, trial."

In this sense **case** has replaced **cause**, from Latin *causa*, meaning "cause, reason, motive, lawsuit," which has given rise to the basic word for "thing" in most of the Romance languages: French *chose,* Italian *cosa,* Spanish *cosa,* Catalan *cosa,* Galician *cousa,* Portuguese *coisa* and even non-Indo-European Basque *gauza* (presumably borrowed from the Latin). Interestingly, perhaps, **case** and **cause** in the sense of "lawsuit" replaced English **sake** (a word of Germanic origin, related to **seek**), which now means "purpose, motive, benefit," as in the expression of impatience, "for heaven's sake." German *Sache*, which has the same origin as English **sake**, still retains the meaning of "lawsuit" together with "thing," or in the plural "clothes." So, according to the German pun, the man who received a summons from the court to appear *In Sachen seines Vaters* ("in his father's lawsuits") mistook that to mean "in his father's things/clothes," and accordingly showed up at court dressed in his father's old clothes!

## Metaphor, language and thought

In 1979, a new movement took off (another metaphor!) among a number of American academics in linguistics, philosophy, psychology and other disciplines and made a meal (yet another metaphor!) – a huge gargantuan meal – of metaphors.

One of the leading figures in this movement, George Lakoff, has identified several "Traditional false assumptions" which this movement has countered. These supposed "traditional false assumptions" are as follows:

- "All everyday conventional language is literal, and none is metaphorical."
- "All subject matter can be comprehended literally, without metaphor."
- "Only literal language can be contingently true or false."
- "All definitions given in the lexicon of a language are literal, not metaphorical."

- "The concepts used in the grammar of a language are all literal: none are metaphorical."[76]

This is really a series of Aunt Sallies, or straw men (two more metaphors!), set up merely for the purpose of being knocked down (yet another metaphor!) These assumptions are certainly wrong, but who actually believes them?

In their place Lakoff opines: "Our ordinary conceptual system, in terms of which we both think and act, is fundamentally metaphorical in nature." True but trite. It is demonstrated by the example of **fast** (above) and many other words throughout this book. Lakoff is probably right, however, in highlighting something that most people, including most linguistics academics and most language courses do not notice. Lakoff also describes as "dead," metaphors that people use without recognizing that they are metaphors – similar to what I call **"frozen metaphors,"** as discussed above.

However, Lakoff also seems to be suggesting that people's mindsets are influenced by the metaphors that they use and appears to condemn certain metaphors of which he disapproves. One metaphor that he singles out for particular disparagement is the "underlying metaphor" that "argument is war" or at least that "argument is struggle." Lakoff gives the following examples:

- He *won* the argument.
- Your claims are *indefensible*.
- He *shot down* all my arguments.
- His criticisms were *right on target*.
- If you use that strategy, he'll wipe you out.

---

[76] George Lakoff, "The contemporary theory of metaphor," in Andrew Ortony (ed) *Metaphor, Language & Thought*, 2nd edition, Cambridge: Cambridge University Press, 1993, p. 204.

**Lakoff comments:**

*"The essence of metaphor is understanding and experiencing one kind of thing in terms of another.* It is not that arguments are a sub-species of war. Arguments and war are different kinds of things – verbal discourse and armed conflict – and the actions performed are different kinds of actions. But ARGUMENT is partially structured, understood, performed and talked about in terms of WAR ... We talk about arguments that way because we conceive of them that way – and we act according to the way we conceive of things."[77]

"Arguments and war are different kinds of things." Really? On a very superficial level that is no doubt true. But as soon as you look just below the surface the similarities become apparent. Arguments, whether public or private, whether in politics, law, academic debate, or a family quarrel, are all forms of expression intended to convince or persuade. If the speaker or creator of a particular argument succeeds in convincing or persuading, then he or she has "won" the argument. In certain areas the parallel with a battle, war or struggle is quite blatant, e.g. Counsel's "closing argument" in a lawsuit.

"The survival of the fittest," a phrase coined by Herbert Spencer as equivalent to Darwin's "natural selection" as part of the Darwinian theory of evolution, sums up the inherent drive of all living creatures, including mankind, to compete with one another. This is reflected in every aspect of human life. Every sport is a battle between two teams, two players or a field of competitors, and winning is often richly rewarded. Politics is a battle between parties, candidates and policies, the chief reward here being the exercise of power. Even art is far from immune from the competitive spirit, with rankings, prizes and rewards.

---

[77] George Lakoff & Mark Johnson, *Metaphors We Live By,* 2nd ed. 2003, University of Chicago Press, p. 4.

Lakoff suggests: "Try to imagine a culture where arguments are not viewed in terms of war, where no one wins or loses, where there is no sense of attacking or defending, gaining or losing ground. Imagine a culture where an argument is viewed as a dance, the participants are seen as performers, and the goal is to perform in a balanced and aesthetically pleasing way."[78] Lakoff seems to be suggesting that this would stop arguments being thought of in terms of conflict. Would it though? Argument is in its very essence competitive, a form of battle. Expressing it as dance would not change that. It would only turn the dance into a representation of conflict. And indeed there are such dances already, like, for example Prokofiev's *Romeo and Juliet* ballet – a translation of Shakespeare's play into dance, but involving no less conflict than the original for all that.

---

[78] Ibid., p. 4.

# CHAPTER 14

# SOUND MOVES

I HAVE ALREADY had occasion to quote Voltaire's remark that: "Etymology is a science in which vowels count for nothing and consonants for very little." At first sight this "sounds" about right, but it has to be remembered that when Voltaire died in 1778, the "science" of etymology, as he describes it with heavy irony, or comparative philology, was as yet in its infancy. Its heyday really began only about half a century later, with the publication of Grimm's Law in 1822. But Voltaire was right to detect a distinction between the handling of consonants and vowels in the "science" of etymology. Grimm's Law, for example, and Verner's Law which acted as a corrective to it, were concerned only with consonants, and the same applies to the second sound shift that differentiated what is now New High German (*Neuhochdeutsch*) from the "Low" Germanic languages such as Dutch, Afrikaans, and the Scandinavian languages. However, vowel changes cannot be ignored.

Sound shift occurs almost imperceptibly over a long period of time. For example, English is undergoing sound shifts even at the present time. For example, **water** is pronounced more like "wadder" in parts of the US, and **bottle** is pronounced "bo'el" (with a glottal stop instead of a /t/ sound) in parts of England. It is important to realize that writing systems and spelling are only approximations (if that) to how a language is actually pronounced. The shifts that occur are shifts in sound, whether they are reflected in the spelling or not.

In Modern Greek, for example, the sound /ee/ as in the English word **feet** can be spelled in six different ways. The reason for this is that

Modern Greek has largely retained the spelling conventions of the Greek of 2,000 years ago. This is helpful for etymology, but it is clear that these six vowels and diphthongs were not always pronounced the same. Greeks are sometimes a bit touchy about this. But when Aristophanes represented the bleating of sheep as "*bê, bê,*" was he suggesting that sheep in his day bleated /vee, vee/, like the Churchillian "V for Victory," which is how it would be pronounced in Modern Greek, or something more like an extended /beh, beh/? Obviously, the latter. Not only has the pronunciation of the vowel shifted, but there has also been a major slide in the pronunciation of the consonant, [b] from a /b/ sound to a /v/ sound. This is a common sound shift, which is found in other languages as well, including Russian. In Modern Greek the sound /b/ occurs only in foreign loanwords and the sound is represented by [mp], as in the Greek word for "beer," spelt *mpyra* but pronounced *byra*. The Cyrillic (Russian) alphabet has actually invented a letter to represent the /b/ sound – a modified version of the letter B with its top "bobble" left open.

Spanish has adopted an almost opposite development, with the letters [b] and [v] both being pronounced as /b/, as in the very common words *vale* ("OK"), *vino* ("wine") and *Habana* (the capital city of Cuba, spelt "Havana" in English). In an intervocalic position (i.e. between vowels) the [v] tends to be pronounced a little more softly, more like /v/, as in *vivir,* from Latin *vivo, vivere* ("to live"). It is important to realize, of course, that, as Spanish is very widely spoken, there are regional differences. One important one is the difference between the Castilian and Aragonese pronunciation of the letter [c-] before an [-e] or an [-i], as for example in the words *hacer* ("to make"), *hacienda* ("estate, fortune"), *sociedad* ("society, corporation"). In Castilian the [c] in all such words is pronounced with a "lisp," like the /th/ sound in English **youth, think, through,** while in Aragonese it is pronounced like the English /s/ sound. Contrary to legend, the Castilian "lisp" did not originate with a lisping king – and in any case a true lisp would presumably have affected the pronunciation of the letter [s-] as well as the [c-], but in fact the [-s] is never "lisped." The Castilian lisp, which originated in the 16th century, is now spoken across most of metropolitan Spain, from Oviedo and Pamplona in the North, through Madrid and Toledo in the centre, and right down to Malaga in the South, with the exception of a pocket around Seville and the whole of Catalonia and the Mediterranean coast down to Valencia and almost to Murcia. The lisp is unknown in the Americas.

A major peculiarity of Spanish is the replacement of Latin initial [f] with [h], as in:

- Latin *facio, facere* >> Spanish *hacer* ("to make"), cf. Portuguese *fazer*, French *faire*.
- Latin *fabulor, fabulari* >> Spanish *hablar* ("to talk, speak"), cf. Portuguese *falar*.
- Latin *filius* >> Spanish *hijo* ("son"), cf. Portuguese *filho*, Italian *figlio*, French *fils*. (The [-s] was deliberately tacked on at the end to differentiate it from *fil* ("thread) from Latin *filum*.)

Note: (a) Despite the replacement of initial Latin [f] with Spanish [h], the [h] is silent. (b) Besides the change from [f] to [h] in Spanish *hijo*, there is also a change from Latin [-iu-] to Spanish [-j-], pronounced as a guttural /ch/ or /kh/ sound. (c) Italian [-gl-] and Portuguese [-lh-] are pronounced the same. In Italian a [-g-] before another consonant and in Portuguese an [-h-] after another consonant add a sort of /y/ sound to that consonant. French has the same convention as Italian, particularly with the letter combination [-gn-], as in French *champagne* ("champagne"), *champignon* ("mushroom"), *gagner* ("to win"), *oignon* ("onion"), *cognac* ("brandy"), *bagnole* ("car, banger, a ride" – slang). The words for "sir" in most of the Romance languages are good examples: Italian *signore*, Spanish *señor*, Portuguese *senhor*, Catalan *senyor*, and also French *seigneur*, under the *ancien régime* before the French Revolution, a feudal lord and used as an honorific form of address, e.g. when King Louis XIV of France successfully claimed the Spanish throne for his grandson, he swept down the grand staircase at Versailles with his grandson on his arm and announced to the assembled foreign ambassadors and dignitaries: *"Seigneurs, voici le Roi d'Espagne."* – "My lords, this is the King of Spain." In all these words the [-gn-], [-ñ-], [-nh-] or [-ny-] are pronounced the same: like the [-ni-] in English **onion**. These words all derive from Latin *senior* "elder," the comparative form of *senex* "old, old man," from which come English **sir** and **sire**.

Note: However, this pronunciation of the [-gn-] in French is not invariable. In words borrowed directly from Latin or Greek the pronunciation of the [-gn-] is, as in English, e.g. *ignition, diagnostique, agnostique.*

In the Romance languages the changes from Latin are largely reflected in the spelling. Thus, from Latin *bonus* ("good") we get French *bon* (nasalized vowel), Italian *buono*, Spanish *bueno* and Portuguese *bom* (nasalized vowel); and from Latin *clavis* ("key") we get French *clef* or *clé*, Italian *chiave*, Spanish *llave* and Portuguese *chave*. Though these words look very different from one another, the changes from Latin all work according to a regular and predictable pattern. In addition, there also are English derivates: **clavicle**, **clavichord**, **autoclave** and **clef** (musical term as in **treble clef**).

From Latin *platea* ("courtyard, open space"), which in turn is from Greek *plateia* ("broad"), come Italian *piazza*, Spanish *plaza*, and French *place*, referring to an "open square," as in the *Place de la Concorde* at the East end of Paris's *Champs-Élysées*. English **place** comes either from the French or directly from the Latin, with a much broader range of meanings developing early on. The OED cites Shakespeare: "In the world I fill up a place, which may be better supplied when I have made it empty."[79] There are also loanwords in the Germanic languages: German *Platz*, Dutch *plaats* (both with meaning "open space, square, place," and in southern dialects of the Dutch word "farm," very common in Afrikaans in the form *plaas*.)

---

[79] Shakespeare, *As You Like It*, Act 1, Scene 2, line 204.

A really important equivalent between the Germanic and Romance languages is initial [w-] and [gu-], as in English **war** and French *guerre*, and Italian, Spanish and Portuguese *guerra*, all meaning "war," from which comes Spanish *guerrilla*, "fighter engaged in irregular warfare," which has been borrowed with the same meaning as English **guerrilla** or **guerilla** – unconnected, except perhaps in behaviour, with **gorilla**, a Greek version of a supposedly African word. Similarly, we have the Germanic **ward**, **warder**, **warden** and the Romanized **guard**, **guardian** and **regard**. Both groups exist in English with different but related meanings. And the Romance languages show French *garder*, Italian *guardare*, Spanish and Portuguese *guarder*. Another doublet from the same origin is English **warrant**, **warranty** on the one hand and, on the other, **guarantee**, **guaranty**, **guarantor**. The reason for these doublets may be the difficulty Romance speakers had in pronouncing the Germanic /w/ sound.

A most puzzling sound equivalent is that between Latin /s/ and Greek /h/, as in Latin *sol* and Greek *helios*, both meaning "sun." As usual, English has the best of all worlds, with **sun**, cognate with German *Sonne*, Dutch *zon*, Afrikaans *son*, Danish, Norwegian and Swedish *sol*, English derivatives from the Latin, such as **solar**, **solarium**, **parasol**, **solstice**, and from the Greek, including **helium**, **heliotrope** – but not **helicopter**, which is from Greek *helix* ("spiral") + *pteron* ("wing").

Similarly, we have Latin *sal, salis* and Greek *hals, halos* ("salt"). English **salt** is Germanic, cognate with German *Salz*, Dutch *zout*, Afrikaans *sout*, Danish, Norwegian and Swedish *salt*. From the Latin we get **salary** (originally, "salt money"), **saline**, **salami**, **salad**, **sauce** (via the French), while from the Greek come **halogen** (lit. "salt producer"), **halide** – but not **halo**, which comes from a different Greek word, *halos* "threshing floor, disk of the sun."

# CHAPTER 15

## TOPS AND TAILS

ONE OF THE chief sources of the richness of English vocabulary is the presence of numerous affixes – prefixes and suffixes – or "tops and tails," which, like the vocabulary generally, are of Germanic, Latin and Greek origin. But, while they undeniably contribute to the richness of the language, these tops and tails are also a source of confusion. For example, **disinterested**, meaning "impartial," is often confused with **uninterested**, meaning "lacking interest"; **awful** describes something really bad, while in colloquial speech **awesome** is used to describe something that fills one with admiration. Both come from awe, meaning "fear" and hence "reverence." **Infamous** is the opposite of **famous**, but only in the sense of **notorious**, a word which itself began life meaning "well known," and still retains that meaning in legal language. Of course, the classic example is that of **inflammable** as distinct from **flammable** and **nonflammable**, which is discussed in greater detail in Chapter 17, A BURNING QUESTION.

**"You turn if you want to – the lady's not for turning."**

This is one of the best-known quotes by Margaret Thatcher, the former British Prime Minister. Inserted into a speech of hers by a speech-writer as a pun on the name of a play by Christopher Fry called *The Lady's Not for Burning*, Margaret Thatcher's remark was in reference to making a U-turn ("You turn...") in policy, against which she firmly set her face.

English contains many words with the underlying meaning of turning derived from Latin *verto, vertere, versum* "to turn," which happen to provide good examples of prefixes and suffixes, or "tops and tails." Before turning to these (feeble pun intended), it is worth noting that English the word **turn** is itself of Latin origin via French: from Latin *torno, tornare, tornatum,* "to turn on a lathe," from *tornus* "a lathe," which in turn is from Greek *tornos* "a lathe." The word **tornado** is from the same origin, via Spanish. These words all derive from a PIE root meaning "to rub, turn," with English derivatives, besides **turn**, including **tour**, **attorney**, **contour**, **detour**.

It doesn't take much to realize that all the following English words are related: **avert**, **aversion**, **advert**, **advertise**, **advertisement**, **convert**, **conversation**, **divert**, **divers**, **diverse**, **diversion**, **evert**, **extrovert**, **introvert**, **invert**, **revert**, **obverse**, **pervert**, **reverse**, **reversionary**, **verse**, **version**, **vertex** and **vertical**. The common concept running through all of them is of "turning" – but what a difference is made by the prefixes and suffixes, or tops and tails! For, all these words are derivatives of the same Latin verb, *verto, vertere, verti, versum*, meaning "to turn." These are the four "principal parts" of the verb, so called because they give us the stem of the verb in each of the different tenses and moods. As a highly inflected language, Latin verbs generally have three different stems: a present stem, a perfect stem and a so-called "supine" stem. *Verto* is technically the first person singular of the present tense meaning "I turn," and *vertere,* is the present infinitive, meaning "to turn." These first two principal parts give us the present stem, *vert-*. The third principal part, *verti*, is the first person singular of the perfect tense, meaning "I turned, I have turned," but, as we do not get any English derivatives from the perfect stem, the third principal part of Latin verbs is normally omitted in this book. But the fourth principal part, or "supine," is often a rich source of English derivatives. The term "supine" literally means "lying flat on its back," though it is not known why it is so called. It is in fact the neuter form of the perfect participle, and in this case it is *versum*, meaning "having been turned," which gives us the supine stem of the word, *vers-*. Cutting through all the technical jargon, we find two different stems for the same Latin verb, *vert-* and *vers-*, from both of which there are English derivatives.

Before turning to these (no pun intended) it is worth mentioning that Latin *verto* also has other cognates in English, including **wring**, and in other languages, such as German *werden,* an auxiliary verb used to form the future tense and passives, as in: *"Ich werde das Buch lesen,"* meaning "I will read the book," and *"Das Buch wird gerade gelesen,"* meaning "The book is being read." Other cognates include Dutch *worden* and Afrikaans *word*, meaning "to become" and also used as an auxiliary verb to form the passive, as in Afrikaans: *"Die boek word gelees"* meaning "The book is being read."

We are now ready to take a look at examples of English derivatives from Latin *verto, vertere, versum* with Latin-based prefixes and suffixes (plus one Greek-based suffix):

- ❖ **Avert**: Literally, "to turn away," with Latin prefix *a-/ab-* "away" as in: "She averted her gaze from the bloody scene."
- ❖ **Advertise**: Literally, "to turn someone's attention towards something," from the Latin prefix *ad-* meaning "to, toward." It is a big concept in modern commercial life, giving rise to **advertisement**, commonly abbreviated to **advert** or simply to **ad. Advertise** is spelt the same way in both British and American English. But there is usually a choice, with American English (and the OED) opting for the *–ize* spelling while British English generally prefers the *-ise* form. Examples abound: **antagonise/antagonize, apologise/apologize, authorise/authorize, digitise/digitize, familiarise/familiarize, specialise/specialize, stabilise/stabilize**. The suffix -ise/-ize is of Greek origin, *-izo, -izein*, giving rise to the **-ize** spelling. The **-ise** spelling comes from Late Latin via French. The meaning, which is the same for both endings, is "to cause, to become," as in **pulverise/pulverize**, literally, "to reduce to powder or dust," hence "to destroy utterly"; **demonise/demonize**, "to turn into a demon, to represent as a demon." More generally, the **-ise/-ize** ending just has the effect of turning a noun or adjective into a verb. Note: Though the **-ise/-ize** suffix is of Greek origin, it can be tacked on to words of non-Greek

origin as well. So, while **antagonise/antagonize, apologise/apologize** and **demonise/demonize** are entirely of Greek origin, all the other examples cited above are of Latin origin. **Advertisement** has the further suffix **-ment**, from Latin *-mentum*, a common ending that turns a verb or adjective into a noun, e.g. **amazement, enjoyment, emolument, fragment, ligament, ointment.**

❖ **Convert**: Literally, "to turn around," with Latin prefix *con-*, literally "together" and by extension "completely." As here, *con-* often just strengthens the meaning in the verb stem. This important and very frequent prefix is from the Latin preposition *cum*, "with, together with," which becomes *com-*, *con-*, *co-*, *col-* or *cor-*, depending on the following sound, with which it blends, e.g. **combat, concur, coexist, collaborate, corroborate.**

❖ **Conversation**: The *con-* prefix again just strengthens the main meaning of the verb, while the *-ion* suffix is a Latin ending creating what the OED calls a "noun of action" from a verb, here the verb to **converse**, referring to the turn and turn about involved in talking.

❖ **Divert**: With the Latin prefix *dis-* or *di-* meaning "away, aside, in different directions" or simply with a negative connotation. So, "to turn aside," as in a traffic **diversion**, but also the figurative meaning "to amuse, entertain."

❖ **Divers** and **diverse**: Originally the same word, meaning literally "turned in different directions." The former (not, of course, to be confused with the plural of the word **diver**, as in "someone who dives under water") is now regarded as archaic. Both **divers** and **diverse** essentially mean "various." Hence **diversity**, "variety," the ending -ty being from the Latin *-tas*, which commonly changes a verb or adjective into an abstract noun.

❖ **Extrovert** and **introvert**: These two psychology terms were popularized by Carl Gustav Jung, meaning literally "turned outward" and "turned inward" respectively, referring to two opposite psychological character types. **Extrovert** was originally spelt **extravert**, with the Latin prefix *extra-*, "outside," while **introvert** is compounded with Latin prefix *intro-*, "inside, within." The spelling **extrovert** was by analogy with **introvert**.

❖ **Obverse** and **reverse**: These are the terms respectively for the "heads" and "tails" sides of a coin. The Latin prefix *ob-* literally means "in the way of, toward," and has given rise to numerous English words, such as: **obdurate, obese, obey, obfuscate, object, objection, objective, oblige, oblique, obliterate**. *Re-* means "back, again" and can therefore have negative connotations. In reference to a coin, the **reverse** is simply the "back" of the coin, or the "tails" side.

- ❖ **Verse**: How is this word connected with the idea of turning? It refers to a line or section of poetry, or a poetic piece of writing, e.g. "a verse translation," as against "a prose translation." According to the OED: "So named from turning to begin another line."

- ❖ **Version**: Literally, "a turning," hence "a translation," as in: "Dryden's version of the Vergil's Aeneid." The ending **-ion** is from the very common Latin suffix *-io, -ionis*, the first of these being in the nominative case or subject form, and the second being in the genitive case or possessive form. The reason both forms are normally shown in dictionaries is that the [-n] at the end of the stem is missing in the subject form but appears in all the so-called oblique cases, i.e. all remaining forms. The stem is also important because it appears in derivatives in English and most Romance languages (Portuguese being the main exception.) So, for example, Latin *natio, nationis*, meaning "race, tribe, nation" becomes: English **nation**, French *nation*, Italian *nazione*, Spanish *nación*, Portuguese *nação*. The reason for the retention of the stem in derivatives is that in Vulgar Latin the accusative case or object form took the place of the subject form. This suffix has the effect of turning a verb or adjective into a noun, usually either a "noun of action" or an abstract noun. Here are some examples of Latin words showing the formation of the stem: *natio, nation-is*; *occupatio, occupation-is*; *reductio, reduction-is*; *receptio, reception-is*.

- ❖ **Vertical**: From Latin *vertex, verticis*, literally, "the turning point," hence the tip of a triangle in geometry. **Vertical** then means "passing through the **vertex**" and hence "straight up and down," as against **horizontal**, which means "running from side to side." The **-ical** ending is a variant on the **-ic** ending, both being from Latin. Sometimes both endings are available for a particular word, but by no means always. Sometimes they are synonymous, but usually not. **Academic** and **academical** are interchangeable in phrases such as "the **academic/al** year." **Academic** is Oxford usage while in Cambridge **academical** is preferred, though in general usage **academic** has prevailed over **academical**. In most cases, however, there is only one form, e.g. on the one hand: **alphabetical, chronological, inimical, theatrical, vertical, zoological**; and on the other hand: **alcoholic, algebraic, bombastic, chaotic, charismatic, demographic, generic, hasidic, homeopathic, majestic, nomadic, paraplegic, systemic**. Where both forms coexist they usually have different meanings: So, **comic** is generally a noun, referring either to a person, as in a **comedian**, or a type of picture-book, though it can also be used as an adjective as **in comic actor, comic monologue, comic relief, comic strip**, whereas **comical** is always an adjective meaning "funny, humorous, amusing."

When a prefix is added to a Latin word, this will result in a sound shift, particularly where the main vowel is an [-a-], and this is carried over to derivatives. So, for example, *capio, capere, captum* "to take," with English derivatives **capture, captive, captor, captivate, caption**, becomes: *accipio, accipere, acceptum; incipio, incipere, inceptum; recipio, recipere, receptum*, with English derivatives **accept, incipient, inception, recipe, recipient, reception**. Notice the sound shift in both the present and supine stems. Similarly, Latin *facio, facere, factum*, ("to make," "to do") with English derivatives **fact, factor, factory, faction**, becomes *afficio, afficere, affectum; conficio, conficere, confectum; deficio, deficere, defectum; efficio, efficere, effectum; inficio, inficere, infectum; sufficio, sufficere, suffectum*, with English derivatives **affect, affection, confection, deficient, deficit, defect, defective, efficient, effect, effective, effectual, infect, infection, sufficient, suffect**. **Affect** and **effect** are often confused, even though their prefixes are quite different. **Affect** is from *ad + facio, facere*, meaning literally "to do to…," whereas **effect** is from *e(x) + facio, facere*, meaning literally "to do out," (but not "to make out" in the American slang sense!), so "to work out, accomplish." **Affect** is chiefly used as a verb, meaning "to influence, to cause a change," as in: "Climate change is believed to affect the polar ice-cap." **Effect** can be used either as a verb or as a noun, e.g. as a noun: "Climate change is believed to have the effect of melting the polar ice-cap." As a verb: "There is some pressure to effect a change in the law." **Affect** is also now used in psychology "to describe the experiencing of feeling or emotion." **Affect** can also have completely different meaning when used in the form **affected**, meaning "artificial, pretended, put on for effect," as in: "He spoke in an affected manner."

The Germanic languages also have prefixes and suffixes, and English, being essentially a Germanic language, is no exception. Here are a few examples:

- **a-**: Adjectives and adverbs formed from nouns: **alive, above, asleep, abroad, afoot, ashore, ahead, aside**. Replacing Middle English "**of**": **abreast, afresh, akin, anew, aware**. Or Old English intensive a- "implying motion onward or away from a position" (OED): **away, abide, arise, awake, ashamed**.
- **be-**: Generally with causative force: **bespatter, besprinkle, bestir**. Or with "privative force": **behead** "to decapitate."
- **by-**: Indicating something outside or additional, as in **bystander, bygones**.
- **by-/bye-**: as in **bylaw** or **bye-law** (Old English *bīlage*) referring to a rule made by a local authority, is cognate with the Danish word *by* ("town or city").
- **un-**: The commonest English prefix, with negative force, cognate with German *un-*, Dutch and Afrikaans *on-* and also Latin *in-*, e.g. English **unable** (but **inability**), **unalienable** (cf. **inalienable**), **uninterested** (cf. **disinterested**), **unapproved** (but **disapproval**), **uncanny, unceasing** (cf. **incessant**), **uncommon, uncouth, unkempt, unqualified, untangle** (cf. **disentangle**), **unturned, untouchable, unusual, unwitting**.
  - According to the American Declaration of Independence, all people have "certain **unalienable** Rights," meaning that, as these rights are God-given, they cannot be taken away by any earthly authority. The basis is Latin *alius*, "other," hence English **alien** ("other, foreign, strange, not one's own") and **alienate** ("to transfer to the ownership of another" (OED), "to take away"). **Inalienable**, with the same meaning, is now the preferred form.
  - **Uncouth** (of a person: lit. "unknown, strange," hence "awkward, uncultured") and **unkempt** (of hair: lit. "uncombed, dishevelled,"

of a person's general appearance: "untidy, rough, neglected") both have negative connotations, but there is no longer a positive adjective corresponding with them, though the words **couth** and **kempt** are sometimes found as modern coinages for humorous effect.

- **Unceasing** and **incessant** are essentially synonymous. **Continuous** is synonymous with both of them, but **continual** is not. **Unceasing, incessant** and **continuous** all refer to an uninterrupted and prolonged occurrence of, say, showers. However, **continual showers** would refer to recurring events rather than to one unbroken one.

- **Unqualified**: An **unqualified** electrician is one lacking formal certification. But an **unqualified success** is not a negative concept at all, meaning as it does "a resounding success." The explanation for this apparent anomaly lies in the origin of the word **qualify**, which comes from Latin *qualis,* "of what kind." Hence, **quality control**. On its own, **quality** generally means "**of high quality**," as in "**a man of quality**."

❖ **-ling**: Suffix creating a diminutive, e.g. duckling, gosling, fledgling, foundling, farthing, diminutive of "fourth," being the name of a quarter of a penny and generally the smallest coin in circulation in England – with the exception of the 9th century **stica** or **styca** (meaning "a piece," related to German *Stück*, Dutch/Afrikaans *stuk* "piece" and *stukkend* "broken, in pieces") or half-farthing, briefly reintroduced in Victorian times. The farthing was last minted in 1961. In South Africa, the farthing normally showed two sparrows on the reverse, from the Biblical verse: "Are not two sparrows sold for a farthing?" (Matthew 10:29.) The Greek word translated as **farthing** is *assarion* (from Latin *as*), representing one tenth of a drachma. The **penny farthing,** which can still be seen occasionally, was an early bicycle, with one very large wheel and one very small one.

❖ **-let**: Ultimately from Latin diminutive *–ellus,* as in *gemellus,* diminutive of *geminus* ("a twin"). In English it is mostly tacked on to words of non-Latin origin, e.g. **piglet, hoglet, booklet, billet,** from **bill,** from Latin *bulla* ("locket, amulet," hence "seal"). Hence in English "any kind of formal document, including both a demand for payment and the payment itself as in "**a dollar bill**," proposed legislation, and (a document assigning) quarters for a soldier." Also, French *billet* "ticket."

- ❖ **-ness**: Cognate with German *-nis*, Dutch and Afrikaans *-nis*, with the effect of turning a verb or adjective into an abstract noun, e.g. **boldness, blindness, craziness, emptiness, forgiveness, goodness** (popularized in the ejaculation (not that kind!) "**Goodness, gracious!**"), **effectiveness, loneliness, promptness, sexiness, thickness, weakness**.

## Greek prefixes

With the fall of Constantinople to the Ottomans in 1453, manuscripts of long lost Classical Greek writings poured into the West. This coincided with the invention of printing. But typographers were baffled by the script of the Greek writings which they were now called upon to set in type. They were confronted not only by an unfamiliar alphabet, but one written in Byzantine monastic script and with curious abbreviations for the many Greek prefixes. So flummoxed were they by this that they simply reproduced the Greek script as they found it without even attempting to decipher the abbreviations. All Greek writings published in the West until about 1820 were printed in this way – and always with a Latin translation on the opposite pages. These Greek prefixes have entered English, not only as part of Greek words but also tacked on to artificially created words, either from Greek or non-Greek stems. Here are some examples:

- ❖ **a-**: A very common negative Greek prefix, as in English: **anarchy, atypical, asexual, amnesia, apolitical, agnostic** ("someone who does not know whether there is a God or not," as against an **atheist**, who is sure there isn't one), **amoral** ("ethically neutral"), as against **immoral**, "unethical, unrighteous, unlawful"). Not to be confused with the Latin and Germanic prefixes *a-* (see above) – not to mention that Greek also has an *a-* prefix of togetherness, as in English **acolyte**, **acoustic**.
- ❖ **anti-**: Common Greek prefix meaning "against," not to be confused with **ante-** from the Latin prefix *ante-*, meaning "before," e.g. English

**antifascist, anti-feminist, antifreeze, anti-hero, antipope, antipodes, antivirus.** Cf. **ante-bellum, antediluvian, antenatal.**

❖ **dys-**: A Greek prefix with negative connotations, but not to be confused with Latin *dis-*, literally "in different directions," hence "apart, away, lacking," e.g. **dysfunctional/disfunctional** – the latter is a variant spelling of the former (OED). Here are some English examples of words with both prefixes. The **dys-** words are noticeably more technical, scientific or medical: **dysentery, dyspepsia, dystrophy, dyslexia**, cf. **dismiss, dispense, disagree, disobey, disconnect, differ.**

❖ **hyper-** and **hypo-** are opposites, meaning "over" and "under" respectively cognate with Latin *super-* and *sub-*. The equivalence between Greek /h-/ (or, more accurately, rough breathing) and Latin /s/ is general.[80] Some English examples of words compounded with **hyper-** and **hypo-** are **hyperglycemia/hypoglycaemia** "high/low blood sugar," **hypertension/hypotension** "high/low blood pressure," **hyperactive, hyperbole, hypodermic** ("under the skin"), **hypochondria** (lit. "under the cartilage of the breastbone," i.e. the liver, gall-bladder and spleen, believed to be the seat of melancholy and "vapours" (OED), hence "unfounded belief that one is sick" (EOL).

---

[80] See Chapter 11, A GREEK DRAMA.

# CHAPTER 16

# IT'S ALL IN YOUR GENES

> The fault, dear Brutus, is not in our stars
> But in ourselves, that we are underlings.
> – Shakespeare, *Julius Caesar*, Act 1, Scene 3, lines 140-141)

TO UPDATE THE question a bit, are your makeup, character and future determined by **nature** or **nurture**? Or, to put it slightly differently, is it all in your **genes**? – not your **jeans**. The word **jeans** in the sense of **denim** trousers evidently comes from a variant of the name of the Italian city Genoa. The word **denim** is short for French *serge de Nîmes*, or serge cloth from the French city of Nîmes.

But what we are dealing with here is something quite different, your **genes** or **genetic** makeup, the words in question belonging to one of the biggest and most important of all Indo-European word families.

The Latin and Greek root **gen-**, the Germanic form of which is **kin-**,[81] is the origin of a vast network of words throughout the Indo-European family. The root essentially means "to produce, give birth to." Hence from the Greek we have English **gene**, **genetic**, **genesis**, **homogeneous** ("of the same kind or origin") – incidentally, not "homogenous," as it is so often mispronounced, though **homogenize** ("to make uniform or similar") is correct; Latin and English **genus** ("class of animals or plants sharing a common origin"); from Latin, English **genius** ("inborn nature, spirit" and hence "inborn or natural intelligence or mental ability"), **ingenious**, **ingenuous** ("of

---

[81] See Chapter 8, A GRIMM TALE.

a noble nature, honourable, innocent," hence **disingenuous**, "dishonest, deceitful"), **genuine** ("natural, not feigned"), **genie**, **genial** ("good-spirited, cheerful, friendly"), **general** and **generally** ("relating to a whole class"), **general** (indicating wide or superior jurisdiction or authority, as in **attorney general** and army ranks **captain general, general, generalissimo**), **generate** ("give birth to, produce"), **generator, generation** ("the process of producing," also "a cohort of people born at the same time," "a period of about 30 years"). From Latin (directly or via French) we get **gentle** ("well bred, of good birth, noble" and by extension "kind, tender, mild"), **gentleman** (referring originally to noble birth), **gentry**, **gentrify, gentile** ("non-Jewish," translated from Hebrew *goy*, "of a [foreign] nation"), **genteel** ("affectedly well-mannered, exaggeratedly polite"), **congenital** (of a disease or physical deformity: "present from birth, hereditary"; of a characteristic or trait "persistent, pathological, chronic," as in **a congenital liar**). Also English **genus** and **generic**. From the related Latin verb *gigno, gignere, genui, genitum* "to give birth to, beget, produce") come English **genital, genitalia, genitive**. The same Latin root, **gen-** (via Old Latin *gnascor/gnasci/gnatus*) gave rise to Latin *nascor, nasci, natus* and hence to English **nature** ("life-giving force, essence"), **natural, naturalize/naturalise, naturalism, naturism, nascent, native** ("born, originating in a place," as in **Native American**), **naïve** (French version of **native**, "natural, simple, childlike, gullible"), **nation** ("population sharing common ancestry"), **national, nationality, nationalize/nationalise, nationalism, cognate** ("sharing the same origin"), **innate, pregnant, miscegenation**.

The PIE root *\*gene-* is the basis of numerous words across the whole Indo-European family, including Greek *genos* "race, birth, descent," **genesis**, a pure Greek loanword, and scientific or medical terms where the /e/ has changed to an /o/ sound, as in **gonad, gonorrhea, gonococcus**.

According to Grimm's Law (see Chapter 8), the Germanic cognate root is *kin-*, from which we get English **kin** ("group of people sharing common origin"), as in **kith and kin**; German and Dutch *Kind* ("child"); English **kind** ("type, sort") and **kind** ("friendly, benevolent," from the idea of treating others as you would family members). Note the similar development of meaning of English **gentle** and **generous** (from the Latin root) and **kind** (from the Germanic root).

# CHAPTER 17

# A BURNING QUESTION

THE ENGLISH WORD **inflammable** is now in disuse because of possible ambiguity. Does it mean "likely to catch fire" or the exact opposite, "fireproof"? Its intended meaning was the former, but there was a danger of its being misunderstood. So we now have **flammable** and **non-flammable**. The basis of all these words is **flame**, from which come **inflame** (usually used in a figurative sense: "to anger, enrage, exacerbate") and **inflammation** (medical: "reddening, swelling").

The problem with **inflammable** arose from the Latin prefix **in-**, which can either be a negative (e.g. **incomplete, indecent, indecisive, indirect, infinite, inopportune**,) or an intensive (e.g. **infuriate, inflame, intense**). Other problematical negatives include **unqualified**, which can either mean "unlicensed, uncertificated," as, for example, in an "unqualified mechanic," or its near opposite, "unreserved, unlimited, unambiguous, positive," as in an "unqualified success."

It is from Latin *qualis* ("of what kind"), hence **quality control** ("testing a product against specification," lit. to find out "of what kind" it is). So to **qualify** literally means "to fulfil a particular condition," which is why **unqualified** can mean "not limited by any condition." **Invaluable** (lit. "which cannot be valued," so "of great value, extremely useful, indispensable"), not to be confused with **valueless**. Ultimately from Latin *valeo, valere, valitum* ("to be well, be strong, have power") and giving rise to English **valid, validate,**

**invalid** ("void, inoperative," or of a person, "disabled, incapacitated"), **valiant**, **equivalent** (lit. "of equal strength").

The Romance languages all have words from this root, most notably Spanish *vale*, used all the time in colloquial speech as equivalent to "OK." This is a comparatively recent development, but *vale* was also the normal Roman way of saying "Goodbye." Cf. *"Ave atque vale!"* ("Hail and farewell!"), which was a standard formula in a eulogy, as used in the Roman poet Catullus' tribute to his brother, who had died prematurely.[82]

Hence **valedictory** and American **valedictorian**, a student who delivers the farewell address at a graduation ceremony. A potentially misleading negative phrase is the somewhat counter-intuitive **no-brainer**, meaning a decision or choice that requires no thought and is therefore obviously correct. An example of a positive wrongly used instead of a negative is the phrase "I could care less" instead of "I couldn't care less," the logic being "I couldn't care less than I do," or in other words, "I don't care at all."

---

[82] Catullus 101.

# CHAPTER 18

# TO THE EGRESS

"TO THE EGRESS" read a sign in P.T. Barnum's American Museum, a collection of curiosities of all kinds. Barnum (1810–91), the archetypal American showman and circus proprietor, was a victim of his own success. So popular was his Museum, situated in New York's Broadway, that customers lingered to gawk at the huge variety of enthralling exhibits, including "the Feejee Mermaid" (actually a dead monkey's head sewn on to a fish's tail), "the bearded lady," "the Siamese Twins Chang and Eng," several beluga whales, dancing bears, a dog-powered loom, waxworks, ventriloquists, and "General Tom Thumb, the Smallest Person that ever Walked Alone." Barnum scratched his head to find a way of flushing the existing customers out to make way for new paying customers queueing up outside. Customers who followed the sign, intrigued by the word **egress** (probably on the assumption that it would lead them to some enormous exotic bird) found themselves outside on the street and having to pay another 25 cents to get back in! **Egress** is simply another word for **exit** (itself a pure Latin word, but one that would have been familiar to any theatre-goer) or **way out** (Anglo-Saxon). **Egress** comes from the Latin (deponent) verb *egredior, egredi, egressus* made up of *e(x)* ("out") plus *gressus* ("go, walk, step"). Related English words include **congress** (*con + gressus*) meaning literally "a going together," and hence "a meeting" or "a representative assembly," as in the "US Congress." Also English **progress, progression, progressive** ("to go forward." Of a disease, "worsening, spreading." Also, "progressive" as a political label); **regress, regression, regressive** (lit. "to go backwards"), **digress, digression** (lit. "to go aside"), **transgress**,

**transgression**, **aggression**, **aggressive**, **ingress**, **ingredient**, **regress**. All these come from Latin *gradus* ("step"), from *gradior, gradi, gressus*, from which we get English **grade**, **retrograde** lit. ("backward step"), **gradation**, **gradient**, **graduate** and **gradual** ("step by step"). An important English derivative, via the French, is **degree**. The prefix **de-** in English as in Latin normally means "down," and, according to the OED, **degree** means essentially "a step in an ascent or descent," as in the phrase "**by degrees**," as in this extract quoted in the OED from Shakespeare's *Othello*: "What wound did ever heale but by degrees?"

Note how the [a] in *gradior* changes to an [e] when compounded with a prefix.

Latin *gradior, gressus* also has many derivatives in the Romance languages, e.g. Spanish *congreso, digression, gradiente, grado* ("degree"), *ingrediente, progreso, regreso* – except as indicated, with the same meanings as their English cognates.

# CHAPTER 19

## LOVE IS ALL YOU NEED

THERE APPEAR TO be two main competing popular philosophies today, one lamenting (or celebrating?) that "Money makes the world go round" and the other proclaiming, in the words of the Beatles song, "Love is all you need." Which is right? This is not the place to go into that. Suffice it to say for now that the English word **love**, a good solid Germanic word, covers a multitude of concepts expressed in other languages by two or more quite different words.

In Classical Greek in particular there are no fewer than four quite distinct words for different types of love:

- *Eros*: This Greek word represents sexual or romantic love, desire or lust, from Greek *eramai* "to love, desire," of uncertain, probably pre-Greek, origin (Beekes). From it come English **erotic**, **eroticism** and other compounds such as **homoerotic** ("homosexual love"). Eros was also the Greek god of love and sex, the son of Aphrodite, goddess of love, beauty and pleasure. Eros, originally represented as a young adult male, later became associated with the cheeky chubby winged young boy familiar from London's Piccadilly Circus. His Roman counterpart is Cupid, or in Latin *Cupido*, meaning "desire, love, passion," whose mother, Venus, was equated with Aphrodite. The Latin word *Cupido* comes from *cupio, cupere* "to desire," which has given us **cupidity** and **concupiscence**, "ardent desire, lust."

- *Philia*: The Greek word for love or affection between friends, *philos* meaning "friend." In English, as a prefix or suffix, **phil-** or **-phile** has two very different connotations, depending on what it is compounded with. It generally has a positive connotation, e.g. **philanthropic** (lit. "loving mankind," hence "highly charitable"), **philhellene** ("lover of things Greek"), **philharmonic** (lit. "love of harmony," hence adopted as part of the title of numerous symphony orchestras), **philology** (lit. "love of letters, learning"), **philosophy** (lit. "love of wisdom"), **philately** (lit. "love of freedom from taxation," meaning stamp-collecting, because cheap prepaid "penny postage" in the form of a postage stamp invented by Sir Roland Hill in 1840 freed the recipient of a letter from the financial burden of having to pay for the postage on receipt), **bibliophile** ("book lover") and **anglophile** ("lover of things English"). However, a **philanderer** (lit. "loving man" refers to a "male flirt" in a disparaging sense), **paedophile** or **pedophile** and **pedophilia** (lit. "child-lover"; "child-love") are used to describe a perverted lust for sex with children. The opposite of Greek *philia* "love" is *phobos*, originally "flight," hence "fear," giving rise to English **phobia**, which generally means "an irrational fear," and is used as a suffix in that sense in many artificially created words, e.g. **agoraphobia** ("fear of open places"), **arachnophobia** ("fear of spiders"), **claustrophobia** ("fear of enclosed spaces"). But -**phobia** can sometimes mean "aversion" rather than "fear," e.g. **xenophobia**, "dislike of foreigners," **homophobia**, "dislike of homosexuals."

- *Agape*: This is the general word for "love" in Modern Greek, but it began in a more restricted sense, used frequently in the New Testament in a Christian religious sense, e.g. *Ho Theos agape estin*, "God is love" (1 John 4). Also, in 1 Corinthians 13, where the word *agape* is used repeatedly in the sense of "charity" (King James Version) or "love" (most other translations). "God so loved the world..." (John 3:16). "Loved" is here *egapesen*, the perfect tense of the verb *agapao*, from *agape*.

- *Storge*: Used particularly of love or natural affection between parents and children.

Latin has two main words that convey the concept of love: *amor* and *caritas*.

*Amor*, from *amo, amare, amatum* "love, like," derivative *amicus* "friend": "The Latin meaning has developed from 'to take the hand of' > 'regard as a friend'." (de Vaan). English derivatives (via French) include **amorous**, **paramour**, **amicable**, and, from the negative, **inimicus** "personal enemy," **inimical** and also **enemy** itself. The words for "love," "friend" and "(personal) enemy" in most Romance languages are derived from these Latin words, e.g.

**French**: "love" *amour*, "friend" *ami*, "enemy" *ennemi*.
**Italian**: "love" *amore*, "friend" *amico*, "enemy" *nemico*.
**Spanish**: "love" *amor*, "friend" *amigo*, "enemy" *enemigo*.
**Portuguese**: "love" *amor*, "friend" *amigo*, "enemy" *inimigo*.

Latin *caritas* ("love, affection, high price"), from Latin *carus, cara, carum* ("dear, precious, valued, costly") has given rise to English **caress**, and via the French, to English **charity**, **cherish**. From PIE *\*qar* (OED, Franck), giving rise to English **whore** ("prostitute") and words with the same meaning in German: *Hure*, Dutch: *hoer*, Danish and Norwegian: *hore*, Swedish: *hora*. According to EOL, Sanskrit *kama* ("love, desire"), as in *Kama Sutra* (ancient Indian textbook on eroticism), is from the same origin.

English **prostitute** ("sex worker") is from Latin *prostituta* ("prostitute, harlot"), which is from *pro + statuo, statuere, statutum* (lit. "to place before, in front," hence "to expose publicly to prostitution"). The more usual Latin word for prostitute is *meretrix,* from which comes English **meretricious** ("alluring by false show of beauty," often applied to artistic or literary style that is "superficially attractive"). *Meretrix* is from *mereo, merere, meritum* ("to deserve, earn"), from which come English **merit** ("worth, just deserts," legal use, "the merits of the case" [always plural]), **meritorious**, **demerit**.

The Greek word for prostitute, *porne*, has given rise to English **pornography** (lit. "writing about prostitutes," hence "portrayal of obscene subjects"). Greek *porne* is from *pernemi* ("to sell"), ultimately, according to EOL, from PIE root *\*per* ("to traffic, to sell"), from which comes Latin *pretium* ("price, value, prize"), from which, via the French, come English **precious**, **appreciate**, **depreciate** (but not **deprecate**), **price**, **priceless**, **prize**, **praise**, **appraise** (but not **apprise**), and **interpret**.

English words related to **love** include not only **lovely**, but also **belief** and **believe**, with German cousins *lieben* "to love," and *glauben* (from Old High German *gilouben*) "to believe," Another member of the family is English *leave* in the sense of "permission," as in "by your leave," formerly used in law as in seeking **leave** of the court, now generally replaced by seeking **permission**. According to the OED, "the root is identical with that of **love, lief, believe**, etc." English **furlough** "leave of absence" is of the same origin. Cf. German *erlauben* "to allow" and *Urlaub* "leave of absence." English **lief** and **liefer**, which have fallen into disuse, meant "rather, more readily." The OED quotes an extract from the Pall Mall Magazine of 1898 reading: "To strip was to confess her sex, than which she would liefer have died." However, equivalent cognates German *lieber* and Dutch and Afrikaans *liewer* are still very much alive.

Latin *libet* "it pleases" is of the same origin, from which we also have **libido**, but this family of words is evidently unrelated to English **liberty** and the whole sub-family of words to which it belongs, including **liberal, liberate, libertarian** (not to be confused with **liberal**), **libertine** ("a person of lax morals"). This sub-family is possibly from PIE *\*leudh-* "people," from which derives the very basic German word *Leute* "people."

English **leave** meaning "to go away" is not related to **leave** meaning "permission," even though its primary meaning of "to allow to remain undisturbed" is not too remote from the meaning of its homonym. Usage includes the sense of "to bequeath a legacy"; "to leave behind," as in "I left my homework on the bus"; "to leave out, leave off, leave it be." Other examples: "Her costume did not leave much to the imagination." Also: "His examination result left much to be desired."

**Leave** meaning "to go away" is related to English **life** and **live** meaning "to remain in existence," which is cognate with other Germanic words for "life," such as German *Leben*, Dutch *leven*, Afrikaans *lewe*, Danish, Norwegian and Swedish *liv(et)*. English **liver**, in reference to the organ in the body, is of the same origin. Hence **liverish**, "feeling bilious, peevish irascible."

## When is a book not a book?

Latin *liber* meaning "book," from which we get **library**, **librarian**, has a completely different origin, from which we also get English **leaf**, plural **leaves**, referring both to the foliage of a tree and also, by extension, to the page of a book.

It is worth noting that in the Romance languages the words related to English **library** do not mean "library" but "bookstore, bookshop," e.g. French *librairie*, Italian and Spanish *libreria*, Portuguese *livraria*. For "library" these languages use a variant of Greek *bibliotheke*, lit. "bookcase, book repository": French *bibliothèque*, Italian, Spanish and Portuguese *biblioteca*. Germanic languages also have variants of the same word for "library," e.g. German *Bibliothek* (as against *Buchhandlung* for "bookstore"), Dutch *bibliotheek* (as against *boekenwinkel* for "bookstore"), Afrikaans *biblioteek* (as against *boekwinkel* for "bookstore"), Danish *bibliotek* (as against *boghandel* for "bookstore"), Norwegian and Swedish *bibliotek* (as against *bokhandel* for "bookstore"). The English word **Bible** is from Latin *Biblia*, which in turn is from Greek *Biblia*, plural of *biblion* "book." Though English no longer has **Bibliotheca**, the original word for "Bible" in Old English, we still have a few words formed from biblio-, such as **bibliophile** ("book lover") and **bibliography** (lit. "the writing of books," hence "list of books referred to, references"). Greek *biblion* is from Greek *byblos* "papyrus," a common writing surface, especially in Egypt. English **papyrus** is the Latin form of Greek *papyros* ("papyrus, a type of reed"), from which comes English **paper**.

English **book** is a Germanic word, cognate with all the words compounded to form the Germanic words for "bookstore" as listed in the previous paragraph: German *Buch*, Dutch and Afrikaans *boek*, Danish *bog*, Swedish and Norwegian *bok*. The main official language of Norway is called *Bokmål* (lit. "book language"), a more conservative variant of which is known as *Riksmål* ("national language"), while the other official language of Norway is known as *Nynorsk* ("new Norwegian").

Some other English words associated with books are:

- **Volume**: Now used to describe one of several separately bound parts of a book, e.g. "Gibbon's *The History of the Decline and Fall of the Roman Empire* is in six volumes." The word **volume**, from Latin *volumen*, originally meant "a scroll" from Latin *volvo, volvere, volutum* ("to roll"), from which there are a large number of English derivatives,[83] either directly or via the French, including: **volume** (also in the general sense of "size, book"), **voluminous, devolve, devolution, evolve, evolution, involve, revolve, revolution, revolver, convoluted, voluble, valve, vault, volte-face,** and **vulva** (originally *volva*, lit. "wrapper," "external female genitals"). The PIE root of Latin *volvo* *\*uel-u-* (de Vaan) or *\*wel-* (EOL), "to wind, revolve" from which comes Greek *eiluo, eiluein* ("to wrap around, envelop"), *helix* ("spiral"), from which we get English **helix** (as in double helix, the key to DNA structure) and also **helicopter** ("twisted, spiral wing"). The Germanic descendants from the same PIE root have given rise to English **wallet, waltz, wallow, well** ("spring, fountain"), **welter, whelk, willow**.

- **Code**: Until the fourth century the normal type of book was a parchment or papyrus scroll (in Latin, *volumen*), which was then replaced by the modern type of book with loose sheets bound together, which in Latin is *codex*, from Latin *caudex* (lit. "a tree trunk, block of wood," hence "wooden writing tablet"), which in turn comes from Latin *cauda* ("a tail"). Hence Latin *codex* referring to a systematic compilation of laws, as in the *Codex Justiniani* ("Justinian's Code") and French *Code Napoléon*. Hence English **codification of laws**. Also **code** as a system of (usually secret) symbols, hence **code-breaker**. Also, **codicil** (lit. "little book," supplement to a will).

- **Folio**: Old-fashioned word for "sheet of paper" in a book, still used in the antiquarian book trade. The number of folios in a book is half the number of pages. **Folio** is from Latin *folium* ("leaf"), from which we have **foliage, defoliate, exfoliate, portfolio, foil** (as in "tin foil"), **trefoil** ("architectural feature in three-clover shape").

---

[83] See Chapter 23, THE PEASANTS ARE REVOLTING.

## The enemy of my enemy is my friend.

"The enemy of my enemy is my friend" is an ancient proverb that can be traced back to a Sanskrit treatise on statecraft known as the *Arthashastra* (lit. "The science of prosperity"). But the concepts of "friend" and "enemy" in the ancient world were more complex than that, and much more recently, too. For example, when Queen Victoria sounded her disapproval of a proposal by Prime Minister Lord Palmerston (1784–1865) to declare war against a "friendly" foreign power, Palmerston is reported to have replied: "Ma'am, nations do not have friends, only interests."

In Latin the word for a public rather than a private enemy is *hostis*, which started life meaning "stranger" and in medieval Latin also came to represent an enemy army or "host" as in old-fashioned English, e.g. "Lord God of Hosts, be with us yet, Lest we forget – lest we forget." (Rudyard Kipling, *Recessional*, 1897).

Latin *hostis* comes from a PIE root that was "the central expression of the guest-host relationship." (Calvert Watkins, *American Heritage Dictionary of Indo-European Roots*). A guest-friend was a stranger with whom there was a reciprocal relationship of guest and host, as exemplified by Odysseus' relationship with the Phaeacians in Homer's *Odyssey*. But of course a stranger could also turn hostile. Hence the double association of the word, with reciprocal hospitality on the one hand and, on the other, with hostility. The English derivatives reflect both these aspects. Thus, both **host** and **gues**t have the same origin, **host** coming from the Latin and **guest** from a Germanic root.[84] So, all these English words are related to one another both semantically and etymologically:

- ❖ From the root of Latin *hostis*: **host, hostile, hostage, hostel, hostelry, hotel** (from French *hôtel*, the circumflex over the [o]

---

[84] See Chapter 8, A GRIMM TALE.

indicating that a letter has dropped out, in this case the [s] in the stem of Latin *hostis*.

❖ From Latin *hostis* + the stem *potis* "able, having the power": Latin *hospes* "guest, host, visitor," English **hospital, hospitality, hospitable, hospice**.

❖ From the Germanic *gæst*: **guest, guest-work, guest-room**.

The same guest-host-enemy concept existed in Classical Greek as in Latin in the word *xenos* "guest, host, stranger," from which come English **xenophobia** ("dislike of strangers") and also **xenon** (lit. "strange," a heavy inert gas).

# CHAPTER 20

# MONEY MAKES THE WORLD GO ROUND

THE ORIGIN OF money is reflected in the derivation of Latin *pecunia*, "money," from Latin *pecu*, "cattle, herd" and *pecus*, "cattle, farm animal." English **fee**, which now refers only to money payment, can be traced back to OE *feoh,* which covered both "livestock" and "money." By Grimm's Law, OE *feoh* is cognate with Latin *pecu*.[85]

From Latin *pecus* we get **pecuniary**, **impecunious**, **peculation**, "embezzlement," and also **peculiar**, lit. "private property," and by extension "unique to one particular person, odd, strange."

**Fee** developed a legal flavour, as in **an estate in fee simple**, meaning "freehold title to land." **Fief** and **feudal**, relating to medieval forms of landholding, are from the same origin.

However, its cousins in the Germanic languages largely retained their agricultural sense, e.g. German *Vieh*, "cattle, beast," Dutch and Afrikaans *vee* "cattle, beast." In Danish the original meaning of *fæ*, "cattle, livestock," and by extension, "mobile wealth, goods, property, riches, money," is now regarded as old-fashioned and the word tends to be used instead as an insulting description of a person as a "fool, idiot, oaf."

---

[85] See Chapter 8, A GRIMM TALE.

None of the words for "money" in the other European languages derive from this root. Instead, what we have is:

- German *Geld*, "money," related to English **yield**, "to give way," and as a noun, "reward, return on investment."
- French *argent*, "money," from Latin *argentum*, "silver." English **argue**, "to provide reasons for or against a proposition," is from Latin *arguo, arguere* from the same root, probably a "denominative verb 'to make bright, enlighten'" (de Vaan). By extension, **argue** can also mean "to **quarrel**," from Latin *queror, queri*, "complain, protest," not to be confused with Latin *quaero (quaeso), quaerere (quaesere), quaesitum*, "to seek, ask, demand," from which we get **query**, **inquire (enquire)**, **quest, question**.
- Cf. French *monnaie*, from which (indirectly) we get **money**, does not mean "money" but "currency." It comes from the name of the Roman goddess *Juno Moneta*, near whose temple was the **mint** where money was coined. The word **mint** ("to make money" and, by extension, "to create, make up"; as an adjective, "perfect, undamaged," as in "this postage stamp is in mint condition") is from Latin *Moneta* via a Germanic borrowing, which has given rise to German *Münze,* Dutch *munt*, Danish *mont*, Swedish *mynt*, Norwegian *mynt* "a coin," while *moneta* itself is the word for "coin" in a number of languages, including Italian and has even been borrowed by Russian, Bulgarian, Polish, Latvian and Lithuanian. In the Romance languages other than Italian the form is slightly different, but the meaning is the same: Spanish *moneda*, Catalan *moneda*, Portuguese *moeda*, Romanian *monedă*.
- **Currency** "monetary denomination," as in: "The US dollar is not only the **currency** of the United States, but also the main international reserve **currency**." By extension, "in circulation, enjoying general acceptance," as in: "The term 'rock 'n' roll,' which was evidently coined in 1934, only gained currency in the 1950s." **Currency** is from Latin *curro, currere, cursum*, "to run," which has numerous English derivatives, including: **current** ("running, flowing," hence "present, happening now," as in "**current** affairs"; as a noun, "the force moving water, air or electricity along"), **concur** ("to run together," so "to agree"), **concurrent** ("running together," as in "**concurrent**, i.e. not consecutive, prison sentences") **occur, recur, excursion, cursive** ("joined up writing that therefore appears to 'run'"), **cursor** (lit.

"runner," a little indicator on a computer showing the user's **current position"**), **precursor** (lit. "one that runs ahead," so "**forerunner**," both parts of which are Germanic equivalents of the two parts of precursor). Also from Latin *curro, currere, cursum*, but via the French, we have **course** (as in a course of study, racecourse, and the common phrases **of course**, or **as a matter of course**, originating from the concept of something "running in a regular and expected manner"), **recourse**, **discourse**, **intercourse** (lit. "running between," hence [frequent] meeting between two people, as in sexual intercourse), **courier**, **succor** ("assistance, aid," from *sub* + *curre*re, lit. "to run from below"). Not from the Latin *curro, currere, cursus*, but from a Celtic cognate to it, (represented by Breton, *karr*, "chariot") via the French, we have **car**, **carry**, **carrier**, **carriage**, **career** ("the course of a person's professional life," but as a verb "to run wildly"), **caricature**, **carpenter** (originally, "wagon-maker"), **charge** (from Latin *carrus*, "wagon," "to load a wagon," hence "to burden, entrust, command, demand payment," accuse," hence "to rush headlong, attack").

❖ **Cattle**: Parallel to English **fee** originating from OE *feoh* (originally "livestock"), which is cognate with Latin *pecu(s)* "cattle," is the word **cattle** itself, from **chattel** ("property other than land"), which, via the French, comes from Latin *capitalis* ("chief, principal"), which in turn is from Latin *caput, capitis* ("head").

❖ **Dollar**: The name for the US currency is an Anglicized version of German *Thaler,* a large silver coin epitomized by the *Maria Theresa Thaler*, which, always dated 1780, became the standard trade currency in large parts of Africa and Asia well into the 20th century and is still produced by the Austrian Mint to this day, now chiefly for collectors. The word *Thaler* was short for *Joachimsthaler*, meaning something coming from Joachimsthal, a town in Bohemia, where the silver was mined from which these coins were minted. *Joachimsthal* means "Joachim's valley," *thal*, or *tal*, as it is now spelled, meaning "valley," cognate with English **dale**.

❖ **Cash**: Ultimately from Latin *capsa* "a box," referring to a money-box and then to the money itself, from Latin *capio, capere, captum* "to take," from which come many English derivatives, including **case** in the sense of "a container, bag."

❖ **Coin**: From Old French *coing* "a wedge, angle, corner," from Latin *cuneus* "a wedge," from which comes **cuneiform,** an early form of writing consisting of wedge-shaped marks on a clay tablet. Invented by the Sumerians of Mesopotamia in the 6th millennium BCE, it was taken over, among others, by the Babylonians, Assyrians, Persians and Hittites. Modern French *coin,* "corner, angle," has retained the essential meaning of Latin *cuneus*. The word for "coin" in French is *pièce*.

# CHAPTER 21

# WHEN DOES A CONVICTION NOT LAND YOU IN JAIL?

"*VENI, VIDI, VICI*" ("I came, I saw, I conquered.") is a boast attributed to Julius Caesar after a short, decisive war. Latin *vinco, vincere, victum* "to conquer" has the stem *vic-*, from which we get the Latin and English **victor** ("winner") and Latin/English **invictus** ("undefeated"), the title of a popular evocative poem ending with the words: "I am the master of my fate: I am the captain of my soul." English **victory** and the name **Victoria** are of the same origin, as is **invincible** ("unconquerable").

Despite a life of crime, Al Capone, the notorious Mafia boss, had no prior **convictions** when he was **convicted** of tax evasion and sentenced to 11 years' imprisonment, resulting in his spending some time as a **convict** in Alcatraz. English **convict** and **conviction** come from Latin *victus* ("defeated, conquered"). The explanation is that being found guilty of a crime is a defeat of sorts. But **conviction** can also mean a "firmly held opinion or belief" of which one is **convinced**. The underlying root of all these English words is Latin *vic-*, or its nasalized form, *vinc-*, meaning to "overcome, conquer, defeat." The prefix **con-** is an intensive, which strengthens the meaning that is already present in the root of the word.[86]

English **evince** and **evict** are from the same root as all these previous words, but this time with the prefix **e-** or **ex-**, meaning "out, out of,

---

[86] For more on this, see Chapter 15, TOPS AND TAILS.

away." **Evict** has again got the concept of conquest, referring as it does to (lawfully) removing a tenant from property. **Evince** (not to be confused with **evidence**, with which it is not related but which has probably influenced its meaning) means to reveal or indicate the presence of a quality or feeling, e.g. "From a very early age Mozart evinced prodigious musical ability without affability." The meaning of **evince** shifted from "to overcome, subdue" to "convince" (or "to overcome by means of argument") to "to prove, show."

English **vanquish**, "to conquer, overcome," is from the same root, and so is French *vaincre*, which shares the same meaning as well. Also from the same root, French has *convaincre*, "to convince." So here, too, we have a shift of meaning from "conquer" in battle to "defeat by argument."

## When does an execution not involve decapitation?

Just as a **conviction** does not always connote condemnation by a court of law, so an **execution**, which can refer to the carrying out of the death penalty, does not necessarily have anything to do with capital punishment. Coming from Latin *ex* ("out") plus *sequor/ secutus* ("follow"), English **execute** essentially means "to follow through, carry out." It can be used in a general sense or in a specific sense, as in the carrying out of a hanging or beheading, the person entrusted with this task being an **executioner**.

From the more general sense, we have the word **executive** denoting the branch of government (as distinct from the **legislature** and the **judiciary**) that carries the law into effect or administers it. An **executive** is anyone in a high administrative or managerial position in a business, and the term **chief executive officer**, usually abbreviated **CEO** is now edging out **managing director** as the designation for the person heading up a company or business entity. An **executor** is someone who has the duty of carrying into effect the wishes of a testator contained in a will. This is a pure Latin word used in English in unchanged form. So a female **executor** is therefore, strictly speaking, **executrix**, which is the Latin feminine form of *executor*. The rise of feminism, together possibly with the comical and vaguely insulting sounding **-trix** ending, has now resulted in female **executors** being referred to informally also as **executors**.

Latin *sequor, sequi, secutus* ("follow") has given rise to a whole slew of English words all with a kernel of meaning related to "following," including: **sequence**, **segue**, **sect**, **obsequious**, **sequel**, **prequel** (a portmanteau word formed from pre "before" + "sequel," so, "a book or movie set prior to the previous one"), **sequester**, **prosecute** ("to pursue legally"), **prosecution**, **prosecutor**, **persecute** ("to pursue unlawfully"), **persecution**, **persecutor**, **pursue** (via Anglo-French *pursuer*, from Latin *persequor, persequi, persecutus* "to follow, chase"), **ensue**, **second** (lit. "following," hence "runner-up," also "one-sixtieth of a minute").

# CHAPTER 22

# TERM LIMITS

TAKE A LOOK at these eight different uses of the English word **term**, **terminology** or **terminological**:

- The U.S. president has a four-year **term**, while a U.S. senator is elected to serve for six years.
- In Britain the academic year generally has three **terms**, whereas in America it is normally made up of two semesters.
- This lease has a 99-year **term**.
- The company's **terms** and conditions were unduly onerous.
- Calling a politician a socialist used to be a **term** of abuse in America.
- The mathematical expression 3x + 2y consists of two **terms**.
- The **terminology** of linguistics has become increasingly technical and opaque.
- "The honourable member is guilty of a **terminological** inexactitude" is a polite way of saying that he is lying.

The English word **term** comes via French *terme* from Latin *terminus*, meaning "end, limit, boundary," probably originally in a very physical sense denoting a boundary post, stone or marker. English **terminus** is used in a similar sense, denoting, for example, the end-point of a bus route. **Terminal**, which has the same origin, exists both as a noun and as an adjective. As a noun it refers to the end-point (or starting point) of a journey, as in an **airport terminal**, denoting a building or facility designated for use by embarking or disembarking passengers. By extension, **terminal** is now commonly used to refer to a computer keyboard and monitor as supposedly the "end-point" in communicating data. As an adjective, **terminal** means "final," most commonly in the expression a **terminal illness**, meaning a fatal illness, or one from which recovery cannot be expected.

The basic underlying concept connecting all these words is, in a broad sense, finality or limit. Hence the first three examples above, and also words such as **short-term**, **long-term**, **terminate**, **termination**, **coterminous** ("having common borders, or of equal length of time or space"). The **terms** of an agreement set out the "limiting" conditions. But what about the last four examples shown above? Latin *terminu*s, denoting a boundary, came to be used for any mathematical expression or indeed any word "used in a definite or limited sense" (OED). English **term** has been used in the same sense since Chaucer in the late 14th century.

In **exterminate** the prefix **ex-** (lit. "out, out of, from") takes the concept of finality to its logical conclusion, so that the word means "to utterly destroy, root out completely."[87]

In **determine**, **determined** and **determination** the prefix **de-** (lit. "down, down from, away") merely has intensive force, strengthening the sense of finality that is already in the stem **term-**. Hence the following examples:

- The jury **determined** that the accused was guilty.
- It was hard to **determine** from which direction the voice was coming.
- Your eye-colour is **determined** by your genes.
- From an early age she was **determined** to become an Olympic gold medalist.
- Her **determination** to win a gold medal was second to none.
- The **determination** of the court was to impose a hefty fine.
- This lease **determines** on the death of the landlord.

The last of these examples has an old-fashioned ring to it, but is still in regular use in legal documents. However, for the sake of clarity, it

---

[87] See Chapter 15, TOPS AND TAILS.

is better to replace it with **terminate**. So the last example becomes: "This lease **terminates** on the death of the landlord. "

German *Termin*, borrowed from Latin *terminus*, is a very common word meaning "an appointment" in the sense of a fixed time scheduled for a meeting. English **appointment** itself, and Italian *appuntamento*, though unconnected etymologically with *Termin*, share the concept of punctuality, by contrast, for example, with French *rendez-vous,* Danish *aftale* and Dutch and Afrikaans *afspraak*, all of which also mean "appointment," but stress the concept of meeting rather than that of punctuality.

# CHAPTER 23

# THE PEASANTS ARE REVOLTING

THIS CHAPTER IS about the family of words related to Latin *volvo, volvere, volutum*, meaning "to roll."

When the news of the fall of the Bastille on 14 July 1789 was broken to Louis XVI of France, the King inquired: *"Est-ce une révolte?"* ("Is it a revolt?"). "No, sire," came the reply, "it's a revolution." Or, in the original French: *"Non, sire, c'est une révolution."* The term *revolution* to refer to the events in France starting in 1789 was quickly picked up in English, and Edmund Burke's Reflection on the Revolution in France appeared in 1790. And the label has stuck.

The English word **revolution**, coming as it does from the same root as the word **revolve**, was originally used in an astronomical sense, referring to the movement of celestial bodies around the earth (as was originally erroneously believed) or (as was proved by Copernicus) around the sun. A **revolving** door is often found in entrances to hotels and certain public buildings and is also used figuratively in a political sense, as in the jibe aimed by one nationality against another, generally to suggest sharp practice: "A Martian can follow you into a revolving door and still come out ahead." The firearm known as a **revolver** is so called because it has a revolving cylinder.

Revolution also came into popular use in the sense of "rotation" with the invention of the gramophone or phonograph record, the earliest of which rotated on a turntable at 78 or 80 **revolutions per minute** (usually abbreviated to **rpm**) and then later at 45 rpm and 33⅓ rpm (for long-playing records, or LPs).

There was nothing sudden or violent about these types of movement. However, the bloodless ouster of King James II and his replacement by the joint monarchy of William III and Mary II in 1688–89 was instantly dubbed a "Glorious Revolution" by its adherents, who wished to stress the non-violent, moderate and indeed conservative nature of the change – by contrast with the bloody Civil War of 1642–49, which had culminated in the execution of King Charles I and which only started being called the English Revolution by Marxist historians like Christopher Hill in the mid-twentieth century.

When the overthrow of a political regime is described as a revolution, this generally carries with it a connotation of a popular uprising. For example, the American War of Independence was referred to by the American "patriots" (as they called themselves) as the Revolutionary War and to a lesser extent as the American Revolution, although the "patriots," who became the "Founding Fathers," were largely drawn from the colonial elite – George Washington himself reputedly being the richest man in America. A very different misapplication of the revolution label was the Bolsheviks' description of their takeover of power in Russia in November 1917 as the "October Revolution," which was wrong not only in terms of the date (because of Russia's retention of the Julian calendar when Western Europe had long discarded it in favour of the Gregorian calendar), but also in its suggestion of having major popular support.

Like revolution, English **revolt** also ultimately derives from Latin *revolvo/revolvere*, meaning "turn back, roll back," via an Italian frequentative form of the verb meaning "to overturn, overthrow." **Revolting** also has quite a different meaning, and the ambiguity is neatly encapsulated in the phrase, "the peasants are revolting," which can refer either to a peasant uprising, or (with **revolting** used as an adjective) it can mean that "the peasants are repulsive or disgusting."

The connection with the concept of "rolling back" is fairly remote but can perhaps be explained as causing onlookers to turn their noses up or possibly to rock back on their heels.

All other English words belonging to this family have meanings more closely related to the core meaning of Latin *volvo/volvere*, "roll." So, revolve means "to roll or turn round." The verb **devolve**, literally "to roll down," and the noun from it, **devolution**, are in common use in business, government and administration. So, in the UK, certain powers are **devolved** from the central government to certain regional authorities. **Convoluted** and **convolution** refer to something that is rolled up in a complicated way, so "wound together, coiled, twisted" as in: "His explanation of the theory was highly convoluted and incomprehensible." **Involve**, literally "to roll in or roll up on itself," now has a largely metaphorical meaning, as in: "Until Pearl Harbor the U.S. Government refused to become involved in World War II." Another member of this family that has become extremely prominent is English **evolve**, literally "roll out, unroll," and, even more so, the noun **evolution**, particularly in the phrase "Darwinian evolution," referring to the development of higher life forms from lower life forms.

English **volume** has two main meanings. The sense of "book" comes from the concept of "roll" or "scroll," from the days when a book was a parchment or papyrus scroll. The concept has been carried over into modern computer language, where one scrolls down to read a document. By extension from the idea of a book, volume came to refer to the measurement of anything occupying space. So, Boyle's Law states that the pressure of a given mass of gas is inversely proportional to its volume. **Voluminous** describes something that occupies a lot of space either literally or figuratively, so "spacious, large, extensive."

The English anatomical term **vulva**, referring to the external female genitalia, is a straight borrowing from the Latin *vulva*, the original form of which was *volva*, a close relative of *volvo, volvere* ("roll"). Over time, the meaning has shifted from "womb, uterus," an internal organ with the connotation of "wrap-around, encompassing," to its external opening.

English **valve**, "a mechanical device that controls the flow of a liquid or a gas," is from Latin *valva*, another member of the *volvo* family, that referred to part of a revolving or folding door. The brand name **Volvo** for a Swedish automobile is particularly apt, being simply the Latin word *volvo*, "I roll."

The perfect participle of *volvo, volvere* is *volutus*, literally meaning "rolled," from which we get **vault**, literally "a curved, arched, concave structure," generally applied to a roof or a ceiling. As a verb, vault means literally "to roll around" and by extension "to jump, leap, surmount," as in pole-vaulting. English (and French) **volte-face**, literally "about-face," refers to a switch or sudden change in someone's opinion or behaviour.

All the examples dealt with so far come from Latin *volvo, volvere*. But there are cognates in other Indo-European languages as well, including the Germanic branch of the family. English **walk** appears to be a member of this branch of the family, from Old English wealcan, "toss, roll." Another member of the family is English **well**, now used chiefly in the sense of a pit or structure dug or sunk in the ground to enable water to be drawn to the surface, from the idea of water literally rolling, hence bubbling or boiling up. As a verb, **well** refers to water gushing or springing into being, particularly in the phrase **welling up**, referring to tears just starting to appear in someone's eye. **Wallow** means literally to "roll around," as in "a hippopotamus wallowing in the mud," and by extension to "wallow in self-pity," where the idea is that the person concerned is almost enjoying a bad situation. From the idea of the rolling or churning of the sea we get **welter**, referring to "a flurry, jumble, mess, confusion," as in "The company was beset by a welter of lawsuits." English **whelk**, related to Dutch *wulk*, is a sea snail which gets its name from its spiral shell and was traditionally sold by street vendors. Hence the disparaging remark that someone is "unable even to run a whelk stall," implying a general lack of competence or ability in the individual concerned. (The [h] in **whelk** is intrusive). **Waltz**, referring to a specific type of dance, can be traced back to Old High German *walzan*, "to roll, whirl, gyrate." It has to be remembered that, as distinct from the much slower and more sedate modern waltz, the original form of the **waltz**, now generally referred to as the **Viennese waltz**, richly deserves the description of whirling or gyrating. So much for the Germanic branch of the family.

At first sight, English **helicopter** may be thought to be connected with Greek *helios*, "the sun," but it actually has a completely different origin: Greek *helix* ("a spiral, twist, curl, coil, whirl") plus *pteron* ("wing"), from the rather strange appearance of its rotor wing. **Helix** itself has entered the English language as a scientific term, as in **double helix**, the description given to the structure of a DNA molecule because of its intertwined double-stranded appearance. But how could these words have any connection with Latin *volvo, volvere*? The key lies in the disappearance of the Greek digamma, representing an initial sound similar to that of initial English [w-]. So the basic Greek word in this connection was originally *weilein*, "to turn, twist, roll," which then lost the digamma to become *eilein*, which unaccountably became aspirated to produce **helix**.[88]

---

[88] See Chapter 11, A GREEK DRAMA.

# CHAPTER 24

## OUR BUSINESS IS RUBBISH

I RATHER LIKE the amusing ambiguous slogan emblazoned on the side of the vans of a British waste-disposal company: "OUR BUSINESS IS RUBBISH." The word **rubbish** of course refers to the fact that the company is concerned with the collection and disposal of **garbage**. But the slogan also has an alternative, jokey, self-deprecating meaning that the company's business is "worthless or unsuccessful" – which the prospective customer is not meant to take seriously.

This is really a slang usage of **rubbish**, as in "I'm **rubbish** at tennis," meaning that I am not a master of that particular sport. It has also become a verb, as in "He **rubbished** the winning painting," meaning *not* that he destroyed the work of art concerned, but simply that he delivered a withering critique of it.

**Rubbish**, according to the OED, is probably related to **rubble** ("broken bricks or stones, debris, from a collapsed or demolished building"), which belongs to the family of words deriving from PIE *\*rump-*, "to break." This is represented in Latin by the verb *rumpo, ruptum* ("break"), which has given rise to several English words, including:

- ❖ **Rupture**, "a break, burst or tear," e.g. of a blood vessel or, as in an inguinal hernia, when part of the intestine protrudes through a weak spot in the abdominal muscle. It can be either a noun or a verb, and in both it can also be used figuratively, e.g. to refer to the break-up of a relationship.
- ❖ **Disrupt**, "to interrupt, cause turmoil." Also in this group **disruptive** and **disruption**.

- **Interrupt**, "to break into," as in **interrupting** a concert or someone's train of thought. Also, the pure Latin phrase **coitus interruptus**, "broken-off sexual intercourse, indicating the withdrawal method of contraception."
- **Abrupt**, "sudden, unexpected, brusque, rude" as in "an abrupt change of subject"; "The Queen in *Alice in Wonderland* has an abrupt manner."

**Garbage**, the main American equivalent of **rubbish**, may possibly be related to **garbled**, "unclear, muddled, confused," as in "a **garbled** message." It has given rise to the computer acronym **GIGO**, or **Garbage In, Garbage Out**, meaning that bad input will result in bad output. **Garble(d)** evidently comes from the Medieval Latin *garbellare* ("to sift"), found in Italian with the same form and meaning, which EOL suggests may come from Latin *cribellum*, diminutive of *cribrum* ("sieve"), which derives from PIE *\*krei* ("to sieve, discriminate, distinguish"). This is a huge word family. But why the change from [c] to [g]?

**Trash**, another American word for **rubbish**, is of unknown origin, but possibly related to Swedish *trasa,* "rags, tatters."

**Junk**, yet another American word for **rubbish**, appears in the 14th century as **junke**, "old cable or rope," possibly from Latin *iuncus*, "reed." By the 17th century its meaning had shifted to refer to rubbish thrown overboard from a ship. It now forms the basis of several much-used popular terms, such as **junk mail**, **junk bond** and **junk food**, this last being a pejorative expression referring to supposedly unwholesome or unhealthy food such as hamburgers, fried chicken and soda. Despite its maritime origins, **junk** meaning "rubbish" is unconnected with **junk** meaning "a Chinese sailboat."

**Refuse** is a classic homonym with two different pronunciations, and meaning both "rubbish" (as a noun) and (as a verb) "to deny, decline, say no," e.g. "He refused to obey his superior officer's orders." Both meanings originate from the same Latin verb, *refundo, refundere, refusum* (from *re + fundo*) "to pour back." To **refuse** in the sense of "to deny, to express unwillingness to do something, to reject," can be understood as coming from the idea of "pouring back" or "throwing back" some request or suggestion. Hence English **refund**, meaning "to pay back," usually in reference to money that has previously been paid. Also, as a noun, e.g. "I got a refund of the money I paid for the defective cell phone." Both meanings of **refuse** are figurative. A **refusenik** was a Russian Jew who was refused permission to emigrate to Israel. The **-nik** suffix is from Russian, indicating a person engaged or involved in something, as in **sputnik**, literally "travelling companion," the name given to the first unmanned satellite launched by the Soviet Union in 1957.

From the supine, or last principal part of the Latin verb *fundo*, namely *fusum*, come such English derivatives as **fuse, fusion, infuse, diffuse, effusive, defuse, confuse**, also **confound, profound, dumbfound**. The underlying concept throughout is of "pouring" in a figurative sense.

**Refuse** is etymologically unconnected with **recuse**, though there is a certain semantic convergence. **Recuse** comes from Latin *recuso, recusare, recusatum*, meaning "to refuse," and its original meaning in English, as in the noun **recusant**, was someone who refused to accept or obey established authority, referring in particular to Roman Catholics who refused to attend Church of England services as obliged to do by law between about 1559 and 1791. Today, however, **recuse** is normally used in reference to someone disqualifying himself from sitting as a judge in a particular case.

**CHAPTER 25**

# DO NOT GIVE ANY MONEY TO SOLICITORS

"DO NOT GIVE any money to solicitors. Their activities are not supported by this facility." This announcement is regularly repeated at LAX (Los Angeles International) and other US airports. In American English, the term **solicitor** refers to someone who **solicits**, in the sense of approaching people to contribute to a charity or a business, or to engage in some illicit activity. In British English, the term has a different meaning, referring to lawyers who do conveyancing and other non-contentious work and who have the right to appear in the lower courts (and in the case of a minority with higher rights of audience, in the higher courts as well, the traditional preserve of barristers). So, as an English barrister I am always somewhat amused to hear this repeated warning against "solicitors."

Solicitors in England used to be known as "attorneys," a term which of course is still used for all lawyers in America. **Attorney** is an honourable term, meaning someone acting on behalf of another, from the law Latin *attorno, attornare*. "to turn towards, to appoint," related to English turn (from Old French *torner*, and Modern French *tourner*, "to turn"). Why and how was the honourable title of "attorney" replaced in Britain in favour of a far less respectable-sounding designation? The reason is that attorneys had such a bad reputation in England that, for example, Dr Samuel Johnson is quoted in the OED as remarking in 1784 that "he did not care to speak ill of any man behind his back but he believed the gentleman was an attorney." Recognizing the problem, in 1873, the English attorneys actually petitioned Parliament to allow them to change their designation to "solicitors."

You really have to be desperate to give up an honourable-sounding title like **attorney** for one like **solicitor** that sounds like a cross between an ambulance-chaser and a prostitute. But in fact the term **solicitor** was already used in 1873 by a smaller offshoot of attorneys who worked in the Court of Chancery (as distinct from the Common Law Courts).

To complicate matters further, the term **attorney** is still used in Britain, not in reference to lawyers, but to someone who is given a **power of attorney** to act and take decisions on behalf of another person. **Attorney** is also used in this sense in the US, often as **attorney-in-fact** to distinguish it from **attorney-at-law**, the full designation for a US lawyer. However, an attorney in this sense is usually a lay person, and its use in Britain has been greatly expanded in recent years by the creation of a special kind of power of attorney to cater for people suffering from mental incapacity. This was originally called an **Enduring Power of Attorney (EPA)** and since 2007 (with some changes), a **Lasting Power of Attorney** or **LPA**.

# CHAPTER 26

## TRUST ME, I'M A DOCTOR

**DOCTOR** IS A straight Latin word meaning "teacher," from Latin *doceo, docere, doctum* "to teach." In both the UK and the US, **doctor** is now primarily used for members of the medical profession, though in American English the more precise term **physician** is still used, which in British English is now generally reserved for specialist or consultant physicians, as distinct from specialist or consultant surgeons. The term **general practitioner** is commonly used in British English as an alternative to **doctor** to refer to a primary care medical practitioner. In French the term *physicien* means a "physicist," and "physician" is *médecin*, *medico* in Italian and *médico* in both Spanish and Portuguese, while German has *Arzt*, and it is *iatros* in Classical Greek and *giatros* in Modern Greek, both of which are pronounced "yatros." German *Arzt* is actually from Greek *archiatros*, meaning "chief doctor," and *iatros* itself is from Greek *iaomai*, "to heal," of uncertain origin. From Greek *iatros* come all the English words ending in **-iatric**, **-iatrician**, **-iatry** and **-iatrist**, such as **pediatrics**, **pediatrician**, **psychiatry**, **psychiatrist**, **podiatry**, **podiatrist**, and also **iatrogenic**, meaning "caused by a doctor," as in an **iatrogenic disease**.

But how did a word meaning "teacher" come to refer to a medical practitioner in the first place? A **doctorate** is the highest university degree in any subject, above the level of Bachelor and that of Master. In most universities in both Britain and America, this degree is called **Doctor of Philosophy** or **Ph.D.**, which almost invariably involves research and the writing of a thesis or dissertation. But qualification as a medical practitioner is not at that level. In the UK, successful medical students are awarded two bachelor's degrees, **Bachelor of Medicine** and **Bachelor of Surgery**, not a doctorate. In fact, in the UK there are very few "Doctors of Medicine" in the strict sense, i.e. people with the university degree of **Doctor of Medicine**, which is a research degree.

The title of "doctor" accorded to medical practitioners in Britain is really just a courtesy title. In previous centuries, most ordinary people never attended university, and the only university graduates that they would be likely to encounter were medical practitioners. So, out of respect these people were accorded the title "doctor" even though they did not actually have a **doctorate**. By contrast, **surgeons**, who doubled as barbers, traditionally were not university-educated. To become a surgeon, you would serve an apprenticeship and then be qualified to set up shop as a barber-surgeon yourself. The red-and-white striped pole that can sometimes still be seen outside traditional barbershops in Britain represent the blood and bandages that were the stock-in-trade of the **barber-surgeon**. This marked dichotomy between **surgeons** and **physicians** is also the reason why, in Britain to this day, while primary care and specialist physicians are accorded the courtesy title of "doctor," specialist surgeons are still called "Mr" (if male), a title which they wear with a form of inverted pride. So, in Britain there is the strange metamorphosis of a medical graduate being called "Dr" straight after qualifying, but then reverting to "Mr" (if male) once his name is added to the specialist register for surgery.

In America the position is quite different. Although the degree that a medical student is awarded on graduating from medical school is also not a research degree, it is officially designated "Doctor of Medicine" or "M.D." right away. So the process is actually the reverse of the British one. By the time the United States came into existence, primary care physicians in Britain were already generally accorded the courtesy title of "doctor." So, cutting the Gordian knot, American medical schools simply designated their degree as a doctorate even though it was not a research degree, and that is still the case today.

# CHAPTER 27

# BEAR WITH ME

ONE OF THE most frequent and most annoying responses I get on the phone is "Bear with me," meaning "Please be patient." English **bear** means literally "to carry," but by extension "to sustain," as in "a **weight-bearing** wall," also "to endure," as "I can't **bear** the pain." Other common expressions include: "the right to **bear** arms," **ball bearings, bear in mind, bear down** and **bear up** "to face up to, to show strength," as in "**to bear up** under the strain." **Bear** can also mean "to give birth," and the words **birth** and **born** are related as well, as indeed is **borne**, which was distinguished from **born** in the 17th century and is used as the past participle of the verb **bear** in senses not related to birth, e.g. "It will not be long before this plane is **airborne**." **Forbear** "to hold back," is not to be confused with **forebear** "ancestor," the "**bear**" part of which is unrelated to that in **forebear**. Also **overbearing**, "domineering, overmastering."

**Bear** belongs to a large and important Indo-European family represented by Latin *fero, ferre* "to bear, carry," Greek *phero, pherein* "to bear," Danish and Norwegian *bære*, "to carry," Swedish *bära* "to carry." German *gebären,* from this root, has the restricted sense of "to bear a child, to give birth." For "to carry" German prefers *tragen,* which comes from a completely different root, probably related to Latin *traho, trahere, tractum* "to draw, drag." English derivatives from Latin *fero* include **defer, deference, differ, difference, differentiate, infer, refer, reference, referee, transfer**. Also **confer, offer, prefer, proffer**.

**Defer** was evidently originally the same word as **differ**, from Latin *dis + fero, ferre*, "to carry apart, in different directions," but from the 15th century came to have a separate identity, meaning "to put off (action), delay, postpone," from which it came to mean "to subordinate oneself to someone else," as in judicial deference to the legislature. **Different** and **difference** are both extremely common English words, e.g. "a distinction without a **difference**." But what about the term **indifferent**? This is not a straightforward negative of **different**, but means "unconcerned" or represents a "couldn't care less" attitude.

**Infer**, from Latin *in + fero, ferre*, lit. "to bring in," hence "to deduce, conclude (from evidence)" is commonly confused with **imply** "to insinuate, hint at," e.g. "I hope you're not **inferring** that I'm lying," a mistake for "I hope you're not **implying** that I'm lying." **Imply** is from Latin *in + plico, plicare*, "to enfold, involve." **Refer**, from Latin *re + fero, ferre*, lit. "to carry back," hence "to send (for treatment), to mention, to classify," is of great practical importance, as in "The GP **referred** the patient to a specialist." "The president did not **refer** once to his notes"; "His résumé did not **refer** to his prison sentence." Hence **reference**, as in "sources consulted in compiling a book," and **referee**, "someone to whom a decision is **referred**," as in many different sports. Cf. **umpire**, with a similar meaning (depending on the sport concerned), from Old French *nonper* "odd number," from Latin *non + par* "not equal," from the fact that an **umpire** was originally a third person who was called upon to adjudicate between two disagreeing arbitrators.

**Confer** is from Latin *con + fero, ferre* (lit. "to carry together"), hence "to consult, discuss together with others," so **conference**, "a formal meeting." **Offer** is from Latin *ob-* ("in the way of") *+ fero, ferre* (to carry"), hence "to present, sacrifice, suggest, propose," also in law, "offer and acceptance" forms the basis of a contract. **Prefer** is from Latin *prae-* ("before") *+ fero, ferre* ("to carry"), so "to like better, to give priority (as in preference shares)," also "to bring forward, lay (charges) against someone." **Proffer** is from Latin *pro-* ("forward")

+ *fero, ferre* ("to carry"), so "to carry forward," hence "**to offer**." **Suffer** is from Latin *sub-* + *fero, ferre* ("to bear from underneath, up"), hence "to be ill, bear, endure, allow." Similarly, **circumference** (lit. "a carrying around") "external boundary."

Most of these words have parallels in the Romance languages, e.g. "to prefer" is *préférer* in French, *preferire* in Italian, *preferir* in Spanish, Portuguese and Catalan, and *prefera* in Romanian.

The English words ending in **-ferous** are also part of this same family, e.g. **odoriferous** (lit. "scent-bearing"), **vociferous** (lit. "voice-carrying," hence "loud, strident, clamorous"), **splendiferous** ("showy, impressive," now used chiefly in a mocking sense); also **proliferate**, from Latin *proles* "offspring" + *fero, ferre* (lit. "to bear offspring," hence "to multiply"), and **prolific** (lit. "producing offspring, fruitful," so "exceptionally productive," as in: "Shakespeare was a prolific writer").

EOL's suggestion that Latin *fur* "thief," from which come English **furtive** and possibly even **ferret** (an allusion to the animal's sly and crafty nature) may be part of this family is not supported by de Vaan, though the semantic connection would presumably be in theft, amounting to "carrying off" stolen property.

Greek *phero, pherein* "bear, carry" gives us **periphery**, from *peri-* "around" + *phero, pherein* "to carry" (lit. "a carrying around," so "an external boundary") and **pheromone**, from Greek *phero, pherein* "to carry" + **hormone** "that which excites," hence "a chemical released by animals that excites other animals of the same species." But in most English derivatives from Greek *phero*, the [e] changes to [o], as in **euphoria** (lit. "bearing well"), **metaphor** (lit. carrying after or in addition), **semaphore** (lit. "signal bearing"), **phosphorus** (lit. "light-bringing, light-producing," a reference to the property of this element to combust spontaneously).

The Latin verb *fero, ferre* is irregular, having as its third and fourth principal parts *tuli* ("I carried, have carried") and *latum* ("having been carried") respectively – which were evidently borrowed from two altogether different verbs. *Tuli* is related to Latin *tollo, tollere, sustuli, sublatum,* meaning "to lift, raise." The last two principal parts showing a close affinity with those of *fero, ferre,* and therefore meaning "to carry from underneath, from below," hence "to lift up, raise, elevate and also "to carry away, remove, do away with." It is important to note that the Latin prefix *sub-,* which usually means "under, underneath," also frequently means "from underneath, from below," with the implication of raising. There are English derivatives with both these senses: in **submarine, subaltern, subdue, submit** and **subordinate**, for example, **sub-** adds a downward force to the meaning of the word to which it is attached. But in such words as **support, sustain, sustenance, subvention, surrogate, substitute**, the force of **sub-** is "from under, from below, up," (OED **sub-**), From the present stem of *tollo, tollere* we get English **extol**, literally "to raise, exalt" in the figurative sense of "to praise, laud, glorify," to which are related **tolerate**, the mythical figure **Atlas**, who was thought of as carrying the world on his shoulders, and **talent**, originating from a Greek word referring to a large sum of money, and hence to "innate ability."

From *latum,* the supine (4th principal part) of Latin *fero, ferre,* come a number of English derivatives, including **elate, dilate, relate, relation, relationship, relative, dilate, dilatory** (from Latin *dis-* "away" + *fero, ferre* "to carry"), so "to put off, delay, postpone." English **late** meaning "delayed, overdue, tardy, recently deceased," is not from the same origin but from a Germanic root meaning "to allow, to let go," as in German *lassen,* e.g. *"lass das sein"* ("let it be, leave that alone"), Dutch and Afrikaans *laat* meaning both "late" (adjective) and "let, allow" (verb), as in *"laat staan"* "leave alone, let be."

**Bear**, "a large mammal," as in a brown, grizzly, polar, koala or panda bear, the last two of which are not really bears at all, hence "a loutish, uncouth person," has no etymological connection with **bear** as a verb (above) but comes from a Germanic root meaning "brown or bright," this latter sense still found in **burnish**. As meaning "brown," we have

German *braun*, Dutch and Afrikaans *bruin*, Danish, Norwegian and Swedish *brun*.

Northern Europe is bear country. My maternal grandmother's family came from a small town in Pomerania (German *Pommern*) in Northern Germany called *Bärwalde* (lit. "bear forest"), which is now part of Poland under the name *Barwice*, but its coat of arms and flag still feature a rather morose-looking black bear standing under a very green tree. Despite its spelling, the German capital, *Berlin*, where my father grew up, is also represented by a bear. The *Berlin* coat of arms and flag feature a fierce-looking black bear rampant (the heraldic word for standing up), and the **bear** has now become a ubiquitous symbol of *Berlin*. So how come the name "Berlin" is spelt the way it is? According to Wikipedia, the name seems actually to derive from the stem *berl-* meaning "swamp" in Old Polabian, an extinct Slavic language. The appearance of a bear on Berlin's coat of arms is therefore what is known in heraldry as "canting arms," (from Anglo-Norman cant "song"), meaning a punning pictorial representation of the name in question, e.g. The coat of arms awarded to Elizabeth the Queen Mother (mother of Queen Elizabeth II), whose coat of arms combined the Scottish lion rampant with a set of bows, reflecting her family name, Bowes Lyon. A rather less attractive escutcheon showing three hogs' heads was awarded to Quintin Hogg, Lord Hailsham, British Lord Chancellor under Edward Heath and Margaret Thatcher. US President Theodore ("Teddy") Roosevelt's coat of arms showed three roses in a field, a translation of his Dutch last name.

**Bare**: When getting the "Bear with me" response on the phone, I am sometimes tempted to reply, "So are you naked, then?" – taking the response to be not **"bear with me"** but **"bare with me,"** which is completely unrelated to **bear** but comes from a Germanic root meaning "pure, sheer, utter," which is reflected in English phrases such as **bare-faced cheek**, the **bare essentials** and **bare necessities**. The German cognate *bar* does not mean "naked," which is represented by *nackt*, but figures particularly in *Bargeld*, "cash."

# CHAPTER 28

# A BATHROOM WITHOUT A BATH

THESE DAYS MOST hotel rooms come with a "private bath" or "private bathroom." But don't call the concierge if you can't locate a **bathtub,** because the chances are there never was one. In American English **bathroom** is a euphemism for **toilet, lavatory, water-closet, WC, bog, loo, restroom, privy, latrine,** or **khazi,** all of which are euphemisms as well. Let's take a look at a few prime examples.

**Toilet**: Like so many euphemisms, this is of French origin. It originally referred to the cloth cover that a lady might place over her dressing table, then to the objects placed upon it and then to the act of applying those to the face and hair. In modern French, *faire sa toilette* mean "to have a wash, to groom oneself, to apply make-up." The origin is **toil**, originally meaning "a net, cloth," then more specifically "a net, snare" for trapping wild game, and now used metaphorically (only in the plural) to refer to "a serious difficulty or intractable situation," e.g. "Hitler was caught in the toils of his own scheming." In Britain, **toilet** still has a whiff (no pun intended) of a genteel "Non-U" euphemism eschewed by the "U" (or upper class) in favor of the slightly more direct **lavatory.**[89]

**Loo**: British slang for "toilet," possibly from the warning cry **gardyloo,** from French *prenez garde à l'eau* or simply *gardez l'eau,* "watch out for the water," a cry predating indoor plumbing uttered by

---

[89] See Nancy Mitford, *Noblesse Oblige,* Oxford: Oxford University Press, 2002 (reprint).

the occupants of an upper floor as they emptied a **chamber pot** on unsuspecting pedestrians below. French *l'eau* "water" is from Latin *aqua*, which is found in English in that form, too.

**Lavatory**: Still in use in Britain, if somewhat old-fashioned. But, strangely, the term of choice for airlines, who use it for the tiny space occupied by a **toilet** seat and a hand basin. It comes straight from the Late Latin *lavatorium*, from Latin *lavo, lavare, lautum (lotum)* "to wash," from which, via the French, we get **launder** "to wash clothes, linen, etc.," **laundry**, which can refer either to "clothes and linen that need washing or have been washed," or to "a room or place dedicated to the washing process." If this is a commercial establishment, it will be known as a **launderette** or **laundromat**. Compare the Germanic word **washing**, also referring to "clothes or linen needing to be washed or having been washed," which comes from the family of words related to **water. Money laundering** is the criminal offence of disguising the source of the proceeds of crime by putting it through apparently legitimate transactions. **Lotion**, "a smooth liquid applied to the skin for cosmetic or medicinal purposes," comes, via the French, from Latin *lotio*, a colloquial form of *lautio*, a contraction of *lavatio*, from *lavatum*, supine stem of Latin *lavo, lavare* "to wash." Latin *lotium*, it is worth noting, means "urine," perhaps a reference to its use as a detergent. The spelling of *lotio* for *lautio* and *lotum* for *lautum* may possibly reflect a more "plebeian" pronunciation or a dialectal variation, the [o] being characteristic of Umbrian, an Italic language related to Latin. Publius Clodius Pulcher, a popular politician of the late Roman Republic, a scion of the ancient patrician Claudian family, changed his name from *Claudius* to *Clodius* to signal his switch from patrician to plebeian. **Lavish**, as an adjective, meaning "rich, sumptuous, luxurious," e.g. "a lavish banquet," also comes, via French, from Latin *lavare* "to wash," the implication being of something on which large sums of money have been spent or poured. Hence the verb, to **lavish** praise or gifts on someone. Compare Germanic **shower**, as in: to **shower** someone with gifts. Another word for "toilet" from Latin *lavare* "to wash" is **latrine**, chiefly in military use, which is probably from Latin *latrina*, a contraction of *lavatrina*.

**Lava**, "molten rock spewed out by a volcano," may also come from Latin *lavare*, but this etymology is not certain.

Besides *lavo, lavare* "to wash oneself, bathe," Latin also has *lavo, lavere* "to wash (something else)" which, according to de Vaan, is related to Greek *louo, louein* "to wash" – though not to Greek *luo, luein*, "loosen," (see below) – and provides us with a number of English words, including **ablution** "washing, ritual purification" (often in the plural, e.g. "morning ablutions") and several other words associated with washing in a more figurative sense, such as **dilute**, **deluge** (lit. "a washing away"), **alluvial** (as in "panning for alluvial gold," which is gold dust "washed along" in a stream or creek).

This root should not be confused with Latin *luo, luere* "to release, suffer, expiate, pay," as in *luere poenas* "to pay the penalty (for a sin or crime)." Etymonline (EOL) derives this from PIE root, *\*leu-*, "to loosen, divide, cut apart," as distinct from *\*leue*, "to wash." Possibly a distinction without a difference? But the Greek representative of this root, *luo, luein*, "to loose, loosen," is probably unrelated to Greek *louo, louein* "to wash." So we may well be dealing with two PIE near-homonyms. The family to which Greek *luo, luein* and Latin *luo, luere* belong has a lot of English members, starting with basic words such as **loose**, **loosen** and also **lose** and **loss** and then, from Latin and Greek, a number of words mostly used in a more figurative sense. From the Latin we have **solve**, **solvent**, **solution**, **soluble**, **dissolve, dissolute, dissolution, resolve, resolute, resolution, absolve, absolute, absolution**. The image common to all these words is one of "loosening," either in a physical sense, as when an aspirin tablet **dissolves** in water and turns the water into a **solution**, or by extension when a problem is **solved** in the sense of being "untied" – think perhaps of "cutting the Gordian knot" – and you have a different kind of **solution**. **Resolve** and **resolution** present a similar image, but they also have an even more figurative meaning as well, as in a New Year's **resolution**. **Absolute** has a wide range of uses, such as **absolute power**, **absolute monarchy**, etc., as in Lord Acton's famous aphorism: "Power tends to corrupt, and absolute power corrupts absolutely." **Absolutely** is much used as an exclamation in colloquial speech to signal strong agreement. "So you think Gladstone was the greatest British Prime Minister?" "Absolutely!"

English derivatives from the Greek *luo, luein* are mostly technical, with some also enjoying a figurative usage: **analysis, analytic, catalyst, dialysis, electrolysis, paralysis**, of which **palsy** (as in **cerebral palsy**) is a contracted form.

One of my favourite examples of language misuse is the true story about the wife of the Oxford historian H. A. L. Fisher in France during World War I. So proud was she of her husband's surprise appointment to the War Cabinet that in her talks all around France during the war to drum up support for the Allied cause, she would make a point of remarking in her best French: *"Mon mari est dans le cabinet de Lloyd George."* The poor woman never understood why this remark was greeted with suppressed giggles by the otherwise sedate French matrons whom she was addressing. What she was intending to convey was simply the fact that her husband was in the cabinet under Prime Minister Lloyd George. However, what her remark meant was: "My husband is in the toilet under Lloyd George." The French word *cabinet* can mean "office" or "surgery," but also (chiefly in the plural) "toilet."

French is particularly richly endowed with words relating to relieving oneself: the word *pissoir* referring to a "urinal" is certainly French in form but more usually used in other languages. Urinals, elaborate versions of which used to adorn the streets of Central Paris, are more usually referred to in French as *Vespasiennes*, named after the Roman Emperor Vespasian (reigned 69–79 CE), who levied a tax on public toilets, and, when twitted for doing so, reportedly held up to his nose a coin derived from that tax and commented, *"Non olet!"* ("It doesn't smell").

As replacements for the *Vespasiennes*, of which there is now only one left in the whole of Paris, some so-called *uritrottoirs* have recently started appearing, open-air urinals painted a bright red with notices pointing to them showing a man fully in view while using one of these contraptions. The term *uritrottoir* is a combination of *urinoir* ("urinal") with *trottoir*, "sidewalk (American), pavement (British)." Not everyone agrees with Paris Mayor Ariel Weil's 2018 description of the *uritrottoir* on Twitter as *"une invention de génie"* ("an invention of genius"). A less controversial arrival on the Paris scene is the *Sanisette,* a completely enclosed self-contained unisex public toilet. There are now about 420 *Sanisettes* in Paris, costing the city over six million euros per year.

We cannot end this survey without mentioning the French slang term *chiotte* ("a crapper"), which is related to English **shit** and German *scheissen. Chiotte* is also an expletive similar to *merde* or the much more polite *sacré bleu!* Strangely enough *chiotte* is also a French slang term for a car.

# CHAPTER 29

# WATER, WATER EVERYWHERE

> Water, water everywhere
> And all the boards did shrink;
> Water, water everywhere,
> Nor any drop to drink.
>
> – Samuel Taylor Coleridge,
> *The Rime of the Ancient Mariner* (1800)
>
> It's a strange world of language in which skating on thin ice can get you into hot water.
>
> – Franklin P. Jones (1908–80)

WATER IS ONE of the most important life-giving resources, and the word itself comes from a PIE root *\*wed-*, which gave rise to Hittite *watar*, Greek *hydor*, Latin *unda* ("wave"), Russian *voda*, and Gaelic *uisge*. For an explanation of how these rather different-sounding words all come from the root *\*wed* see Chapter 8, A GRIMM TALE.

This root is represented in the Germanic languages by English **water**, **wet**, **wash**, **whisky/whiskey**, **vodka** and possibly even **winter** (OED). Germanic cognates include Dutch and Afrikaans *water*, Icelandic *vatn*, Swedish *vatten*, Danish *vand*, Norwegian *vann*, German *Wasser* – all meaning "water." Note the introduction of an intrusive [-n-] or *nasalization* in Danish and Norwegian, and the shift from [t] in the Low Germanic languages to [-ss-] in Modern German (technically Neuhochdeutsch or New High German) – *die zweite Lautverschiebung*, or second sound shift – as explained in Chapter 8, A GRIMM TALE.

In Latin, this root is represented by *unda,* whose primary meaning is "wave," but which also has the poetic meaning of "water." English derivatives from it include: **undulate, redundant, abundant, abound, surround** (not related to **round** or **around**) and also **redound** (not to be confused with **rebound**).

Greek *hydor, hydatos* "water" has given rise to English **hydrate, hydration, dehydrate, carbohydrate**. In Modern Greek the word for water, *nearon,* is short for *nearon hydor* "fresh water."

The usual Latin word for water is of course *aqua,* which is from a different PIE root altogether. It is used in that same form, **aqua**, in English in a technical sense. English derivatives **abound** (pun intended): **aquatic, aquarium, aqueous, aqueduct**. And Romance derivatives, all meaning "water," include: Italian *acqua,* Spanish *agua,* Portuguese *agua,* Catalan *aigua,* French *eau,* found in English expressions such as **eau de Cologne, eau de toilette** and **eau de vie** (lit. "water of life" and hence "brandy").

# CHAPTER 30

# A FEW CONTRANYMS

THE RICHNESS OF English vocabulary has inevitably resulted in certain words having more than one meaning – and sometimes even meanings that are so different from one another as to be virtual opposites. These are termed **contranyms** or **contronyms** (plus an assortment of other labels). I have picked just a few of the more confusing ones here plus some of my favourite terms at the end.

- **Cleave** can mean either "to split or divide," or the opposite, "to cling, stick together." These are two separate verbs with completely different origins and even different grammatical forms. The past tense of the one meaning "to split" is **cleft** (as in "cleft palate") and its past participle is **cloven** (as in "cloven hoof"), whereas the past tense and past participle of cleave meaning "to cling" is usually simply **cleaved**. Words related to cleave meaning "to split" include **clever** (evidently with an original sense relating to manual dexterity) and also **clove**, as in "a clove of garlic," a small bulb cut from a compound bulb of garlic. It derives from PIE *gleubh-* "to tear apart, cleave," giving rise to Greek *glyphe* "a carving," from which we get **glyph** (a typographical term meaning "a symbol"), and **hieroglyphic** (lit. "sacred carving").

- **Cleave** meaning "to cling" is best known from the King James Bible: "Therefore a man shall leave his father and mother, and shall **cleave** unto his wife and they shall be one flesh." (Gen. 2:24). Possibly related to **clay**, from the family represented by Latin *gluten* "glue, paste," which has entered English directly as **gluten**, as in "gluten-free bread," and from which we get **glue**.

- **Smart**, "to feel a sharp, burning pain"; as an adjective, "well dressed, intelligent, clever, from an original physical meaning, "biting, severe, sharp." These two meanings are very different, but not opposites, and both have same origin. **Outsmart**, **smart phone** and the phrase **smart as a whip**, "quick-witted, bright," are good examples of how the meaning slid from literal sharpness to intellectual ability or mental **acuity**. Cf. **clever** (above) and **acuity** (below), both of which also refer to mental qualities but have an underlying physical meaning. **Smart** derives from PIE *mer- "to harm," which has given rise to German *Schmerz*, Danish and Norwegian *smerte*, and Swedish *smärta*, all meaning "pain"; and English **murder**, German *Mord*, Dutch and Afrikaans *moord*, Danish and Norwegian *mord*, Swedish *mörda*, all meaning "murder," Also Greek *brotos* "mortal" and Latin *mors, mortis* "death," Latin *morbus* "illness" and possibly Latin *mordeo, mordere, morsum* "to bite." From Latin *mors, mortis* we get **mortal**, **immortal**, **amortize** (lit. "to kill," hence "to write-down the cost of intangible business assets"), **mortuary**, **mortify** (lit. "to make dead," hence "to humiliate, shame, embarrass"), **mortgage** ("lit. "dead pledge"); from Latin *mordeo, mordere, morsum*, we get English **mordant**, **remorse** ("a feeling of deep regret"), **morsel** ("a small bite"); and from Latin *morbus* we get **morbid** (medical, "diseased," hence "morbid curiosity," an unhealthy, prurient interest).

❖ **Acuity** "sharpness": like both clever and sharp, this has a figurative meaning overlaid on top of a disused literal meaning. From PIE *ak-, represented by Latin *acus* "needle," Greek *acme* "point, summit," *akros* "at the topmost point," *oxys* "sharp," German *Eck* "corner." From or related to Latin *acus* we have English **acute**, **acumen**, **acupuncture**, **acid**, **acerbic**. From Greek *acme* we have English **acme** "pinnacle" (a favourite name for small businesses advertising in alphabetically-arranged classified ads) and also, strangely, **acne** (a corruption of **acme**, referring to a rash of "pointed" pimples on the face).

❖ **Conviction** can refer either to "a finding of guilt in a court of law" or "a strongly held belief," as in: "Do you have the courage of your **convictions**?" Both come from Latin *com-* + *vinco, vincere, vici, victum*, "to conquer, defeat," of which the best-known use was Julius Caesar's famous boast, *Veni, vidi, vici,* "I came, I saw, I conquered." The common element connecting a firm belief with a finding of guilt is the concept of proof, which in turn rests on the idea of a successful fight or struggle. **Victor**, **victory**, **convict**, **convince** and **invincible** all derive from the nasalized present stem or from the non-nasalized supine stem of this same Latin word. **Evict** "to overcome by removing from property," rests on the concept of conquest, whereas **evince** "to constitute evidence of something," is based more on the concept of proof, as in: "Converts tend to evince great enthusiasm for their new religion." **Province**, "an administrative division of a country," is from Latin *provincia*, which is probably not from the same origin, although it may at first sight appear to be connected with the concept of conquest, but the original meaning of Latin *provincia* was "a sphere of duty," and **province** is still used in this sense in English today: "Negotiating international deals is outside his province."

❖ **Commit** can mean either "to perpetrate a crime"; "to make a definite decision," as in: "The automobile manufacturer has now **committed** itself to making only electric vehicles" or "to send," as in: "Please **commit** this formula to memory." Both come from Latin *com + mitto, mittere, missum*, which has numerous derivatives, including **mission, missionary, admit, admission, commission, intermission, omit, omission, permit, permission, remit,** and **remission**. The semantic link with the concept of "send" is often quite tenuous, but it is essentially present in all these derivatives. **Remit**, for example, generally means "to send a payment," while **remission**, as in "her cancer was in **remission**," means that the disease has been, as it were "sent back or sent away." **Mission**, literally "a sending," is used in reference to a religion's proselytizing activities, or an envoy sent to represent one country in another, and is also used figuratively to mean the chief goal of a business or organization, or, in more informal usage, a really difficult task, as in: "Getting that toaster to work was quite a mission."

❖ **Mean** has several quite diverse **meanings**. In the sense of "to intend, to signify, to be equivalent to," it is of Germanic origin, cognate with German *meinen* ("think, opine"). From a different Germanic root **mean** can also be used in reference to "stingy or low dishonourable behaviour or trickery," e.g. **mean-spirited**. But a completely different **mean** is from Latin *medius* "middle," as in the mathematical calculation similar to but different from **median** and **average** (a word of uncertain origin, possibly Arabic), e.g. If we have a set of numbers, say 2, 4, 5, 6, 8, 10, 25 and 60, the **mean** or **average** is 30, calculated by adding all the numbers together (= 120) and dividing them by the size of the set, 8 (so, 15). The **median** (also from Latin *medius)* of this set is calculated by adding the middle two numbers and dividing by 2.

So, 6 + 8 = 14 ÷ 2 = 7. If the set consists of an odd number of figures, the **median** is the central one, regardless of value. So, in the set 5, 10, 15, 25, 65, the **average** or **mean** is 24, but the **median** is 15. By extension, the Latin-based adjective **mean** has come to be used in such compound words as **meanwhile** and **meantime**. By a further extension, the Latin-based noun has come in the plural, **means**, to have the sense of "method, way, resources, wherewithal" as in "by all means," signifying strong assent or certainty. Also such uses as in: "She is a woman of considerable means" and "The end justifies the means."

❖ **Dear**, of Germanic origin, means both "expensive, costly" and "beloved." The link between these two senses is the concept of "precious." The Germanic cognates are confined to the meaning of "expensive, costly": German *teuer*, Dutch and Afrikaans *duur*, Danish and Norwegian *dyrt*, Swedish *dyr*. The etymologically unrelated Latin word *carus, cara, carum* shows the same semantic duality, as do its Romance derivatives: Italian *caro*, Spanish and Portuguese *caro*, French *cher*. The change from Latin [ca-] to French [che-] is quite regular, cf. Latin *caput* ("head") >>French *chef* ("boss"); Latin *capra* >> French *chèvre* (both "goat"); Latin *casa* ("hut") >> French *chez* ("at the house of, "as in the phrase *"on est chez nous,"* "We are at home"); Latin *scala* ("ladder") >> French *échelle* ("ladder"). However, Latin [ca-] sometimes changes to French [cha-], as in: Latin *cambio, cambire* ("to exchange, barter") >> French *changer* ("to change"); Latin *canto, cantare* >> French *chanter* (both "to sing").

❖ **Enjoin** is from Latin *in + iungo, iungere, iunctum*, lit. "to join in," hence "to attach," and by extension "to attack" – **attach** and **attack** being etymological doublets. **Enjoin** can have both the two opposite meanings of "to direct or order someone to do something," OR "to prohibit," the negative meaning being more often expressed by the noun **injunction**.

❖ **Sanction** has a similar double meaning, both "to allow, permit" and as a noun "legal authority," and on the other hand also "to penalize," and as a noun, "a penalty." From Latin *sanctio* ("an establishing, ordaining, or decreeing as inviolable under penalty of a curse; a decree, ordinance, sanction,"[90] which in turn is from Latin *sacer, sacra, sacrum*, "holy,

---

[90] Lewis & Short.

sacred," cognate with Greek *hagios* with the same meaning. Note the equivalence of Latin [s-] to Greek [h-] (rough breathing).

❖ **Principal** and **principle**, which are often confused, have the same origin: Latin *primus* ("first") + *capio, capere* ("to take"), **principal** meaning "chief, most important," both as an adjective and as a noun, as in "school principal" and "principal ballerina," while **principle** exists only as a noun, meaning "fundamental concept, code of conduct," sometimes contrasted with **practice**, e.g. "Your proposal is acceptable in principle, but its practicality remains to be tested." Cf. Groucho Marx's remark: "Those are my **principles**, and if you don't like them, I have others."

❖ "**Untold suffering seldom is.**" (Franklin P. Jones). This is a pun on the word **untold** and therefore on the verb of Germanic origin **to tell**, which originally meant "to count," as in a **bank teller**. By extension it came to mean to **recount**, giving an **account** of, or relating or narrating a **tale**, which is cognate with **tell**. So, what the aphorism is saying is that those who complain of **untold** suffering, meaning "uncounted, limitless" suffering, do not refrain from whining about it. German shows a similar relationship between "to count" and "to recount" in *zählen* "to count" and *erzählen* "to recount, relate, narrate, tell."

❖ **Apprise/appraise**: These two words are often confused, but they are quite distinct in both origin and meaning. **Apprise** is, via the French, from Latin *apprehendo, apprehendere, apprehensum*, meaning "to take hold of, grasp," often in a figurative sense, hence English **apprise** means to inform, notify." **Apprehend, apprehension** can of course be used in either a literal or figurative sense, as in **apprehending** a thief or in having a certain amount of **apprehension** about the likely spread of a newly discovered virus. **Appraise**, on the other hand, is from Latin *pretium* ("price, value, worth"), and so means "to value, set a price on," Hence, an **appraisal** and **sworn appraiser**.

❖ **Appreciate**, which is also from Latin *pretium* "price, value," means "to increase in value." But it also means "to estimate aright"; "to esteem adequately or highly, to recognize as valuable or excellent, to find worth or excellence in."[91] As in: "I really appreciate all the help that you have given my son." And similarly, with **appreciation**, **appreciative**.

- **Aggravate**, from Latin *gravis* "heavy, serious," means "to make worse, more serious," but it is often misused in colloquial speech to mean "to bother, annoy," as in "you are aggravating me."

- **Paralegal**: A warning against home-made etymologies. In the TV series *King of Queens*, the wife's ill-educated father calls to speak to his daughter while she is at work as a legal secretary. To the father's surprise, the call is answered by a male voice. "And what is your position over there?" asks the inquisitive old man. "I am a **paralegal**," comes the reply. "Oh, I really admire the wonderful work that you people do – and all in a wheelchair!" The old father has presumably heard words like **paraplegic** and **paralympic** and jumped to the conclusion that any word beginning with **para-** must refer to disabled people who are unable to walk. In fact, of course, the prefix **para-** is from the Greek preposition *para*, meaning "beside, alongside, beyond, contrary to" as in **paragraph, paramedic, paranormal, parapsychology, paradigm, paradox, parameter.** So a **paralegal** is simply an assistant to a lawyer. This Greek-based **para-** is not to be confused with the Latin-based **para-**, from Latin *paro, parare, paratum*, "to prepare, make ready," from which come such words as English **parasol, parachute, parapet, Parabellum** (a well-known type of World War I machine gun, named from the Latin adage: *Si vis pacem, para bellum*, ("If you want peace, prepare for war").

- **Echo tria orchidia**: A warning against repeating foreign phrases without understanding what they mean. In the movie *My Big Fat Greek Wedding*, the "Anglo" bridegroom is told by the bride's brothers to greet the wedding guests with the words: *Echo tria orchidia*. The result is great mirth at his expense, because what this Greek phrase means is "I have three testicles." English **orchid** is so called because of its root's supposed resemblance to a human testicle. Another English derivative is **orchidectomy**, the technical medical term for the Latin-based **castration**.

---

[91] OED.

# CHAPTER 31

# ALL THAT ALGEBRA

COMPARATIVE PHILOLOGY, AS it used to be called, is a study of languages with a view to determining their relationship, if any, to one another and tracing their origins. It is now rebranded as "comparative linguistics," though that is not really quite the same animal, as I show below. The recognition of linguistic relatedness goes back to ancient times. The Romans were well aware that their Latin language was related to Greek, and medieval speakers of the Romance languages were conscious that their languages were related to one another and were all modern forms of Latin. But it was not until the 17th century that there was any recognition of the existence of what is now called the Indo-European family of languages. Probably the earliest writer to identify this family was the Dutch scholar Marcus van Boxhorn (1612–53), who held, quite correctly, that Greek, Latin, Persian, German, Dutch, and the Slavic, Baltic and Celtic languages all had a common ancestor, which he called "Scythian." It was the recognition by Sir William Jones (1746–94) of Sanskrit, the ancient Indian language, as cognate with Latin and Greek that proved to be the key to an understanding of the Indo-European family of languages. But it was only in the 19th century that comparative philology came into its own, particularly with the discovery of Grimm's Law by Jacob Grimm in 1822 and refined by Verner's Law in 1877, which established a system of regular correspondences between certain sounds in the Germanic languages on the one hand and Latin and Greek on the other.[92]

In the 20th century, efforts were intensified on reconstructing Proto-Indo-European (PIE), the common ancestor of the whole Indo-European family of languages, which is not recorded in writing. Reconstructing this language has resulted in a number of new theories, including the many variants of so-called "laryngeal theory," which posits three or even four different /h/ sounds in this unrecorded language – the pronunciation of which is disputed! As a result of this and other developments in what is now called "comparative linguistics," the subject has become esoteric, highly theoretical and involving a good deal of speculation, and is not concerned with the learning of actual languages. It has even developed a whole language of its own, presumably with a view to enabling it to claim the title of a science. This has resulted in making it inaccessible to all but its own small circle of adherents – and even to traditional scholars of comparative philology.

### "I can't understand all that algebra."

Among these was the great "Joppy," Norman Brooke Jopson (1890–1969) of my college, St John's College, Cambridge, Professor of Comparative Philology in the University of Cambridge from 1937 to 1955, who lamenting the direction that the subject had taken, would remark, "I can't understand all that algebra."

Joppy had a love of language, not in a general or theoretical sense, but of actual individual languages, and was reputed to be able to speak pretty well any European language plus a good few others besides. When introduced at a college dinner to a lady guest purporting to be Hungarian, Joppy immediately broke into Hungarian and a conversation in Hungarian ensued, during which Joppy remarked to

---

[92] See Chapter 8, A GRIMM TALE.

the guest that for a Hungarian she had a remarkably strong Romanian accent. This was a reflection of the fact that Hungarian speakers living in Transylvania, Romania, despised the Romanians and would often try to pass as Hungarians. But Joppy had no interest in politics, and his remark was not intended as an insult.

Joppy came up to St John's as a Scholar in 1909, and a brilliant first class in French and German was followed by an equally distinguished performance in Sanskrit and Comparative Philology. Then, after a spell studying Indo-European philology in Vienna, Czech in Prague and Russian in St Petersburg, he returned to Britain, on the outbreak of World War I in 1914. He was snapped up by the Postal Censorship office, which gave him the opportunity to widen his already extensive knowledge of languages. He used to say that the two commonest languages he encountered used as ciphers during the War were Latin followed by Welsh. His knowledge of Slovene gave him the position of chief interpreter to the British delegation in the 1920 Carinthian plebiscite commission, which decided the boundary between Austria and Yugoslavia. So much did Joppy endear himself to the Slovenes that his name was included in the *Slovene Dictionary of National Biography*.

Between 1922 and 1936, Joppy served as Reader in Comparative Slavonic Philology in the University of London and was then elected to the newly created Chair of Comparative Philology in Cambridge in 1937. World War II found him back at the Postal Censorship Office, where he appropriately became Head of the Uncommon Languages Department. After the war, he returned to Cambridge, retiring from his professorship in 1955, but remaining a resident Fellow of St John's for the rest of his life.

"If Jopson had any knowledge of the laryngeal theory or of the general principles of structural linguistics, this had no effect on the content of his lectures," wrote Sir John Lyons in 2004 in his obituary of W. Sidney Allen, Joppy's successor as Professor of Comparative Philology, continuing: "On the other hand, his presentation of what was still the generally accepted version of the phonological and morphological structure of PIE and of the prehistoric stages of Greek, Latin and Sanskrit and the other Indo-European languages (Slavonic, Celtic, etc.) was greatly enlivened by his humorous anecdotes of one kind and another and his own facility in a wide range of modern languages upon which he could draw relevantly at the drop of a hat."[93]

"Reconstruction" of Proto-Indo-European (PIE), which interests me as little as it did Joppy, is not only highly speculative, but also of very little practical value. The "reconstructed" PIE words (or rather, "lexemes") and roots do not lead to identifying cognates derived from them. Quite the reverse, in fact: the "reconstructions" are reached by working backwards from known cognates. So a "reconstruction" is, so to speak, supposedly the lowest common denominator of all the cognates. Yet, there are usually several variant forms of each particular "reconstruction," many of which are unpronounceable, and the ubiquitous "laryngeal" /h/ sounds make them all the more so. All three (or four) of these numbered sounds, were supposedly guttural, but there is no agreement on how they were actually pronounced. Many of the "reconstructions" are hard to imagine ever forming part of an actual spoken language. So, in this book I have referred to PIE reconstructions as seldom as possible. But here, just to give you a flavour of what they are like, are a few examples, all of which are prefixed by * to indicate that they are unattested by any record:

- ❖ *$séh_2u$-l (de Vaan) ("sun"): Latin *sol*, Greek *helios*, Lithuanian *saulė*, German *Sonne* and English **sun**, all of which not only have the same meaning, "sun," but are all etymologically cognate as well, i.e. share the same origin. That is clear from the rules governing sound shift in the various languages. For example, the initial /h-/ "rough breathing" in Greek being equivalent to /s/ in the Latin and Romance, Germanic and the other Indo-European sub-groups.

---

[93] Sir John Lyons, Obituary of Prof. W. Sidney Allen, https://thebritishacademy.ac.uk/sites/default/files/138p003.pdf.

## ALL THAT ALGEBRA

- *$h_1ouHd^{h}$-r* (de Vaan) ("udder"): Latin *uber* (as a noun, "udder"; as an adjective "abundant, rich"), Greek *outhar*, German *Euter*, English **udder**. All mean "udder," with Latin *uber* having the added figurative meaning of "rich, abundant," from which comes the legal term *uberrima fides*, meaning "utmost good faith," applied particularly to insurance contracts.

- *$d^hg^h$-ôm* (de Vaan) ("earth, soil"): Latin *humus* and *homo* ("man"), Greek *chthon*, the second part of German *Bräutigam*, Middle English *gome*, and the second component of Modern English **bridegroom**. The basic concept is that of "earth" in the sense of soil, and by extension to man as an "earthling."

The new trends in comparative linguistic study are visible in the papers read to the Philological Society, established in its present form in 1842, which prides itself on being "the oldest learned society in Great Britain devoted to the scholarly study of language and languages." I am a member of the Society, but rarely attend meetings, despite the excellent sandwiches served beforehand.

## "Suppletion"

A recent paper by Richard S. Kayne titled "What is Suppletion? On *goed and on went in Modern English," published in the *Transactions of the Philological Society*, is fairly typical of the type of research done nowadays. "Suppletion," a term first attested by the OED in a 1933 article, is the replacement of the forms of one word with those of another in certain situations, especially the replacement of certain tenses of a verb with forms drawn from a different verb – what we used to refer to simply as "irregular verbs." The example focused on in the paper is the verb **go**, which, instead of *goed as its past tense, has **went**, which is actually the past tense of a completely different verb, **wend**. Here is the abstract of that paper:

"The term 'suppletion' is appropriate to *went/*goed*, but only if that term is taken to be an informal descriptive term that hides a rich set of phonological and morphosyntactic properties that underlie each of *went* and *goed* taken separately. No direct blocking relation between *went* and **goed* is called for. The notion of verbal theme vowel is central." What exactly does this mean? All it seems to be suggesting is that the form **goed* as the past tense of **go** is not prevented just because there exists an alternative past tense, **went**. The explanation offered by Kayne for the non-existence of the form **goed* is that "go belongs to the class of English verbs that does not allow a theme vowel to be merged just above it." (Richard S. Kayne, "What is Suppletion? On **goed* and on *went* in Modern English," *Transactions of the Philological Society*, Vol. 117, 2019, Number 3, pp. 434-454.)

All this smacks of making a gargantuan meal out of a very small snack. The plain fact of the matter is that in a number of languages some of the commonest verbs have their present tense drawn from one stem and their past tenses from another, e.g. Latin *fero, ferre, tuli, latum* ("to carry"). This verb apparently has three different stems, a present stem, perfect stem and supine stem, though the last two stems are actually the same. The supine was previously *tlatum*, evidently related to *tuli*, which comes from the Latin verb *tollo, tollere, sustuli, sublatum* ("to raise, lift"), the last two principal parts of which are clearly related to those of *fero*, and the meaning "raise" is of course related to "carry." A number of other languages, including French, Italian, Spanish, Portuguese and German, also have suppletive verbs, none of which, however, are cited in Kayne's paper. In many languages the commonest adjectives are also suppletive, notably in English **good/better/best**, and equivalents in Latin: *bonus/melior/optimus,* Greek: *agathos/beltion/beltistos*, French: *bon/meilleir/le mieux*, Italian: *buono/meglio/il migliore and ottimo (il migliore* means "the best," while *ottimo* means" very good, excellent," Spanish: *bueno/mejor/el mejor*, Portuguese: *bom/melhor/o melhor*, German: *gut/besser/beste*. None of these suppletive forms are mentioned by Kayne. The simple question, which Kayne does not ask, is why suppletion is a feature of such common verbs and adjectives in so many languages? It must surely be connected with the fact that they *are* so common – and their forms are so diverse as to blow Kayne's "theme vowel" theory out of the water. I like to think of it in terms of wear and tear. A rug that experiences a lot of wear may need patching up, while one that is in an isolated spot will not. Similarly, words meaning "to be," "to go," or "good" obviously get a lot of wear and tear. It's as simple as that. But a mistake with this sort of thing is not fatal. One of my favourite "wrong" expressions, which one sometimes hears uttered by non-English speakers, is "**very better**." There is no misunderstanding what is meant, though it is clearly incorrect. One could formulate a rule to the effect that **very** is never used together with a comparative. So, you can say "very good," "very old," "very pretty," "very ugly," but if you want to use these adjectives in an extreme comparative sense, you have to insert "much" between "very" and the comparative, e.g. "very much better," "very much older," "very much uglier." But mistakes with suppletives are not confined to non-native speakers. I can't count the number of times I have heard "you was" as a regular expression by native English speakers. It would of course be simpler just to abolish suppletion, which has happened, for example, in Afrikaans, which has ditched the Dutch verbal inflections altogether. Compare the Dutch present tense of the verb "to be": *ik ben/jij bent/hij is/wij zijn/jullie zijn/ze zijn*, with the Afrikaans: *ek is/jy is/hy is/ons is/julle is/hulle is*. In short, in Afrikaans *is* is used unchanged throughout.

## Word order conundrum

Let us look at another fairly typical Philological Society paper: "The Old Sardinian Condaghes: a syntactic study," Sam Wolfe, *Transactions of the Philological Society* Vol. 113, 2015, No. 2, pp. 177-205.) I rather suspect that this paper, by a member of Joppy's and my alma mater, St John's College, Cambridge, would have qualified as an example of what Joppy referred to as "all that algebra." The abstract reads in part as follows:

"This article presents findings of a syntactic study of two Old Sardinian legal documents. It is proposed that Old Sardinian had a verb-initial syntax, which at face-value appears quite distinct from the verb-second (V2) syntax reported elsewhere in Old Romance. It is suggested, however, that this verb-initial order is derived by V-to-C movement, a feature which is inherited from late Latin and represents a synchronic point of continuity in the syntax of Old Romance varieties." Under "Background" we read that Old Sardinian generally "patterns with the rest of Old Romance. It will be seen however that the remaining parametric makeup of Old Sardinian appears quite distinct from other Old Romance varieties, leading to an information structure sensitive VSO/SVO [verb-subject-object/subject-verb-object] alternation rather than the form of V2 syntax which is found elsewhere. The central focus of this article will be the position occupied by the verb and the position(s) occupied by overt subjects."

Cutting through all the "algebra," what this paper seems to be saying is that, unlike V2 word order (that is, with the verb in the second position) typical of Old Romance languages generally, Old Sardinian sometimes departs from this word order, and this exception "is inherited from late Latin." This is neither a particularly startling nor a particularly illuminating point.

Some background information would have made this paper much more interesting and also more helpful than it is. An obvious starting point, which was perhaps taken for granted by Sam Wolfe, is that Latin, including Late Latin, i.e. post-classical written Latin from the third to the sixth centuries, was a highly inflected language, whereas the Romance languages are much less inflected, as nouns do not decline, though verbs continue to conjugate. It is an elementary but fundamental point that in Latin, as a highly inflected language, meaning is determined by inflectional endings rather than position, so that word order is flexible and can be varied for emphasis. In the Romance languages, by contrast, meaning is largely determined by word order. And the same of course applies to English, except where either the subject or the object is inflected.

Romance linguists often consider Old Sardinian to be closer to Latin than the other Romance languages, indicating that it was a very conservative language. Professor Mario Pei estimated that Sardinian (that is, modern Sardinian) was only 8% away from Latin, as compared with 12% for Italian, 20% for Spanish and a whopping 44% for French.[94] If this is the degree of conservatism of modern Sardinian, how much more so must Old Sardinian have been? This is not speculation. It is confirmed by no less an authority than Dante Alighieri himself in his treatise, *De Vulgari Eloquentia*, in which he said that the Sardinians lacked a vernacular of their own and so resorted to aping Latin instead.[95] This conservatism may well account for Old Sardinian word order flexibility when the other Romance languages had abandoned it. Yet Sam Wolfe provides none of this information in his 29-page paper!

---

[94] Pei, Mario (1949), "A New Methodology for Romance Classification," *WORD* 5 (2), pp. 135-146.
[95] Bk I.xi.7.

# CHAPTER 32

# ENVOI

THIS BOOK IS about English etymology, or word origins, and the relationship between English and the other Indo-European languages, especially Latin together with its daughter Romance languages, and the Germanic languages, English being at bottom a Germanic language itself. But it is not an academic treatise on the theory of the subject. Concerned with vocabulary rather than grammar or syntax, it shows how you can improve your English vocabulary by means of etymological links between words, and also how you can use English etymological links to unlock vocabulary in other languages. So the book should be helpful to you whether you are a native English speaker or not. However, while aiming to be practical and instructive, the book makes no claim to be a language learning course of any kind. And, without seeking out curious and quirky word origins for their own sake – a feature of all too many popular books – I hope you find the book entertaining and engaging as well as useful and educational in the best sense of the word.

# Glossary

I HAVE TRIED to write this book in the most down-to-earth language possible, so as to be accessible to readers regardless of their background. I have also made a point of explaining any even remotely technical terms in the text itself. Nevertheless, just to make assurance double sure, I have put into this Glossary any term that I thought could conceivably cause puzzlement to anyone. But I hope that will not make anyone feel that they are being talked down to. Believe me, that is certainly not the intention!

## Conventions

- Key English words are printed in **bold**.
- Words in all other languages are printed in *italics*.
- An asterisk (*) in front of a word means that it has been reconstructed.
- English translations are printed between inverted commas, except where the translation is more of an explanation.
- The translation of a verb is always preceded by "to."
- Except where otherwise indicated, "Greek" refers to Classical Greek.
- Greek words are transliterated into the Roman alphabet, generally keeping as closely to the original Greek orthography as possible and using [ch] for the letter [χ] (chi).
- Except where otherwise indicated, the name of a language refers to its modern form.
- Except where otherwise indicated "Norwegian" refers to *Bokmål* (as distinct from *Nynorsk*).

## Terminology

- **Noun:** The name of a person, institution or place ("proper noun") or of any animate or inanimate object, activity or concept ("common noun"), e.g. **cat, book, athletics, equality**.
- **Pronoun:** A word standing in for a noun, e.g. "Please read the **book** and let me know what you think of **it**." The word **it** is a pronoun, taking the place of **book**.
- **Verb:** A "doing" word, e.g. **to dance, to run, to think, to decide**.
- **Adjective:** A word that describes a noun, e.g. **black, old, genuine, deceitful**.
- **Inflection:** A modification of or ending tacked on to a word to reflect some grammatical function, e.g. in English, the change from **he** to **him** to indicate whether the word is the subject or object of the sentence.
- **Declension:** A type of inflection as it applies to nouns, pronouns and adjectives. So, for example, the well-known schoolboy Latin declensions, which British Prime Minister William Gladstone claimed to have been beaten into every bone in his body, e.g. *mensa, mensa, mensam, mensae, mensae mensa* (declension of *mensa* "a table").
- **Conjugation:** A type of inflection as it applies to verbs, e.g. French conjugation of the present tense of *être* ("to be"): *je suis, tu es, il/elle est, nous sommes, vous êtes, ils/elles sont*. Note: In French *on est*, which literally means "one is" has come in practice to mean "we are," as in the phrase, *on est chez nous* ("we are at home"), a charming phrase, which has however been appropriated as a slogan by a French political party.
- **Nominative:** The subject form, as in English **she**, as distinct from the object form, **her**.
- **Accusative:** The object form, as in English **him**, as distinct from the subject form, **he**.
- **Case:** In grammar, this refers to the particular forms taken by a noun, pronoun or adjective. German, for example, has four cases: nominative, accusative, genitive (possessive) and dative (indirect object, "to" or "for," e.g. Ich gab **ihm** das Buch, "I gave the book **to him**," or "I gave **him** the book."
- **Oblique case:** This is the term used in grammar to refer to any case other than the nominative. The word **case**, from Latin *casus*, means

# Glossary

literally "a falling," and the nominative was visualized as standing straight, with all the other cases "falling" obliquely away from it.

- **Infinitive**: The "to" form of a verb, e.g. **to run, to sing, to dance, to think, to believe**. Different languages have different signal endings for the infinitive, and some have different tenses of the infinitive, e.g. Latin *amare* ("to love" – present infinitive; *amavisse* "to have loved," – perfect infinitive). In Classical Greek, the present infinitive (active) ends in *-ein*, as in *lambanein* "to take," but Modern Greek, surprisingly, does not have infinitives at all.
- **Principal parts**: This term applies particularly to Latin verbs, e.g. the principal parts of the verb "to make," are: *facio* ("I make" – present tense), *facere* ("to make" – present infinitive), *feci* ("I made" – perfect tense), *factum* ("having been made" – perfect participle –"supine"). The principal parts are so called because they provide a snapshot of all the stems of the verb concerned. The first and second principal parts provide the present stem, the third provides the perfect stem and the fourth what is called the "supine" stem. Only the first two and fourth principal parts provide English derivatives, so in this book I generally refer to Latin verbs in terms of principal parts one, two and four.
- **Cognate**: A word sharing the same origin as another word, from Latin literally "born together," e.g. Latin *cor, cordis*, the stem of which is *cord-*, has the Greek cognate *kardia* and the English cognate **heart**, all of which mean "heart."[96]
- **Derivative**: A word that is a descendant of another word. So, while English **heart** is cognate with Latin *cor, cordis*, English **cordial, accord, record** are derivatives from the Latin word.
- **Loanwords**: These are words "borrowed" from another language, without of course any intention of giving them back. A loanword may either be exactly the same as in the original language, or its meaning and/or spelling may be altered. Italian loanwords in English include: **opera, broccoli, ghetto, gusto, nostalgia**, all of which retain their original form and meaning. However, in these Italian loanwords either the meaning or the form, or both, have been altered in English: **dilettante** (in Italian it means simply "amateur"), **imbroglio** (Italian

---

[96] See Chapter 8, A GRIMM TALE.

meaning, "cheat"), **novel** (Italian *novella*, "tale"), **stucco** (Italian "plaster"), **umbrella** (Italian *ombrello*).
- **Calque**: a loanword, the components of which are translated back into words in the borrowing language, e.g. German *Fernsprecher* (lit. "far speaker") is a calque of English **telephone** (from Greek, lit. "far sound, far voice"), German *Wolkenkratzer* (literal translation into German of English **skyscraper**), and English expressions such as **running dog**, **look-see**, **paper tiger**, **chop chop** and **long time no see** are all Chinese calques, their components being translated back into English from Chinese originals.
- **Grimm's Law**: See Chapter 8.
- **Verner's Law**: See Chapter 8.
- **Lexeme**: An item of vocabulary, generally the same as a word.

## Abbreviations

- BCE    Before Common Era
- CE    Common Era
- cf.    compare with
- i.e.    id est = "that is"
- IE    Indo-European
- IPA    International Phonetic Alphabet
- lit.    literally
- PIE    Proto-Indo-European
- viz.    videlicet, short for Latin videre licet, meaning "it is permitted to see," hence "namely, that is to say."

# References

THE REFERENCE BOOKS and sources consulted in the writing of this book are far too numerous to list. This is a list of only some of the most frequently consulted reference works, together with their abbreviations where relevant.

OED – *Oxford English Dictionary*, 2nd ed., Clarendon Press, 1989.

EOL – Harper, Douglas, *Online Etymology Dictionary* – etymonline.com.

AHDIER – *American Heritage Dictionary of Indo-European Roots*, ed. Calvert Watkins, New York: Houghton Mifflin Harcourt, 2000.

Beekes – Beekes, Robert, *Etymological Dictionary of Greek*, Leiden: Brill, 2010.

de Vaan – de Vaan, Michiel, *Etymological Dictionary of Latin & other Italic Languages*, Leiden: Brill, 2008.

Lewis & Short – Lewis, Charlton & Short, Charles, *A Latin Dictionary*, Oxford, OUP, 1880.

Liddell & Scott – Lidell, Henry & Scott, Robert, *A Greek-English Lexicon*, 9th ed., Oxford: Clarendon Press, 1996.

Dr Johnson – Johnson, Samuel, *A Dictionary of the English Language*, London, 1755.

MW – *Webster's Third New International Dictionary*, Springfield, Mass: Merriam-Webster, 2002.

Buck – Buck, Carl Darling, *A Dictionary of Selected Synonyms in the Principal Indo-European Languages*, University of Chicago Press, (1949) 1988.

Wiktionary – wiktionary.org. *The free dictionary*.

Barnhart – Barnhart, Robert, *Dictionary of Etymology*, ed., H. W. Wilson & Co., 1988.

Klein – Klein, Ernest, *A Comprehensive Etymological Dictionary of the English Language*, Amsterdam, Elsevier, 1971.

Liberman – Liberman, Anatoly, *Analytic Dictionary of English Etymology*, University of Minnesota Press, 2008.

Pokorny – Pokorny, Julius, *Indogermanisches Etymologisches Wörterbuch*, Tübingen: A. Francke Verlag, 1959.

Ringe, Don, *From Proto-Indo-European to Proto-Germanic*, Oxford, 2006.

Kluge, Friedrich, *Etymologisches Wörterbuch der deutschen Sprache*, Berlin: Walter de Gruyter, 2002.

Meyer-Lübke, W., *Romanisches Etymologisches Wörterbuch*, 7th ed., Heidelberg: Winter, 2009.

Roberts, Edward, *A Comprehensive Etymological Dictionary of the Spanish Language with Families of Words Based on Indo-European Roots*, 2 vols., Xlibris LLC, 2014.

Dauzat, Albert, *Dictionnaire Étymologique de la Langue Française*, Paris: Larousse, 1938.

Picoche, Jacqueline, *Dictionnaire Étymologique du Français*, Paris: Le Robert, 2002.

Drosdowski, Günther, *Duden Etymologie: Herkunftswörterbuch der deutschen Sprache*, Mannheim: Dudenverlag, 1989.

Brodsky, David, *Spanish vocabulary: an etymological approach*, Austin: University of Texas, 2008.

Clackson, James, *Indo-European Linguistics: An Introduction*, Cambridge: Cambridge University Press, 2007.

McPherson, Fiona, *Indo-European Cognate Dictionary*, Wellington, New Zealand: Wayz Press, 2018.

# English Word Index

A-, 192
Aardvark, 168
Abdomen, 167
Abide, 190
Ability, 102
Able, 102
Ablution, 238
Abound, 242
Above, 190
Abreast, 190
Abroad, 190
Abrupt, 225
Absolute, 238, 239
Absolutely, 239
Absolute monarchy, 239
Absolute power, 239
Absolution, 238
Absolve, 238
Abundant, 242
Academic, 188
Academical, 188
Accept, 32, 43, 89, 189
Accomplice, 36
Account, 53, 247
Accountancy, 53
Accountant, 53
Acerbic, 244
Achieve, 53
Acid, 244
Acme, 244
Acne, 244
Acolyte, 192
Acoustic, 192

Actual, 92
Actually, 92
Acuity, 244
Acumen, 244
Acupuncture, 244
Acute, 244
Address, 86
Admiral, 169
Admission, 245
Admit, 245
Advert, 185, 186
Advertise, 185, 186
Advertisement, 185, 186, 187
Aero-, 160
Aerobics, 160
Aerodrome, 73, 160
Aerodynamics, 160
Aeronautics, 160
Aeroplane, 160
Aerospace, 160
Affect, 189, 190
Affected, 190
Affection, 189
Affidavit, 101
Affirm, 101
Afoot, 190
Afresh, 190
Age, 137
Aggravate, 248
Aggression, 200
Aggressive, 200
Agnostic, 192
Agoraphobia, 202
Ahead, 190

Aid, 39
Air, 160
Airborne, 231
Airdrome, 73
Airport, 73, 160
Airport terminal, 216
Akin, 190
Alcohol, 169
Alcoholic, 189
Algebra, 169
Algebraic, 189
Alien, 190
Alienate, 190
Alive, 190
Allergic, 78
Allergy, 78, 161
Alliance, 100
Alluvial, 238
Ally, 100
Alphabetical, 189
Altogether, 137
Amazement, 187
Amicable, 202
Amnesia, 192
Amoral, 192
Amorous, 202
Amortize, 244
Analysis, 239
Analytic, 239
Anarchist, 160
Anarchy, 160, 192
Anew, 190
Anglophile, 202
Angst, 169
Animal, 166

265

Answer, 137
Antagonise/antagonize, 186, 187
Ante-, 192
Ante-bellum, 193
Antediluvian, 193
Antenatal, 193
Antenna, 167
Anti-, 192
Antifascist, 193
Anti-feminist, 193
Antifreeze, 193
Anti-hero, 193
Antipodes, 193
Antipope, 193
Antivirus, 193
Anus, 167
Aperitif, 168
Apolitical, 192
Apologise/apologize, 186, 187
App, 35
Application, 35
Applied, 35
Applied psychology, 35
Apply, 35
Appointment, 218
Appraise, 203, 247
Appraisal, 247
Appreciate, 247
Appreciation, 248
Appreciative, 248
Apprehend, 247
Apprehending, 247
Apprehension, 247
Apprise, 203, 247
Aqua, 237, 242
Aquarium, 242
Aquatic, 242
Aqueduct, 242
Aqueous, 242
Arachnophobia, 202
Arch-, 160
Archaeology, 160

Archaic, 160
Archbishop, 160
Archduke, 160
Archenemy, 160
Archipelago, 160
Archrival, 160
-arch/-archy, 160
Argue, 210
Argued, 139
Arise, 190
Aristocracy, 160
Aristocrat, 160
Around, 242
Artificial preservatives, 91
Asexual, 192
Ashamed, 190
Ashore, 190
Aside, 190
Ask, 139, 140
Asleep, 190
Assist, 39, 90, 168
Ate, 139
Atheist, 192
Atlas, 234
Attach, 246
Attaché, 168
Attack, 246
Attend, 90, 168
Attorney, 25, 185, 227
Attorney general, 195
Atypical, 192
Authorise/authorize, 186
Auto-, 88
Autobiography, 160
Autoclave, 182
Autocracy, 160
Autocrat, 160
Automobile, 88
Avant-garde, 168
Average, 245, 246
Aversion, 185

Avert, 185, 186
Awake, 190
Aware, 190
Away, 190
Awesome, 184
Awful, 184
Back-flip, 139
Bagel, 128, 169
Baguette, 168
Ball bearings, 231
Ballet, 168
Bandied words, 139
Bank teller, 247
Bar, 150
Barbarian, 61
Barbaric, 61
Barbarism, 61
Barbarous, 61
Bar code, 150
Bare, 235
Bare with me, 235
Barrier, 150
Based, 159
Bathos, 91
Bathroom, 236
Bathtub, 236
Be-, 40, 190
Bear, 30, 37, 46, 114, 231, 234, 235
Bear down, 231
Bear in mind, 231
Bear up, 231
Bear with me, 235
Becalm, 40
Beef, 84
Beeves, 84
Befall, 139, 174
Befuddle, 40
Beg, 139
Beginning, 156
Behave, 40
Behead, 190
Beheading, 102
Behest, 139
Behind bars, 150

# English Word Index

Behold, 40
Beholden, 40
Behoove, 40
Belief, 203
Believe, 203
Belittle, 40
Beluga, 169
Berate, 40
Beret, 168
Besmirch, 40
Bespatter, 190
Besprinkle, 190
Bestir, 190
Bible, 205
Bibliography, 205
Bibliophile, 202, 205
Bibliotheca, 205
Bidding, 139
Bill, 191
Billet, 191
Biltong, 168
Bio-, 160
Biochemistry, 160
Biodiversity, 160
Biography, 160
Biology, 160
Birth, 37, 231
Bishop, 164
Bless, 93
Blindness, 192
Bog, 236
Boldness, 192
Bombastic, 189
Bon voyage, 168
Book, 205
Booklet, 191
Born, 231
Borne, 231
Bot, 80
Bottle, 179
Bovine, 74
Brawny, 140
Breach, 34
Break, 34
Bride, 41

Bridegome, 41
Bridegroom, 41, 253
Bridegroome, 41
Brother, 38, 114, 119, 122
Brunette, 168
Brydegrome, 41
Buckram, 169
Burden, 37
Bureau, 168
Burnish, 234
Bus, 146
Butter, 164
By-, 190
By degrees, 200
Bygones, 190
Bylaw, 190
Bystander, 190
Cab, 30, 31, 89
Calf, 85
Calorie, 88
Calque, 169, 262
Camel, 47
Camp, 85
Camping, 85
Campus, 85
Capable, 89
Capacious, 31
Capacity, 31
Capital, 53
Capital punishment, 102
Capitation, 53
Capitulate, 53
Captain, 53
Captain general, 195
Caption, 31, 189
Captivate, 189
Captive, 189
Captor, 189
Capture, 31, 89, 189
Car, 88, 211
Carbohydrate, 242

Cardiac, 116
Career, 88, 211
Caress, 203
Cargo, 88
Caricature, 211
Carpenter, 211
Carriage, 88, 211
Carrier, 211
Carry, 88, 211
Cartwheel, 139
Case, 89, 139, 174, 175, 211
Case-law, 89
Cash, 211
Castration, 248
Catalyst, 239
Cathedral, 152, 164
Catholic, 101
Cattle, 53, 211
Cause, 174, 175
Cavalcade, 74, 75
Cavalier, 74, 75
Cavalry, 74
Cavalryman, 74
Cerebral palsy, 239
Chafe, 88
Chair, 152, 153, 164
Chaise longue, 153
Chamber pot, 237
Champagne, 168
Chant, 75
Chaotic, 189
Chapter, 53
Charge, 88, 211
Charismatic, 189
Charity, 203
Chassis, 89
Chattel, 53, 211
Chauffeur, 88, 168
Chef, 53
Cherish, 203
Chic, 168
Chief, 53

267

Chief executive officer (CEO), 214
Chiffon, 169
Chiro-, 160
Chiropodist, 160, 163
Chiropractor, 160
Chivalrous, 75
Chivalry, 75
Chronological, 189
Church, 164
Chutzpah, 128, 169
Circumference, 233
Circumstance, 104
Claustrophobia, 202
Clavichord, 182
Clavicle, 182
Clay, 243
Cleave, 243
Clef, 182
Cleft, 243
Cleft palate, 243
Clever, 243, 244
Cliché, 168
Clinical diagnosis, 159
Clove, 243
Cloven, 243
Cloven hoof, 243
Coarse, 96
Code, 206
Code-breaker, 206
Codicil, 206
Codification of laws, 206
Coexist, 187
Cognate, 195
Coin, 212
Coitus interruptus, 225
Collaborate, 187
Color-fast/colour-fast, 173
Colloquium, 166
Combat, 187

Comedian, 189
Comic, 189
Comical, 189
Comic actor, 189
Comic monologue, 189
Comic relief, 189
Comic strip, 189
Commission, 245
Commit, 245
Committed, 245
Common, 138
Commonly, 138
Common people, 139
Common sense, 90, 139
Commune, 138
Communicate, 138
Communication, 171
Communism, 138
Community, 138
Complement, 28
Complex, 36
Complicate, 36
Complicated, 36
Complicit, 36
Complicity, 36
Compliment, 28
Comply, 36
Computation, 53
Compute, 53
Computer, 53
Con, 101, 213
Coined, 210
Consecutive, 210
Concord, 116
Concordat, 116
Concourse, 88, 96
Concupiscence, 201
Concur, 88, 187, 210
Concurrent, 210
Confection, 189

Confer, 37, 231, 232
Conference, 37, 232
Confidant, 101
Confide, 101
Confidence, 101
Confirm, 101
Confound, 226
Confuse, 226
Congenital, 195
Congress, 199
Con man, 101
Connoisseur, 168
Conservation, 91
Conservative, 91, 103
Conserve, 91, 103
Consist, 104
Consistency, 104
Consolidate, 101
Constable, 104
Constituent, 104
Constituency, 104
Constitute, 104
Constitution, 103, 104
Continual, 191
Continuous, 191
Contour, 185
Contranyms, 243
Contronyms, 243
Convent, 29
Convention, 29
Conventional, 29
Convenient, 29
Convenyent, 29
Conversation, 185, 187
Converse, 187
Convert, 187
Convict, 213, 244
Convicted, 213
Conviction, 213, 214, 244
Convince, 213, 244

# English Word Index

Convoluted, 206, 221
Convolution, 221
Cooperate, 77
Cooperative, 77
Copius, 78
Copy, 78
Cordial, 116
Corridor, 88, 96
Corroborate, 187
Coterminous, 217
Count, 53
Coup, 89, 165
Coup d'état, 88
Coupe, 88
Couple, 139
Courier, 88, 96, 211
Course, 88, 96, 211
Couth, 191
-crat/-cracy, 160
Craziness, 192
Create, 39, 122, 157
Created, 156, 157
Creation, 157
Creature, 157
Cuneiform, 212
Cupidity, 201
Currant, 96
Currency, 88, 96, 210
Current, 88, 96, 210, 211
Curriculum, 96
Cursive, 88, 210
Cursor, 88, 210
Cursory, 88
Curt, 130
Cyber-, 161
Cyber-cafe, 161
Cybernetics, 161
Cyber security, 161
Cyberspace, 161
Dais, 125
Dale, 211

Daresay, 140
Daughter, 121
De-, 200, 217
Deal, 124
Deal with, 124
Dear, 246
Decapitation, 53, 102
Deceive, 32, 89
Deck, 103
Decline, 174
Deem, 140
Defect, 189
Defective, 189
Defence, 103
Defend, 103
Defense, 103
Defer, 37, 231, 232
Deference, 37, 231
Deficient, 34, 157, 189
Deficit, 157, 189
Defoliate, 206
Defuse, 226
Degree, 200
Dehydrate, 242
Deify, 157
Deism, 157
Deity, 157
Delict, 145
Delinquent, 145
Deluge, 238
Demerit, 203
Demo-, 160
Democracy, 160
Democrat, 160
Demographic, 189
Demographics, 160
Demonise/demon-ize, 186, 187
Demotic, 160
Denim, 194
Deploy, 36
Deprecate, 203
Depreciate, 203
Desert, 91, 103

Deserve, 91
Desk, 125
Despair, 146
Desperate, 146
Dessert, 91, 103
Detect, 91, 103
Detection, 103
Detective, 103
Determination, 217
Determine, 217
Determined, 217
Detour, 25, 185
Devil, 121, 124
Devolution, 206, 221
Devolve, 206, 221
Devolved, 221
Diabolical, 121
Dialysis, 239
Differ, 37, 193, 231, 232
Difference, 37, 231, 232
Different, 232
Differential, 37
Differentiate, 231
Diffidence, 101
Diffident, 101
Diffuse, 226
Digitise/digitize, 186
Digress, 199
Digression, 199
Dilate, 234
Dilatory, 234
Dilute, 238
Dining saloon, 89
Direct, 86
Dis-, 193
Disagree, 193
Disapproval, 190
Disc/disk, 125
Disconnect, 193
Disentangle, 190
Disingenuous, 195

269

Disinterested, 184, 190
Dish, 125
Discord, 116
Discount, 53
Discourse, 96, 211
Discursive, 88
Discus, 125
Dishearten, 116
Dismiss, 193
Disobey, 193
Dispense, 193
Display, 36
Disrupt, 225
Disruption, 225
Disruptive, 225
Dissolve, 238
Dissolute, 238
Dissolution, 238
Divers, 185, 187
Diverse, 185, 187
Diversion, 185, 187
Diversity, 187
Divert, 185, 187
Divine, 157
Divinity, 157
Dole, 124
Dole out, 124
Dollar, 211
Dollar bill, 192
Door, 115
Door-jamb, 85
Dossier, 168
Double Dutch, 130
Double helix, 162, 223
Dreck, 128
Dress, 86
Dressed, 86
Drift, 124
Drink, 130
Drive, 124
Drome, 73
Dromedary, 73
Drone, 73
Drug, 139

Dumbfound, 226
Duplex, 36
Duplicate, 36
Duplicitous, 36
Duplicity, 36
Dutch, 130, 131
Dynamic, 161
Dynamite, 161
Dynamo/dynamo-, 161
Dys-, 193
Dysentery, 193
Dysfunctional/disfunctional, 193
Dyslexia, 193
Dyspepsia, 193
Eager, 56
Earth, 158
Easy, 56
Eat, 38, 120, 122, 130, 139
Ecclesiastical, 164
Eco-, 161
Ecology, 161
Econometric, 161
Economist, 161
Economize, 161
Economy, 161
Ecstasy, 104
Effect, 189
Effective, 189
Effectiveness, 192
Effectual, 189
Efficient, 34, 93, 157, 189
Effusive, 226
Egoism, 96
Egotism, 96
Egregious, 166
Egress, 199
Elate, 234
Electrocardiogram (ECG/EKG), 116
Electrolysis, 239
Elite, 168
Elope, 131

Embarrass, 150
Embarrassed, 150
Emolument, 187
Empathetic, 91, 92
Empathy, 92
Emptiness, 192
Employ, 36
Employee, 36
Employer, 36
Employment, 36
Encamp, 85
Encyclopaedia/encyclopedia, 163
Endlessly, 137
Enemy, 202
Energetic, 78
Energy, 78, 161
Engine, 89
English Revolution, 220
Enjoin, 246
Enjoyment, 187
Ensue, 215
Entrepreneur, 69
Envy, 92
Equestrian, 74
Equine, 74
Equivalent, 198
Erg-, 161
Ergon, 161
Ergonomics, 78, 161
Erotic, 201
Eroticism, 201
Ersatz, 168
Establish, 104
Estate, 104
Etymology, 28, 31
Euphoria, 37, 233
Evade, 166
Eventual, 93
Eventuality, 93
Eventually, 93
Evert, 185
Evidence, 214
Evil genius, 90

Evict, 213, 214, 244
Evince, 213, 214, 245
Evolve, 206, 221
Evolution, 206, 221
Ex-, 213, 217
Ex cathedra, 152
Except, 32
Exception, 32
Excursion, 210
Execute, 101, 102, 214
Executed to death, 102
Execution, 101, 102, 214
Executioner, 214
Executive, 101, 214
Executor, 214, 215
Executrix, 215
Exfoliate, 206
Exhibit, 103
Exit, 199
Expedient, 117
Expedite, 116
Expedition, 117
Expeditious, 117
Explicate, 36
Explicit, 36
Exterminate, 217
Extol, 234
Extrovert, 185, 187
Facade, 168
Fact, 157, 166, 189
Faction, 157, 189
Factor, 189
Factory, 157, 189
Faith, 101
Faithful, 101
Faithfully, 101
Familiarise/familiarize, 186
Famous, 184
Farm, 101
Fart, 120

Farthing, 191
Fast, 172, 173, 174, 176
Fast friends, 173
Fastness, 173
Father, 38, 118, 119, 122
Faux pas, 168
Feat, 157
Federal Bureau of Investigation (FBI), 102
Federal Government, 102
Federal marshal, 76
Federal Reserve, 102
Federation, 102
Feds, 102
Fee, 209, 211
Feet, 179
-ferous, 233
Ferret, 37, 233
Feudal, 209
Few, 139
Fiancé, 101
Fidelity, 101
Fiduciary, 101
Fief, 209
Field-marshal, 76
Fight, 139
Figurative, 171
Figure of speech, 172, 173
Finished, 139
Fire, 38, 122
Firm, 101
Firmament, 101
Fish, 87
Fit, 29, 30
Fitted, 30
Flame, 197
Flammable, 184, 197
Floor, 49, 72

Flora, 73
Floral, 50, 73
Florid, 50, 73
Florist, 50
Flower, 73
Foil, 206
Foliage, 206
Folio, 206
Foot, 114, 115, 116
Footstool, 153
Forbear, 231
Forebear, 231
Forerunner, 211
Forfeit, 93, 102
Forfend, 103
Forgiveness, 192
Form, 73
Fought, 139
Fraction, 34
Fracture, 34
Fragile, 34
Fragment, 34, 187
Frail, 34
Frangible, 34
Frankfurter, 169
Frozen metaphor, 172, 173, 174, 176
Furlough, 204
Furtive, 233
Fuse, 226
Fusion, 226
Gambol, 85
Gammon, 85
Garbage, 224
Garbage In, Garbage Out (GIGO), 225
Garble, 225
Gardyloo, 236
Gather, 138
Gen-, 194, 195
Gene, 194
General, 195
Generalissimo, 195
Generally, 195
Generate, 195

Generation, 195
Generator, 195
Generic, 189, 195
Generous, 196
Genesis, 194, 195
Genetic, 194
Genial, 90, 168, 195
Genie, 195
Genital, 195
Genitalia, 195
Genitive, 195
Genius, 90, 194
Genteel, 195, 236
Gentile, 128, 195
Gentle, 195
Gentleman, 195
Gentrify, 195
Gentry, 195
Genus, 194, 195
Geo-, 161
Geography, 161
Geology, 161, 163
Geophysics, 161
Geopolitical, 161
Glue, 243
Gluten, 243
Gluten-free, 243
Glyph, 243
Go, 131, 253, 254
Goal, 139
God, 157
God complex, 36
Gome, 41
Gonad, 195
Gonococcus, 195
Gonorrhea, 195
Good/better/best, 254
Goodness, 192
Goodness, gracious, 192
Gorilla, 183
Gov/gov'nor, 161
Govern, 161
Government, 161

Governor, 161
Goy, 128, 195
Gradation, 200
Grade, 200
Gradient, 200
Gradual, 200
Graduate, 200
Great, 130
Greatly, 137
Grit, 130
Groom, 41
Groom of the stool/stole, 153
Gross, 130
Guarantee, 183
Guarantor, 183
Guaranty, 183
Guard, 183
Guardian, 183
Guerilla/guerrilla, 183
Guest, 115, 207
Guest-room, 207
Guest-work, 207
Gym, 162
Gymnasium, 162
Gymnastic/gymnastics, 162
Gymno-, 162
Gym shoes, 162
Gym teacher, 162
Gyn-, 164
Gynaecologist/gynecologist, 164
Gynaecology/gynecology, 164
Habit, 103
Habitat, 103
Habitation, 103
Hairdressing salon, 89
Hale, 138
Halide, 183
Halo-/halo, 162, 183
Halogen, 162, 183

Handle, 139
Handsome, 42
Hard and fast, 173
Harm, 137
Hasidic, 189
Have, 32, 40, 42, 43, 89
Haven, 32
Head, 38, 53, 122
Headache, 54
Heading, 54
Headlight, 54
Headlong, 54
Head over heels leap, 139
Heal, 138
Health, 138
Heart, 38, 115, 116, 122
Hearten, 116
Heartening, 116
Heartfelt, 116
Hearty, 116
Heave, 32, 40
Heave-ho, 40
Heaven, 157, 158
Heaven forfend!, 103
Heavy, 32
Heli-, 162
Helicopter, 132, 162, 183, 206, 223
Heliotrope, 183
Helipad, 162
Heliport, 162
Helium, 163, 183
Helix, 132, 162, 206, 223
Help, 39
Henchman, 76
Hibernate, 159
Hierarchy, 160
Hieroglyphic, 243
Hi-fi, 101
High quality, 191
Himalayas, 159

Hinterland, 169
Hippocratic Oath, 74
Hippodrome, 73
Hippopotamus/hippo, 74
Hoglet, 191
Hold, 40, 42
Holdup, 40
Holocaust, 101, 138
Hologram, 101, 138
Holograph, 138
Holy, 138
Homeopathic, 163, 189
Homeopathy, 42, 163
Homoerotic, 201
Homeostasis, 163
Hominid, 163
Homo-, 42, 163
Homo erectus, 163
Homogeneous, 42, 163, 194
Homogenize, 194
Homograph, 42, 163
Homonym, 42, 163
Homophobia, 202
Homophone, 42, 163
Homo sapiens, 41, 139, 163
Homosexual, 42, 163
Hope, 130
Horizontal, 188
Hormone, 233
Horse, 73, 75
Hospice, 208
Hospitable, 208
Hospital, 208
Hospitality, 208
Host, 115, 207

Hostage, 207
Hostel, 207
Hostelry, 207
Hostile, 115, 207
Hotel, 168, 207
Human, 41
Hurt, 137
Hydrate, 242
Hydration, 242
Hydro-, 163
Hyper-, 193
Hyperglycemia, 193
Hypo-, 193
Hypoglycemia, 193
-iatric, 229
-iatrician, 229
-iatrist, 229
Iatrogenic, 229
Iatrogenic disease, 229
-iatry, 229
-ical, 188
Ichthyologist, 87
Ichthyology, 87
Immoral, 192
Immortal, 244
Impecunious, 209
Impede, 116
Implicate, 36, 37
Implication, 37
Implicit, 36, 37
Imply, 37, 232
In-, 197
Inability, 190
Inalienable, 190
Inception, 43, 157, 189
Incessant, 191
Incessantly, 137
Incipient, 43, 157, 189
Incomplete, 197
Indecent, 197
Indecisive, 197
Indifferent, 37, 232

Indirect, 197
Infamous, 184
Infect, 189
Infection, 189
Infer, 37, 231, 232
Inferior, 167
Inferring, 232
Infidel, 101
Infinite, 197
Infirm, 101
Infirmary, 101
Inflame, 197
Inflammable, 184, 197
Inflammation, 197
Inflect, 174
Infuriate, 197
Infuse, 226
Ingenious, 194
Ingenuous, 194
Ingredient, 200
Ingress, 200
Inhibit, 103
Inimical, 189, 202
Inimicus, 202
Initiate, 157
Initiation, 157
Injunction, 246
Injure, 137
Innate, 195
Inopportune, 197
Inquire (enquire), 210
Insouciant, 101
Institute, 104
Institution, 104
Integument, 103
Intense, 197
Intercourse, 96, 211
Intermission, 245
Interpret, 203
Interrupt, 225
Introvert, 185, 187
Invalid, 198
Invaluable, 197

Invert, 185
Invictus, 213
Invincible, 213, 244
Involve, 206, 221
-ion, 188
Irrationality, 91
-ise/ize, 186
Jam, 131
Jeans, 194
Judiciary, 214
Jump, 127
Junk, 225
Junk bond, 225
Junk food, 225
Junk mail, 225
Kaput, 168
Kempt, 191
Khazi, 236
Kibitz/kibbitz, 128
Kibbutz, 128
Kin-, 194, 195
Kin, 195
Kind, 196
Kindergarten, 168
Kith and kin, 196
Kitsch, 168
Knee, 115
Knight, 41
Kosher, 128, 169
Labor, 76
Labor-intensive, 76
Laborious, 76
Labor of love, 76
Labor the point, 76
Labor union, 76
Laissez-faire, 168
Lamb, 85, 86
Languid, 146
Late, 234
Latex, 167
Latrine, 236, 237
Launder, 237
Launderette, 237
Laundromat, 237
Laundry, 237

Lava, 238
Lavatory, 236, 237
Lavish, 237
Law, 139
Lax, 145
Laxative, 145
Leaf/leaves, 205
League, 100
Leap, 131
Lease, 146
Leash, 146
Leave, 204
Legal, 100, 163
Legible, 163
Legislation, 163
Legislature, 214
Legitimate, 163
Lemon, 169
-let, 191
Lethargy, 161
Liable, 100
Liason, 100
Liberal, 204
Libertarian, 204
Libertine, 204
Liberty, 204
Libido, 204
Librarian, 205
Library, 93, 205
Lief, 204
Liefer, 204
Lien, 100
Ligament, 100, 187
Ligature, 100
Listen, 127
Liturgy, 79, 161
Liver, 204
Liverish, 204
Loanwords, 168
Logic, 163
Logical, 163
Logistics, 163
Logo-, 163
Loneliness, 192
Long-term, 217
Loo, 236

Look, 127
Loose, 238
Loosen, 238
Lope, 131
Lose, 238
Loss, 238
Lotion, 237
Loud, 127
Love, 201, 204
Lovely, 203
Loyal, 100, 163
Majestic, 189
Make, 121, 130
Mammoth, 169
Man, 23
Manage, 139
Managing director, 214
Manifold, 36
Maneuver, 77
Man of quality, 191
Manure, 77
Mare, 76
Marshal, 76
Marxist principles, 157
Massage, 168
Matter of course, 211
Mattress, 169
Mazel tov, 128
Mean, 245, 246
Meaning, 73, 245
Means, 246
Mean-spirited, 245
Meantime, 246
Meanwhile, 246
Median, 245, 246
Mensch, 128
-ment, 187
Menu, 168
Meretricious, 203
Merit, 203
Meritorious, 203
Metallurgy, 79

Metaphor, 37, 171, 173, 233
Metonymy, 171
Mint, 210
Miscegenation, 195
Mischief, 53
Mischievous, 53
Misogynist, 164
Mission, 245
Missionary, 245
Monarchy, 160
Money, 210
Money laundering, 237
Morbid, 244
Mordant, 244
Morsel, 244
Mortal, 19, 244
Mortgage, 244
Mortify, 244
Mortuary, 244
Mother, 38, 122
Motorcade, 75
Motor car, 88
Move, 27
Multiple, 36
Multiplicity, 36
Multiply, 36
Murder, 244
Murmur, 167
Muscular, 140
Mutton, 85
Naches, 128
Naive, 195
Naked, 162
Nascent, 195
Nation, 188, 195
National, 195
Nationalism, 195
Nationality, 195
Nationalise/ nationalize, 195
Native, 195
Native American, 195
Natural, 195

Naturalism, 195
Naturalise/ naturalize, 195
Nature, 194, 195
Naturism, 195
Neologisms, 159
-ness, 192
New, 38, 122
-nik, 226
Nobility, 160
No-brainer, 198
Nomadic, 189
Non-flammable, 184, 197
Non-stop, 137
Notorious, 184
Nuclear energy, 78
Nude, 162
Obdurate, 188
Obese, 188
Obey, 188
Obfuscate, 188
Object, 188
Objection, 188
Objective, 188
Oblige, 188
Oblique, 174, 188
Obliterate, 188
Obsequious, 215
Observatory, 103
Observe, 103
Obstacle, 104
Obstinate, 104
Obverse, 185, 187
Occur, 88, 210
Octopus, 117
Odiferous, 233
Oedipus complex, 36
Of course, 211
Offer, 37, 231, 232, 233
Office, 78, 102
Official, 78, 92, 102
Officiate, 78

Officious, 78, 92, 102
Ointment, 139, 187
Oligarchy, 160
Omen, 167
Omission, 245
Omit, 245
Omni-, 146
Omnibus, 146
Omnipotent, 146
Omniscient, 146
Omnivorous, 146
Onion, 182
On the dole, 124
Onus, 167
Open, 120
Opera, 77
Operate, 77
Operation, 77
Operational, 77
Operative, 77
Operator, 77
Ops, 77, 167
Optimal, 77
Optimism, 77
Optimist, 77
Optimum, 77
Opulence, 77
Opulent, 77
Opus, 77
Orchid, 248
Orchidectomy, 248
Organ, 78, 161
Organism, 79
Organisation/ organization, 79
Organise/organize, 79
Orgy, 79, 161
Orphan, 80
Orthopedic, 163
Osteopath, 160
Outsmart, 244
Overbearing, 231
Ovine, 74
Ox, 84

Oy vey, 129
Paediatrician/pediatrician, 163
Paedo-/pedo-, 163
Paedophile/pedophile, 163, 202
Palindrome, 73
Palsy, 239
Paper, 205
Papyrus, 205
Para-, 248
Parabellum, 248
Parachute, 248
Paradigm, 248
Paradox, 248
Paragraph, 248
Paralegal, 248
Paralympic, 248
Paralysis, 239
Paramedic, 248
Parameter, 248
Paramour, 202
Paranormal, 248
Parapet, 248
Paraplegic, 189, 248
Parapsychology, 248
Parasol, 168, 183, 248
Parent, 93, 168
Pâté, 158
Pathetic, 91, 92
Pathos, 91
Patron, 93
Pavement, 158
Peculation, 209
Peculiar, 209
Pecuniary, 209
Pedal, 116, 163
Pedestrian, 116, 163
Pediatrics, 229
Pedicure, 163
Pedigree, 117
Pedology, 163
Pedometer, 163
Pedophilia, 202
Penis, 168
Penny farthing, 191
Per annum, 167
Perfectly, 137
Perfidy, 101
Pericarditus, 116
Pericardium, 116
Periphery, 233
Permission, 204, 245
Permit, 245
Persecute, 215
Persecution, 215
Persecutor, 215
Perverse, 185
Pheromone, 233
Phil-, 201
Philanderer, 202
Philanthropic, 201
Philately, 202
Philharmonic, 202
Philhellene, 201
Phile-, 201
Philip, 74
Philology, 202
Philosophical theory, 159
Philosophy, 139, 202
Phobia, 202
Phosphorus, 37, 233
Physician, 229
Pig, 84
Piglet, 191
Place, 164, 182
Placid, 166
Plait, 36
Pleat, 36
Plexus, 36
Pliable, 36
Pliant, 36
Ply, 36
Plywood, 36
Podiatrist, 160, 229
Podiatry, 117, 163, 229
Podium, 117
Pogrom, 169
Pole-vaulting, 222
Porcine, 74
Pork, 84
Pornography, 203
Portfolio, 206
Practice, 247
Praise, 203
Pray, 139
Precedent, 102
Precious, 203
Precipice, 53
Precipitate, 53
Precipitation, 53
Precursor, 211
Prefer, 37, 231, 232
Pregnant, 195
Prequel, 215
Preservative, 91, 168
Preserve, 103
President, 102
Price, 203
Priceless, 203
Principal, 156, 247
Principle, 156, 247
Privy, 236
Prize, 203
Procreate, 157
Profound, 226
Progress, 199
Progression, 199
Progressive, 199
Prohibit, 102
Prohibition, 102
Proliferate, 233
Prolific, 233
Proffer, 37, 231, 232

# English Word Index

Promptness, 192
Prosecute, 215
Prosecution, 215
Prosecutor, 215
Prostate, 104
Prostitute, 104, 203
Prostitution, 104
Prostrate, 104
Protect, 103
Province, 245
Psychiatrist, 229
Psychiatry, 229
Pulverise/pulverize, 186
Pursue, 215
Putz, 129
Qualify, 191, 197
Quality, 191
Quality control, 191, 197
Quarrel, 210
Queen, 164
Query, 210
Quest, 210
Question, 140, 210
Quid, 98
Re-, 188
Realise/realize, 92
Realpolitik, 169
Reason, 139
Reasonable, 91
Rebound, 242
Recap, 53
Recapitulate, 53
Recapitulation, 53
Receive, 32, 89
Reception, 32, 43, 189
Recipe, 43, 189
Recipient, 43, 189
Record, 116
Recount, 53, 247
Recourse, 88, 96, 211
Recreation, 157

Recruit, 157
Recur, 210
Recusant, 226
Recuse, 226
Redound, 242
Redundant, 242
Refer, 37, 231, 232
Referee, 231, 232
Reference, 37, 231, 232
Referred, 232
Refund, 174, 226
Refuse, 174, 225, 226
Refusenik, 226
Regal, 100
Regard, 183
Regime, 168
Regress, 199, 200
Regression, 199
Regressive, 199
Reject, 174
Relate, 234
Relation, 234
Relationship, 234
Relative, 234
Relax, 145
Release, 146
Relic, 145
Relinquish, 145
Remission, 245
Remit, 245
Remorse, 244
Replica, 36
Replicate, 36
Replied, 137
Reply, 36
Reservation, 91, 103
Reserve, 91, 103
Reservoir, 103
Resist, 104
Resistance, 104
Resolute, 238
Resolution, 238, 239

Resolve, 238
Restaurant, 168
Restitution, 104
Restroom, 236
Retrograde, 200
Return, 25
Reverse, 185, 187
Reversionary, 185
Revert, 185
Revolt, 219, 220
Revolting, 220
Revolution, 206, 219, 220
Revolutionary War, 220
Revolutions per minute (RPM), 219
Revolve, 206, 219, 221
Revolver, 206, 219
Revolving, 219, 222
Revolving door, 219
Ricochet, 168
Road, 158
Robot, 80
Round, 242
Roundhead, 75
Royal, 100
Rubbish, 224, 225
Rubbished, 224
Rubble, 224
Rucksack, 168
Run, 131
Run hard, 173
Running, 173
Rupture, 224
Safe, 101
Sage, 139
Sake, 175
Salad, 183
Salami, 183
Salary, 183
Salient, 138
Saline, 183

277

Salon, 89
Saloon, 88, 89
Saloon bar, 89
Salt, 183
Salubrious, 101
Salutary, 101
Salute, 101
Salvage, 101
Same, 42, 162
Sanction, 246
Satin, 169
Sauce, 183
Save, 101
Scathe, 137
Scathing, 137
Scat, 128
Schadenfreude, 168
Scroll, 221
Sebaceous, 139
Second, 215
Second sound shift, 116
Sect, 215
Seek, 175
Seem, 42
Seemly, 42
See to it, 139
Segue, 215
Semaphore, 233
Senator, 166
Sense, 90
Sensibility, 90
Sensible, 90, 91, 168
Sequel, 215
Sequence, 215
Sequester, 215
Serf, 91
Servant, 91, 103
Serve, 91, 103
Service, 91, 103
Servile, 91
Sexiness, 192
Shape, 39, 123, 127

Shave, 39, 123
Sheep, 85
Shit, 240
Shirt, 130
Short, 130
Short-term, 217
Shower, 237
Shtick/shtik, 129
Shtook/shtuck, 129
Shtum, 129
Sidewalk, 158
Silhouette, 168
Similar, 42
Simile, 172
Simpatico, 91, 92
Simple, 36, 17, 42
Simplicity, 36
Simulate, 42
Simultaneous, 42
Sincere, 157
Sinewy, 140
Single, 42
Singlet, 42
Singleton, 42
Singular, 42
Sir, 182
Sire, 182
Skirt, 130
Slack, 146
Slacks, 146
Sleep, 146
Smart, 243, 244
Smart as a whip, 244
Smart phone, 244
Snack, 129
Soap, 139
Sociology, 163
Solar, 36, 183
Solar energy, 78
Solarium, 183
Solar plexus, 36
Solder, 101
Soldier, 101
Solicitor, 101
Solicitous, 101

Solid, 101
Solidarity, 101
Solemn, 101
Solemnly, 101
Solstice, 183
Soluble, 238
Solution, 238
Solve, 238
Solved, 238
Solvent, 238
Some, 42
Somersault, 138
Sophisticated, 139
Sophistry, 139
Souvenir, 168
Soviet, 169
Sow, 84
Specialise/specialize, 186
Spiel, 169
Splay, 36
Splendiferous, 233
Sputnik, 226
Squabbled, 139
Stabilise/stablize, 186
Stand, 104
Standard, 104
State/states, 19, 100, 101, 102
State of the Union, 102
Stranglehold, 40
Static, 104
Station, 104
Statistic, 104
Statue, 104
Status, 104
Statute, 104
Steadfast, 173
Stica/styca, 191
Stool/stole, 153
Stool-pigeon, 153
Stop, 137
Sub-, 234
Subaltern, 234

# English Word Index

Subdue, 234
Submarine, 234
Submit, 234
Subordinate, 234
Substitute, 104
Subterranean, 158
Succor, 211
Suet, 139
Suffect, 189
Suffer, 233
Sufficient, 189
Sun, 183, 252
Superb, 166
Supple, 139
Suppliant, 139
Supplicate, 139
Support, 234
Suppose, 140
Surrogate, 234
Surround, 242
Swear, 137
Swine, 84
Sworn appraiser, 247
Subservient, 91
Subsist, 104
Subsistence, 104
Substance, 104
Substitute, 234
Subvention, 234
Suffer, 37
Sufficient, 34, 157
Sure, 138
Surgeon, 161
Surgery, 79, 160, 161
Sustain, 234
Sustenance, 234
Swallowed, 139
Sympathetic, 91, 92
Synergy, 78, 161
Systemic, 189
Tachycardia, 116
Take care of, 139
Take over, 139

Tale, 247
Talent, 234
Taxi, 89
Taxicab, 89
Taximeter, 89
Technological phenomenon, 159
Telephone, 169
Tell, 247
Term, 216, 217
Terminal, 216, 217
Terminate, 217, 218
Termination, 217
Terminological, 216
Terminology, 216
Terminus, 216
Terms, 217
Terrace, 158
Terra firma, 101
Terrain, 158
Terrier, 158
Terrine, 158
Territory, 158
Testoon, 153
Teuton/Teutonic, 130,
That, 130
Thatch, 103
Theatrical, 189
Theism, 157
Thickness, 192
Thin, 114
Think, 180
Thorough, 138
Thoroughly, 137
Threesome, 42
Through, 138, 180
Tide, 121
Tile, 103
Timber, 121
Toil, 236
Toilet, 236, 237
Tolerate, 234
Topic, 164

Tornado, 185
Tour, 25, 185
Tower, 25
Transfer, 231
Transgress, 199
Transgression, 200
Trash, 225
Travail, 79
Treble clef, 182
Tree, 38, 122
Trefoil, 206
Tripod, 117
-trix, 215
Tureen, 158
Turn, 25, 185
Turret, 25
Tush/Tushie/Tushy, 129
Two, 139
Type, 164
Typesetting, 164
Typewriter, 164
Typist, 164
Udder, 253
Umpire, 232
Un-, 190
Unable, 190
Unalienable, 190
Unanimous, 102
Unapproved, 190
Uncanny, 190
Unceasing, 190, 191
Uncommon, 190
Uncommonly, 138, 139
Uncouth, 190
Undulate, 242
Uninterested, 184, 190
Union, 102
Union Army, 102
Unique, 102
Unison, 102
United, 102

279

United States, 100, 101, 102, 230
Unity, 102
Universal, 102
Universe, 102
University, 102
Unkempt, 190
Unqualified, 190, 191, 197
Unreasonableness, 91
Unscathed, 137
Untangle, 190
Untold, 247
Untouchable, 190
Unturned, 190
Unusual, 190
Unwitting, 190
Utterly, 137
Valedictorian, 198
Valedictory, 198
Valiant, 198
Valid, 197
Validate, 198
Valueless, 197
Valve, 206, 222
Vanquish, 214
Vault, 206, 222
Veal, 85
Veldt, 168
Vent, 109
Ventilate, 109
Ventilation, 109
Verboten, 168
Verily, 137
Verse, 185, 188
Version, 185, 188
Vertex, 185, 188
Vertical, 185, 188, 189
Very, 137, 255

Very better, 255
Vicinity, 161
Victor, 213, 244
Victoria, 213
Victory, 213, 244
Viennese waltz, 223
Villa, 168
Vociferous, 37, 233
Vodka, 169, 241
Voice, 46
Volte-face, 206, 222
Voluble, 206
Volume, 206, 221
Voluminous, 206, 221
Volvo, 222
Vulva, 206, 221
Walk, 131, 222
Wallet, 206
Wallow, 206, 222
Wallowing, 222
Waltz, 206, 222, 223
Wanderlust, 168
War, 183
Ward, 183
Warden, 183
Warder, 183
Warrant, 183
Warranty, 183
Wash, 241
Washing, 237
Water, 38, 44, 121, 122, 179, 237, 241
Water-closet, 236
Way out, 199
WC, 236
Weakness, 192
Weather, 109

Weight-bearing, 231
Well, 206, 222
Welling up, 222
Weltanschauung, 169
Welter, 206, 222
Wend, 253
Went, 253, 254
Wet, 241
What, 130
Whelk, 206, 222
Whisky/whiskey, 241
Whole, 138
Wholly, 137
Whore, 203
Wi-Fi, 101
Wikipedia, 163
Willow, 206
Wind, 109
Window, 109
Wine, 161
Winsome, 42
Winter, 241
Withstand, 104
Woe, 129
Wood, 46
Work, 38, 76, 78, 122, 161
Works, 80
Wring, 186
Xenon, 208
Xenophobia, 202, 208
Yet, 46
Yield, 210
Young, 38, 122
Youth, 180
Zeitgeist, 168
Zoological, 189

# Subject and Name Index

Acton, Lord, 239
Aeneid (The), 188
Aetheling, Edgar, 83
Africa, 108, 211
Afrikaans language/Afrikaners, 74, 80, 81, 104, 106, 118, 120, 122, 124, 125, 132, 133, 134, 149, 168, 179, 182, 186, 255
Ainu language, 47, 48
Akbar (Mughal Emperor), 64
Alcatraz, 213
Alice in Wonderland, 136, 137, 225
Alighieri, Dante, 144, 145, 257
Allen, W. Sidney, 251
Alphabets, 44
American Declaration of Independence, 190
American English, 83, 128, 129, 158, 186, 225, 227, 229, 236
American Federation of Labor (AFL), 76
American Revolution/American War of Independence, 220
The Americas, 108, 181
Amish/Pennsylvania Dutch, 131
Andorra, 154
Anglo-Norman French/Old Norman French, 82, 83, 84, 99, 100, 235
Anglo-Saxon (Old English), 38, 82, 83, 84, 99, 121, 122, 141, 156
Aphrodite/Venus, 201
Aquitani (tribe), 155
Arabic, 26, 167, 169, 245
Aramaic, 46
Arbiter, Gaius Petronius, 143
Arthashastra, 207
Aristophanes, 180
Asia, 108, 211

Assyrians, 212
Asterix, 154
As You Like It, 182
Ataturk, Mustapha Kemal, 44
Atticus (friend of Cicero), 143
Augustus, 84, 98, 142, 148
Aurelian (Roman emperor), 155
Austen, Jane, 90, 91
Austria, 120, 125, 126, 127, 211, 251
Avestan (Zoroastrian language), 107
Babylon/Babylonians, 61, 212
Balearic Islands, 154
Balochi language, 107
Baltic languages, 55, 66, 68, 107, 110, 111, 249
Bantu languages, 134
Barnum, P.T., 199
Barwice, Poland, 235
Basque language/Basque people, 26, 47, 48, 105, 148, 149, 155
Bastille, 219
Bavaria, 126
Bayeux Tapestry, 83
Beatles (The), 201
Bears, 235
Beethoven, Ludwig van, 91
"Bei Mir Bistu Shein" (Yiddish song), 45
Belgae (tribe), 155
Belgium, 95, 120, 125, 130, 131, 132
Bengali, 107
Ben-Gurion, Amos, 136
Ben-Gurion, David, 136
Berlin, 162, 235
Berwick, Rachel (artist), 65
Berwick, Robert (computer scientist), 61, 62

Bible, 94, 112, 122, 143, 149, 156, 191, 202, 205, 243
Black, Paul, 66
Black Sea, 108
Bloomfield, Leonard, 55
BMW (Bayerischer Motoren Werke), 80
Bohemia, 211
Bopp, Franz, 111
Boroditsky, Lena, 69
Bowes-Lyon, Elizabeth (The Queen Mother), 235
Bow-wow theory (Cuckoo theory), 62
Boxhorn, Marcus van, 55, 111, 249
Boyle's Law, 221
Brazil/Brazilian Portuguese, 58, 150, 151, 152
Breton language, 106
Britain (Britannia), 99, 120, 146, 227, 228, 229, 230, 236, 251, 253
British English, 158, 186, 227, 229, 236,
British Parliament, 228
Broadway, 199
Bulgarian, 106
Burke, Edmund, 219
Bush, George W., 69
Byrd, Andrew, 110
Byron, Lord (George Gordon), 172
Caesar, Julius, 26, 46, 142, 154, 155, 213, 244
Calques, 135, 169
Cambridge University, 94, 103, 188, 250, 251
Canada, 25, 88
Capek, Karel, 80
Capone, Al 77, 213
Caracalla, 103
Caribs, 64, 65
Carinthian plebiscite of 1920, 251
Carroll, Lewis, 136, 137
Castilian lisp, 180
Catalan language/Catalonia, 26, 75, 95, 106, 142, 144, 154, 156, 181
Catullus, 198
Çelebi, Evilya, 111
Celtic languages, 54, 55, 68, 106, 110, 111, 148, 249, 252
Champs Elysees, 85, 182

Chang and Eng (Siamese twins), 199
Charles I of England, 75, 220
Chaucer, Geoffrey, 173, 217
Chester, 83
Chinese, 16, 26, 55, 72
Chomsky, Noam, 22, 55, 56, 57, 58, 59, 61, 62
Chomskyan/generativist linguistics, 33, 55, 56, 57, 58, 59, 61, 62
Church of England, 226
Cicero, Marcus Tullius, 28, 46, 51, 142
Cisalpine Gaul, 154, 155
Clackson, James, 109
Claudius, 99
Code of Justinian, 206
Colchester (Camulodunum), 99
Coleridge, Samuel Taylor, 241
Common Law Courts, 228
Common Sense, 90
Comparative Linguistics, 249, 250
Comparative Philology, 32, 55, 179, 249, 251
Constitutio Antoniniana, 103
Copenhagen, 134
Copernicus, 219
Cornish language, 106
Couerdoux, Gaston-Laurent, 111
Court of Chancery, 228
Cuba, 46
Cuneiform, 212
Cupid/Eros, 201
Curzon, Lord, 146
Cyrillic alphabet, 180
Czech, 80, 106, 251
Dahlhoff, Nick, 17
Danish language/Danes/Denmark, 106, 120, 122, 124, 134, 209
Darwin, Charles, 62, 177
Davos World Economic Forum, 15
The History of the Decline and Fall of the Roman Empire, 206
Deism, 157
Descartes, Rene, 26, 97
Deutsche Grammatik, 111, 112
Deutsches Wörterbuch, (DWB), 112
De Vulgari Eloquentia (treatise by Dante), 144, 257
Die Afrikaanse Patriot, 132
The Divine Comedy, 144, 145

## Subject and Name Index

Doner, Tim, 52
Dulwich, 161
Dutch language, 52, 55, 74, 80, 81, 106, 111, 116, 118, 120, 120, 122, 124, 126, 130, 131, 132, 133, 149, 151, 166, 167, 179, 182, 249, 255
Dutch universities, 94
Early Modern English, 83
The Economist, 68
Edward the Confessor, 83
El Cid, 148, 149
Enduring Power of Attorney (EPA), 228
Egypt/Egyptian language, 54, 205
England/ the English people, 38, 82, 83, 84, 99, 130, 153, 154, 191, 227
English Civil War/English Revolution, 220
English Renaissance, 83
Enlightenment, 100
Erdoğan, Recep Tayipp, 44
Estonian, 26, 105
Etruscan alphabet/language, 46, 47
Etymology, 28, 31, 179, 258
Europe, 108
European Parliament, 15
European Union (EU), 125
Evangelical Christians, 87
Everett, Daniel, 56, 57, 58
Fall of Constantinople (1453), 192
Farlow, Sue (parrot fancier), 65
Fell, Matthew, 14
Finnish language, Finland, 26, 105, 134, 135
Finno-Ugric languages, 105
First World War, 239, 251
Fisher, H.A.L, 239
Flemish (Dutch dialect), 122, 131, 132
Franco, Francisco, 53
Franklin, Benjamin, 26
Franks, 155
Frederick the II (the Great) of Prussia, 13
French language/French people/France, 14, 16, 20, 21, 24, 25, 26, 27, 47, 66, 69, 75, 79, 80, 82, 85, 88, 90, 91, 92, 93, 95, 99, 100, 103, 105, 106, 107, 125, 130, 131, 141, 144, 146, 147, 150, 152, 154, 155, 156, 157, 158, 164, 165, 166, 168, 169, 181, 182, 185, 186, 202, 203, 211, 212, 229, 236, 239, 240, 251, 254, 257
French Revolution, 181, 219
Freud, Sigmund, 96
Fry, Christopher, 184
Furst, Bruno, 50
Gaelic, Irish, 106
Gaelic, Scottish, 106
Galba (Roman emperor), 43
Gallic Wars (The), 154
Gascon language, 149
Gaul/Gauls, 75, 154, 155
Genoa, 194
The Germania, 123
Germanic languages/words, 21, 24, 27, 38, 39, 66, 68, 81, 87, 106, 110, 112, 113, 114, 115, 116, 117, 118, 119, 122, 123, 124, 131, 137, 147, 149, 153, 166, 182, 183, 184, 190, 194, 195, 205, 209, 222, 223, 241, 246, 250, 252, 258
German language/Germans/ Germany, 13, 14, 17, 18, 25, 45, 55, 69, 72, 74, 75, 79, 80, 106, 107, 111, 112, 114, 116, 118, 119, 120, 122, 123, 124, 125, 126, 127, 129, 130, 132, 132, 138, 147, 162, 168, 169, 175, 179, 186, 229, 235, 241, 247, 249, 251, 254
Gibbon, Edward, 206
Gladstone, William 70, 239
Glorious Revolution, 220
Glottochronology, 65, 66
Godwinson, Harold (Harold II of England), 83
Gothic language, 119
Grammar, 17, 18, 24, 25, 26, 27, 28, 55, 56, 258
Granada, 149
Gray Goose Laws, 134
Great Bible, 95
Greek language (Ancient and Modern)/Greeks/Greek alphabet, 34, 46, 47, 49, 53, 54, 55, 66, 70, 74, 83, 84, 87, 93, 94, 106, 108, 110, 111, 112, 113, 114, 115, 116, 117, 118, 119, 159, 160, 161, 162, 163, 164,

283

165, 166, 179, 180, 182, 183, 184, 186, 187, 191, 192, 193, 194, 195, 201, 202, 203, 204, 205, 208, 223, 229, 234, 238, 2423, 247, 248, 249, 250, 252
Greene, Robert Lee (moderator), 69
Greenwich, 161
Gregorian Calendar, 220
Grimm, Jacob and Wilhelm, 55, 111, 112, 118, 123, 249
Grimms' Fairy Tales, 112
Grimm's Law, 32, 43, 53, 55, 111, 112, 113, 114, 115, 116, 117, 118, 119, 120, 123, 179, 195, 209, 249
Gujarati, 107
Haarhoff, Theo, 151
Hadrian, 148
Ham (son of Noah), 60
Hasidic Jews (Haredim), 45, 127
Hastings, Battle of, 83
Havana, 31, 46, 180
Heath, Edward, 235
Hebrew alphabet/language, 24, 25, 46, 47, 64, 67, 128, 129, 149, 158
Hellenic languages, 68
Helsinki, 135
Henry VII of England, 83
Henry VIII of England, 95
Herod I of Judaea, 84
Herodotus, 47, 63
Hill, Christopher, 220
Hill, Sir Roland, 202
Himalayas, 159
Himba, 70
Hindi, 26, 107, 167
Hippocrates, 74
Hitler, Adolf, 85, 236
Hittite language/Hittites, 108, 212
Hobbes, Thomas, 94
Hogg, Quintin, 235
Holocaust, 127
Homer, 70
Hopi language/people, 69, 71
Horace, 96, 142
Horses, 73, 74, 75, 76
Huguenots, 132
Humboldt, Alexander von, 64, 65
Hungarian language/Hungarians/ Hungary, 26, 79, 105, 250, 251

Ibbotson, Paul, 59
Iberian language/Iberian peninsula, 148
Icelandic language/Icelanders/ Iceland, 119, 120, 124, 134, 135, 136
Iliad (The), 70
India, 111, 167
Indo-Aryan languages (Indic languages), 68, 107, 110
Indo-European language family, 54, 66, 106, 107, 108, 110, 111, 112, 122, 194, 195, 222, 231, 249, 250, 251, 252, 258
Indonesian language/Indonesians/ Indonesia, 44, 52, 53, 54, 132, 166, 167
Industrial Revolution, 83
Invictus, 213
Iranian languages, 107, 110
Irish English, 24
Israel, 127, 226
Italian language/Italy, 14, 26, 66, 75, 79, 95, 106, 125, 142, 144, 145, 146, 147, 153, 154, 156, 157, 165, 181, 203, 210, 225, 229, 254, 257
James II of England, 220
James IV of Scotland, 63
Japanese, 26, 55
Japheth (son of Noah), 60
Jerome (Saint), 94, 143
Jesus Christ, 87
Jews, 45, 127, 150, 226
Joachimsthal/Joachimsthaler, 211
Johnson, Samuel, 227
Jones, Franklin, 241, 247
Jones, Sir William, 54, 55, 111, 249
Jopson, Norman Brooke ("Joppy"), 33, 250, 251, 252, 255
Julius Caesar, 194
Jung, Carl Gustav, 36, 187
Juno Moneta, 210
Julian Calendar, 220
The Kama Sutra, 203
Kayne, Richard, 253, 254
Kennedy, John F., 95
Kentucky, University of, 110
Khoekhoe (Hottentots), 132
King Kong, 97
King of Queens, 248

## Subject and Name Index

Kipling, Rudyard, 207
Korean, 26, 47, 48, 69
Krantz, Judith, 129
Kurgan theory, 108
Kruskal, Joseph, 66
Kurdish language, 107
Ladino language, 45
Lakoff, George, 175, 176, 177
Language Transfer (language learning company), 20, 21
Languedoc, 144
Laryngeal theory, 108, 109, 110, 250, 251, 252
Lasting Power of Attorney (LPA), 228
Latin/Latin alphabet, 25, 26, 33, 34, 45, 46, 49, 53, 54, 55, 66, 75, 79, 82, 85, 94, 95, 96, 97, 98, 99, 100, 106, 108, 110, 111, 112, 113, 114, 115, 116, 117, 118, 119, 122, 137, 141, 142, 143, 144, 145, 146, 147, 149, 150, 151, 154, 155, 156, 157, 158, 159, 161, 162, 163, 164, 165, 166, 167, 174, 175, 181, 182, 183, 184, 185, 186, 187, 188, 189, 191, 192, 193, 194, 195, 197, 199, 200, 202, 203, 205, 206, 207, 208, 213, 215, 217, 221, 222, 224, 233, 237, 238, 242, 244, 245, 246, 247, 248, 249, 250, 251, 252, 253, 254, 256, 257, 258
Latvian, 107, 210
Leviathan, 94
Lexicostatistics, 65, 66
Liechtenstein, 120, 125, 126, 127
Lisbon, 153, 154
Lithuanian, 107, 210
Livy, 142
Lloyd George, David, 146, 239
Loanwords, 168
Lomonosov, Mikhail, 111
London (Londinium), 99
London Underground, 88
Los Angeles International Airport (LAX), 227
Louis XIII of France, 96
Louis XIV of France, 181
Louis XVI of France, 219
Low German (Plattdeutsch), 120, 123, 124, 126, 129, 130
Luther, Martin, 173
Luwian, 108
Luxembourg, 125
Lycian, 108
Lyons, Sir John, 251
Macbeth, 42
Madagascar, 132
Madrid, 181
Malaga, 181
Malay language, 44
Manchester (Mamucium), 99
Manx language, 106
Marathi, 107
Maria Theresa Thaler, 211
Marx, Groucho, 157, 247
Marx, Karl, 157
Mary II of England, 220
Maypore language/tribe, 64, 65
Mein Kampf, 85
Melchert, H. Craig, 110
Metaphors, 171, 172, 173, 174, 175, 176, 177
Metonymy, 171
Middle English, 83
Milan, 153
Modern English, 83, 84, 99
Moldova, 155
Monogenesis, 65
Moors, 148
More, Sir Thomas, 102
Mozambique, 150
Mozart, Wolfgang Amadeus, 214
Murcia, 181
My Big Fat Greek Wedding, 49, 159, 248
Namibia, 132
Naples, 147
Napoleon, 73
Napoleonic Code, 206
National Geographic Society Genographic Project, 48
Native Americans, 103
Nazis, 138
Neanderthals, 63
Nero, 143, 148
Netherlands, the, 120, 123, 130, 131, 132
Nimes, 194
Noah, 60

285

Norman Conquest of England/ Normandy/Normans, 82, 83, 84, 86, 87, 99
Norwegian language/Norwegians/ Norway/ 06, 120, 122, 124, 134, 205
Nova Vulgata translation of the Bible, 94
Occitan (Provencal), 142, 144, 154
Oceania, 108
October Revolution, 220
Odysseus, 207
The Odyssey, 70, 207
Old Norse, 119, 134, 135
Old Sardinian language, 255, 256, 257
Olympic Games (ancient), 74
Orinoco River, 64
Oswald, Lee Harvey, 95
Othello, 200
Ottoman Turks, 192
Oviedo, 181
Oxford University, 94, 188
Paine, Thomas, 90
Pakistan, 167
Pall Mall Magazine, 204
Palmerston, Lord, 207
Pamplona, 181
Paris, 239, 240
Parrots, 64, 65
Pashto language, 107
Patronymic naming system, 135, 136
Pei, Mario, 23, 257
Persian language (Farsi)/Persia, 54, 55, 107, 111, 167, 212, 249
Phaeacians, 207
Phillip II of Macedon, 74
Philological Society, 253, 255
Philology, 32
Phoenician alphabet/language, 46, 47
Phoenix Sky Harbor Airport, 71
Phrygian language, 63
Piccadilly Circus, 201
Pimsleur (language learning company), 19
Pirahã language/people, 57, 58
Place de la Concorde, 182
Plautus, 142
Poema del Cid, 148

Polabian language (extinct Slavic language), 235
Polish language/Polish people/ Poland, 13, 106, 210, 235
Pomerania, 235
Pompadour, Madame de, 89
Pope Gregory I, 38
Portuguese language/Portugal, 26, 75, 95, 106, 142, 148, 150, 151, 152, 153, 156, 157, 158, 165, 181, 203, 229, 254
Postal Censorship Office, 251
Prague, 251
Prokofiev, Sergei, 178
Protestants/Protestantism, 95, 112
Proto-Germanic, 119, 123, 124, 130
Proto-Indo-European, (PIE) 66, 68, 106, 108, 109, 110, 111, 112, 113, 117, 118, 123, 250, 252
Provence, 154
Psammetichus (Egypt. pharaoh), 63
Pulcher, Publius Clodius, 237
Punjabi, 107, 108
Purnavarman (Indian king), 53
Pyrenees, 154
Quakers, 128
Quebec, 88
Rask, Rasmus, 111, 123
Rasputin, 90
Reagan, Ronald, 69
Recessional (Kipling), 207
Reconquista, 148
Recursion, 56, 57, 58
Reflection on the Revolution in France, 219
Renfrew, Colin, 108
The Restoration, 83
Richards, Olly, 29, 30
Richelieu, Cardinal, 96
Riebeeck, Jan van, 132
Rime of the Ancient Mariner, 241
Roman Catholic Church/Roman Catholics, 94, 143, 226
Romance languages, 21, 68, 106, 110, 142, 144, 146, 147, 148, 149, 156, 157, 158, 175, 181, 182, 183, 188, 198, 200, 205, 210, 233, 242, 246, 249, 252, 256, 257, 258

## Subject and Name Index

Romanian language/Romanians/ Romania, 75, 79, 95, 106, 142, 147, 155, 156, 157, 158, 251
Rome/Roman Empire/Roman Republic/Romans, 94, 99, 103, 130, 143, 145, 148, 155, 156, 198, 237, 249
Romeo and Juliet, 178
Rosetta Stone (language learning company), 16, 17, 18, 19
Roosevelt, Franklin, 124
Roosevelt, Theodore, 235
Ruhlen, Merritt, 67
Russian language/Russia, 69, 106, 107, 108, 169, 180, 210, 220, 226, 251
St Albans (Verulamium), 99
St. John's College, Cambridge, 250, 251, 255
St. Petersburg, Russia, 251
Samaritans, 46
Sami (Lapp) language, 105
Samoyedic languages, 105
Sanskrit, 49, 53, 54, 107, 108, 110, 111, 112, 113, 114, 115, 117, 118, 119, 167, 207, 249, 251, 252
Sao Paolo, 152
Sapir, Edward, 68
Sapir-Whorf hypothesis (Whorfianism), 24, 68, 69
Sardinian language/people, 257
Sassetti, Filippo, 111
Satyricon, 143
Saudi Arabia, 135
Saussure, Ferdinand de, 55
Scandinavian languages/ Scandinavia, 120, 134, 135, 179
Scientific American, 59
Scotland, 99
Scruples, 129
"Scythian" language, 55, 111, 249
Second sound shift (zweite Lautverschiebung), 114, 116, 119, 119, 120, 123, 130, 134, 179, 241
Second World War, 251
Seneca, Lucius Annaeus, 148
Sense and Sensibility, 90
Serbo-Croatian, 106
Seville, 181
Schlegel, Friedrich, 111
Schleicher, August, 110
Schools/universities, foreign language teaching in, 13, 14, 15
Shakespeare, William, 42, 182, 194, 200
Shem (son of Noah), 60
Shillibeer, George, 146
Simile, 172
Simons, Andreas, 82, 141
Simonides of Ceos, 51, 52
Sir Gawain and the Green Knight, 41
Slavic languages, 55, 66, 68, 106, 110, 111, 249, 252
Slovak, 106
Slovene language/Slovenia, 106, 251
Solicitors, 227, 228
South Africa/South Africans, 132, 134, 149, 151, 191
South African Act, 1909, 133
South Tyrol (region of Italy), 125
Soviet Union, 155, 226
Spanish language/Spain, 14, 17, 18, 26, 48, 72, 75, 95, 105, 106, 142, 144, 147, 148, 149, 150, 151, 151, 152, 154, 156, 157, 165, 180, 181, 198, 203, 229, 254, 257
Spencer, Herbert, 177
Stalin, 76
Standard German (Neuhochdeutsch), 119, 120, 123, 125, 127, 129, 130, 179, 241
Stone Age, 106
Strabo, 47
Structural linguistics, 251
Subject-null languages, 26, 27
Sumerian language/Sumerians, 47, 212
Suppletion, 253, 254
Suriname, 130
Swadesh, Morris, 65
Swahili, 44
Swedish language/Swedes/ Sweden,106, 107, 119, 120, 122, 124, 129, 134, 135
Swiss German/Switzerland, 120, 126, 127
Syntax, 22, 27, 258
Tacitus, 43, 123, 142
Tchaikovsky, Pyotr, 91
Terence, 144

Teutons/Teutonic, 130
Thatcher, Margaret, 184, 235
Theism, 157
The Lady's Not for Burning, 184
Theodosius (Roman emperor), 148
Thermopylae, Battle of, 52
Thrace, 155
Thumb, Tom, 199
Tiro (Cicero's secretary), 142
Tito (leader of Yugoslavia), 76
Tocharian (Tokharian), 108
Toledo, 181
Tomasello, Michael, 59
Tottenham Court Road, 152
Tower of Babel, 49, 60, 61, 63, 65
Trajan, 98, 148, 155
Transactions of the Philological Society, 253, 255
Transalpine Gaul, 155
Transylvania, 251
Trask, Larry, 58
Trimalchio's Dinner, 143
Trump, Donald, 77, 98
Tuscany, 145
Turkish language/Turkey, 16, 44, 72, 108
Twitter, 240
Tyndale, William, 95
Ukraine/Ukrainian language, 106, 108, 127
Umbrian language, 237
United Nations, 15
United States Congress, 101
United States Constitution, 100, 101
United States of America, 101, 102, 128, 131, 179, 227, 228, 229, 230
United States President, 101, 216
United States senators, 216
University of London, 251
"U" & "Non-U" language, 236
Uralic language family, 105
Urdu, 107, 167
Utopia, 102
Valencia (city and region of Spain), 154, 181
The Vatican, 94
Venezuela, 64
Verner, Karl, 118

Verner's Law, 118, 119, 120, 123, 179, 249
Versailles, 181
Vespasian, 157, 239
Victoria, Queen of Great Britain, 207
Vienna, 251
Viennese Waltz, 223
Vietnamese language, 44
Viola, 85
Viola da gamba, 85
Violin, 85
Virgil (Vergil), 142, 152
Visigoths, 148
Vocabulary, 55, 56, 59, 258
Voltaire, 179
Volvo, 222
Vorarlberg (Austrian state), 126
Vulgar Latin, 26, 142, 143, 150, 156
Vulgate translation of the Bible, 94, 143
Walter, Henriette, 82
Washington, George, 220
Welsh language/Wales, 99, 106, 251
Weil, Andre, 240
Whorf, Benjamin, 68, 69
Williams, Joseph, 141
William the Conqueror (William I of England), 83
William III of England, 220
Witenagemot (Anglo-Saxon assembly), 83
Wolfe, Sam, 255, 256, 257
Wolfe, Tom, 57, 58
Woolwich, 161
Yiddish, 45, 126, 127, 128, 129, 135, 169
York (Eboracum), 99
Yoruba, 44
Young, Thomas, 111
Yugoslavia, 251
Zulu, 44

www.ingramcontent.com/pod-product-compliance
Lightning Source LLC
Chambersburg PA
CBHW071144160426
43196CB00011B/2009